Complete
MathSmart®

Grade 10

To Our Valued Customer:

To express our gratitude for your support, we would like to invite you to join our "**Popular Canada Parents' Club**" program for free. By scanning the QR code above and signing up, you will enjoy these exclusive benefits:

- 50% off all future online purchases of *Complete Canadian Curriculum* and 30% off any other Popular titles through the Popular Book Company (Canada) Limited website

- notification emails with information about our new releases, contests, and exclusive offers

- FREE printable worksheets on various core subjects

- access to educational resource videos provided by certified Canadian teachers

- access to fun, educational workshops by Canadian teachers on online platforms

- entry into our quarterly contests for a chance to win an iPad or workbooks

Join thousands of Canadian parents and see how we are making children's learning fun and rewarding today!

Your Partner in Education,
Popular Canada Team

Printed in China

ISBN: 978-1-77149-221-8

ISBN: 978-1-77149-221-8

Overview

Complete MathSmart is our all-time bestselling series. *Complete MathSmart* Grade 10 is designed to strengthen students' math foundation, and allow them to learn the key concepts and demonstrate their understanding by applying their knowledge and skills to solve real-world problems.

This workbook covers the three strands of the Mathematics curriculum:
- Quadratic Relations of the Form $y = ax^2 + bx + c$
- Analytic Geometry
- Trigonometry

This workbook contains eight chapters, with each chapter covering a math topic. Different concepts in the topic are each introduced by a simple example and a "Try This" section to give students an opportunity to check their understanding of the concept. The basic skill questions that follow lead up to application questions that gradually increase in difficulty to help students consolidate the concept they have learned. Useful hints are provided to guide students along and help them grasp the essential math concepts. In addition, a handy reference containing definitions and formulas is included to provide quick and easy access for students whenever needed.

A cumulative review is provided for students to recapitulate the concepts and skills they have learned in the book. The questions are classified into four categories to help students evaluate their own learning. Below are the four categories:
- Knowledge and Understanding
- Application
- Communication
- Thinking

The review is also ideal as testing practice to prepare students for the Math examination in school.

At the end of this workbook is an answer key that provides thorough solutions with the crucial steps clearly presented to help students develop an understanding of the correct strategies and approaches to arrive at the solutions.

Complete MathSmart will undoubtedly reinforce students' math skills and strengthen their conceptual foundation that is a prerequisite for exploring mathematics further in their secondary programs.

Contents

ISBN: 978-1-77149-221-8

Chapter 6: Solving Quadratic Equations

Chapter 7: Triangles and Trigonometry

Chapter 8: Acute Triangle Trigonometry

1 Basic Skills

Words TO LEARN

BEDMAS:

an acronym to help remember the order of operations

> **B**rackets
> **E**xponents
> **D**ivision
> **M**ultiplication
> **A**ddition
> **S**ubtraction

Algebraic expression:

an expression that consists of constants, variables, and operations

e.g. $2a + 16b$
$x^2 + 3x - 4$

Linear equation:

an equation that represents a straight line on a graph

e.g.

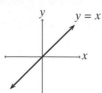

1.1 Order of Operations

Example

Evaluate the expression.

$12 - (2 + 3)^2 \div 5$

$= 12 - 5^2 \div 5$ ← brackets

$= 12 - 25 \div 5$ ← exponent

$= 12 - 5$ ←——— division

$= 7$ ←——— subtraction

Try This

$(-1 + 4)^2 \div (2 + 1) - 7$

$= \boxed{}^2 \div \boxed{} - 7$

$= \boxed{} - 7$

$= \boxed{}$

$16 \div (3^2 - 5) + (3 - 5)^2$

$= 16 \div \boxed{} + (\boxed{})^2$

$= \boxed{} + \boxed{}$

$= \boxed{}$

Evaluate.

① $8 \times 2 \div 4^2 - 1$

② $17 - 18 \div (2 + 1)^2 + 2^2$

③ $-3 + (5 + 2 \times 3) - 2(-17)$

④ $(9 - 5)^2 - (9^2 - 5^2)$

⑤ $(-2 - 1) \times 6^2 \div 4$

⑥ $(-7 + (-3)) \div (2^2 + 5 \div 5)$

     ISBN: 978-1-77149-221-8

Evaluate each of the following expressions.

Expressions with Fractions

⑦ $\left(\dfrac{5^3}{5^2} - 2\right) \times \left(\dfrac{2}{3}\right)^2$

⑧ $(-6)^2 - 16 \times 2^{-3}$

⑨ $\left(\dfrac{(2 - 3 \times 2 + 8)^2}{-2 + 3^2 \times 2}\right)^{-1}$

⑩ $\left(\left(\dfrac{(-5)5^{-1}}{(\frac{1}{3})^{-2}\, 9^{-1}}\right)^{-3}\right)^{-1}$

⑪ $\left(\dfrac{1}{6} - 3^{-1} + 3 \times 6^{-1}\right) + \left(\dfrac{1}{2}\right)^2$

Expressions with Square Roots

⑫ $\dfrac{\sqrt{(6 - 3)(-1 + 4)}}{27(3)^{-1}}$

⑬ $2\left(-\sqrt{9^2 \times 5^2}\right) - \left(\sqrt{\dfrac{1}{9}}\right)^{-2}$

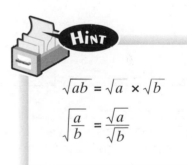

⑭ $\left(\dfrac{\sqrt{9} + \sqrt{4}}{\sqrt{9 + 4}}\right)^2$

⑮ $\sqrt{\dfrac{(-2)^2 - 3}{(\frac{1}{3})^{-2} - 5}}$

⑯ $(17^0 - \sqrt{144} \times 12^{-1})(1319^{3^2 - 2^3})$

Determine whether each number sentence is true or not.

⑰ Does $(8 - 4)^2 = 8^2 - 4^2$?

⑱ Does $(\sqrt{2})^3 = 2\sqrt{2}$?

⑲ Does $\sqrt{\dfrac{(-2 + 9)^2}{(9 - 2)^2}} = 1$?

⑳ Does $\sqrt{(-2 - 6)^2} = \sqrt{(-2)^2} - \sqrt{6^2}$?

Solve the problems. Show your work.

㉑ Adam scored 78 marks on his assignment. He then received 2 extra marks for answering a bonus question correctly. However, 10% of his total marks were deducted because he handed in the assignment late. What is his final score?

㉒ Jason receives a 20% employee discount at the store he works at. On Boxing Day, he receives a $20 voucher as well. Jason wants to buy a jacket that costs $168. Will it be cheaper if the employee discount is applied before using the voucher or after?

㉓ Adam says, "I'm 12 years old. Take my age and divide it by 3. Find its square root and then raise it to the power of 6 and subtract it by 2. The answer is Grandpa's age." How old is Adam's grandfather?

ISBN: 978-1-77149-221-8

1.2 Algebraic Expressions

Evaluate each algebraic expression.

① $3(a - 2) - 8$ $a = 4$

② $\dfrac{x^3 - x^2}{6}$ $x = 3$

③ $(10 - 1\frac{1}{2}j)^{-2}$ $j = 6$

④ $2m + 6n$ $m = 0.5$ $n = -1$

⑤ $pq - (\frac{p}{q})^2$ $p = 2$ $q = -1$

⑥ $\dfrac{c^2}{d} \times (c - d)$ $c = -5$ $d = 10$

⑦ $8\sqrt{s} + st$ $s = 9$ $t = \frac{5}{6}$

⑧ $(x^3 y)^{-2}$ $x = -2$ $y = \sqrt{25}$

⑨ $\sqrt{-gh} - g^{-2}h$ $g = -2$ $h = 8$

Simplify each algebraic expression.

⑩ $3k^2 - 6k + 7k^2 - 5$

⑪ $2(3a^2 + 1) - 7(a - 4)$

⑫ $2d(d + 2) + 5(d - 2)$

⑬ $2x + 5y + 7z - 2y - 3x - 4z$

⑭ $4x^2 + 12xy - 3y^2 - 5xy$

⑮ $j^3 + k(3j^2 + 3jk + k^2)$

⑯ $a^2(a + b^2) - b(a^2b - c)$

⑰ $-d(e^2 + 1) + 4e^2(d + 1)$

Simplify and evaluate.

⑱

	$6p(2p + 3q) - 7pq$	$\frac{3}{4}l + 5\frac{1}{3}w - \frac{1}{8}l - \frac{1}{6}w$	$a(a^3 - b) - (a^4 - 6b)$
simplify			
evaluate	$p = -3 \quad q = 2$	$l = -8 \quad w = \sqrt{36}$	$a = -9 \quad b = 3^{-1}$

Write an algebraic expression each for the perimeter and area of the shapes. Then evaluate when *x* = 1.5.

⑲   *P*:   *A*:

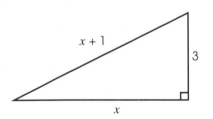

⑳   *P*:   *A*:

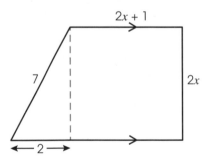

㉑   *P*:   *A*:

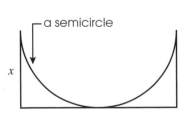

ISBN: 978-1-77149-221-8

Check the correct algebraic expression for each scenario. Then evaluate it.

㉒ Peter is p years old. He says, "Take my age, double it, take away 6, and then square it. The answer will be my uncle's age." How old is Peter's uncle?

Ⓐ $2(p - 6)^2$ Ⓑ $(2p - 6)^2$

If Peter is 7 years old, then his uncle is _____ years old.

Evaluate $(p = 7)$

㉓ A badminton player is practising serving. She serves b shuttlecocks on the first day and she serves 25% more shuttlecocks each day that follows. How many shuttlecocks will she serve in 3 days?

Ⓐ $x + 1.25x + 1.25x$ Ⓑ $x + 1.25x + (1.25)(1.25x)$

If she serves 16 shuttlecocks on the first day, she will serve

_____ shuttlecocks in 3 days.

Evaluate $(b = 16)$

Solve the problems.

㉔ n is a number. What is the difference between the number added to itself and then squared, and 1 less than twice the number? Write an algebraic expression. Find the difference if $n = -9$.

_____

㉕ Brandon has $\$b$. Matthew has $\$100$ more than $\frac{1}{4}$ of what Brandon has. How much do they have in all? Write an algebraic expression. Find the total amount if b is 32.

_____

㉖ To find the sum of n consecutive positive integers (starting from 1), add the smallest and largest numbers, multiply the sum by n, and then divide it by 2. What is the sum? Write an algebraic expression. Find the sum if n is 99.

_____

1.3 Equations

Solve the equations.

① $3x + 5 = 20$

② $-x - 1 = 28$

③ $6a - 12 = 3a - 6$

④ $8p + 4 = 16p$

⑤ $2p + 6 = 3(p + 1)$

⑥ $\frac{1}{3}(a + 6) = 3(\frac{1}{10}a + 3)$

⑦ $\frac{n}{4} + \frac{2}{3} = \frac{n}{2} - \frac{23}{6}$

⑧ $8x - 4 = 2(x + 1)$

⑨ $6(x + 2) = 3(x - 3)$

⑩ $(\sqrt{x})^2 = \frac{-x - 3}{2}$

⑪ $\frac{1}{4} + \frac{1}{3} = \frac{7}{12}x$

⑫ $\sqrt{(x + 2)^2} = 3x + 12$

Solve each equation. Then check your answer by substitution.

⑬ $12x - 4 = 11x$

⑭ $7(a - 2) = 5(a + 4)$

⑮ $\frac{a}{5} - \frac{1}{15} = \frac{a}{3} - \frac{1}{3}$

Check

LS	RS
$12x - 4$	$11x$
$= 12 \times \boxed{} - 4$	$= 11 \times \boxed{}$
$= \boxed{}$	$= \boxed{}$

Check

Check

ISBN: 978-1-77149-221-8

Solve for each unknown with the given information.

⑯ 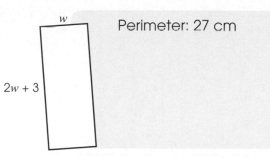 Perimeter: 27 cm

⑰ 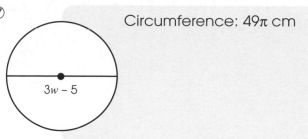 Circumference: 49π cm

⑱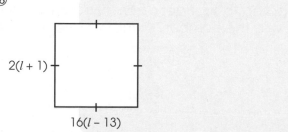

⑲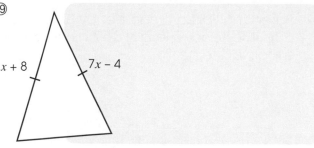

⑳ 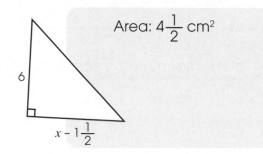 Area: $4\frac{1}{2}$ cm²

㉑ 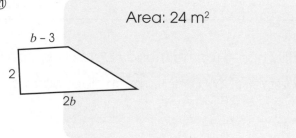 Area: 24 m²

Answer the questions.

㉒ Consider the equation below.

$$x + 2(x - 1) = \frac{1}{2}(6x - 1) - \frac{3}{2}$$

Laura thinks that the solution is $x = 1$, but Alex argues that $x = 3$. Who is correct? Explain.

㉓ Consider the equation below.

$$7x - 6(3x - 2) = 2(7 - 5x) - x$$

David says that the solution is $x = 0$, but Daniel thinks there is no solution. Who is correct? Explain.

ISBN: 978-1-77149-221-8

Set up an equation for each scenario. Then solve it.

㉔ The sum of two numbers is -21. One number is half of 2 less than 3 times the other number. What are the numbers?

_____

㉕ Jared multiplied a number by 3. He was then supposed to subtract 6 from it, but he added 6 to it instead. He got 159 as an answer. What was the number? What answer was he supposed to get?

_____

㉖ Billy has $\frac{3}{4}$ of the money Derek has, and Derek has $\frac{7}{9}$ of the money Jason has. If they have a total of $680, how much does each person have?

_____

㉗ In a 100-m dash, Andre finished 0.1 s slower than Sophie and Yasmine finished 0.04 s after Andre. If their average time was 9.88 s, how long did it take Sophie to finish the dash?

_____

㉘ Three pieces of string form a triangle. The medium one is 2 cm longer than the shortest one and the longest one is 1 cm shorter than twice the medium one. The perimeter of the triangle is 21 cm. What are the side lengths of the triangle?

_____

Identify the form of each equation.

① $y = 3x - 2$ •

$y - 2 = -\dfrac{1}{4}(x - 4)$ •

$3x - y - 2 = 0$ •

$y - 4 = 3(x - 2)$ •

$4x + y - 3 = 0$ •

$y = -\dfrac{1}{2}x$ •

• Slope y-intercept Form

• Standard Form

• Point-slope Form

 HINT

• **Slope y-intercept Form**
$$y = mx + b$$
slope y-intercept

• **Standard Form**
$$Ax + By + C = 0$$

• **Point-slope Form**
$$(y - y_1) = m(x - x_1)$$
slope

Rewrite each equation in slope y-intercept form. Then match each equation with its graph.

② Ⓐ $2x - y + 3 = 0$

Ⓑ $3x + 4y - 8 = 0$

Ⓒ $y - 5 = -3(x + 2)$

Ⓓ $4x = 2y - 3$

Ⓔ $y - 1 = \dfrac{1}{4}(x + 1)$

Ⓕ $y - 1.5 = 1.5(x - 4)$

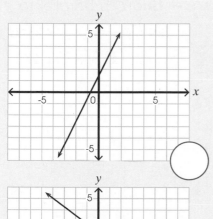
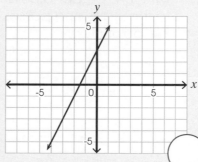
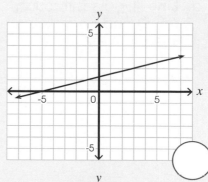
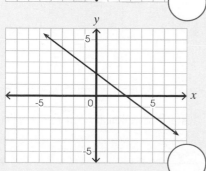
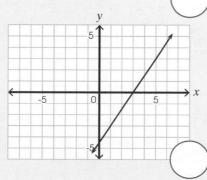
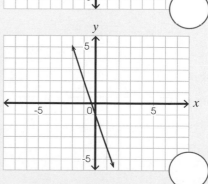

**Identify the slope and *y*-intercept of each equation.
Then graph it and answer the questions.**

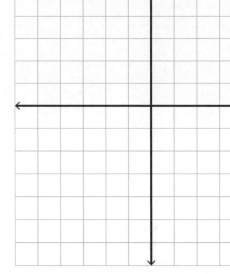

③ $2y = 8x + 6$

④ $y - 3x = 1$

slope: _____

slope: _____

y-intercept: _____

y-intercept: _____

⑤ $x + 4y - 4 = 0$

⑥ $3x - y - 2 = 0$

slope: _____

slope: _____

y-intercept: _____

y-intercept: _____

⑦ Compare the slopes of the lines described below.

a. lines that are parallel _____

b. lines that are perpendicular _____

Write the equation of each line in standard form.

⑧ a. **Line *A*** passes through (-1,-1) and is parallel to line $y = 3x - 2$.

Line *B* is perpendicular to the *x*-axis and passes the point (1,2).

Line *C* is parallel to the line $y = -\frac{1}{3}x - 4$ and its *x*-intercept is at (-6,0).

_____   _____   _____

b. Do any of the equations represent lines that are perpendicular? Explain your reasoning.

_____

_____

   ISBN: 978-1-77149-221-8

Identify whether each statement is true or false.

⑨ A vertical line always has exactly one x-intercept.

T / F

⑩ The lines $y = 4x - 5$ and $2x - 0.5y + 1.8 = 0$ will never intersect.

T / F

⑪ The b in slope y-intercept form of a line is the same as the B in standard form.

T / F

⑫ The y-intercept of $Ax + By + C = 0$ is $-\dfrac{C}{B}$.

T / F

⑬ Given $Ax + By + C = 0$, if $A > 0$, $B < 0$, and $C < 0$, then the line will have a positive y-intercept.

T / F

Write a linear equation for each problem. Then graph it.

⑭ Wilson's office is 60 km away from his home. He drives home from work at a constant speed of 80 km/h. Represent his distance from home over time.

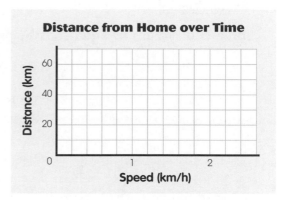

_____

⑮ To make iced tea, Doris mixed black tea with green tea. Represent the amount of each type of tea used to make 1 L of iced tea.

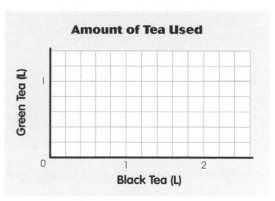

_____

⑯ Joyce was playing a game at a carnival. Hitting a red target gets 3 points and hitting a blue target gets 2 points. She needs 18 points to win a prize. Show the different ways she can win the prize.

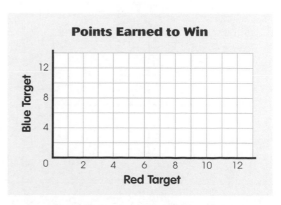

_____

ISBN: 978-1-77149-221-8

2 Systems of Linear Equations

Words TO LEARN

System of linear equations: a set of two or more linear equations

Solution (to a set of equations): a point where a set of equations intersects

Substitution: replacing a variable with a constant or an algebraic expression

Elimination: eliminating a variable from a set of equations

2.1 Graphing Systems of Linear Equations

Example

Solve the system of equations by graphing.

$$y = \frac{1}{2}x - 3 \qquad -x - y = 0$$

slope y-intercept form: $y = -x$

Solution:

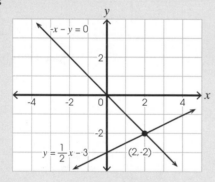

The solution is (2,-2).

TRY THIS

Solve by graphing.

$$y = -x + 3 \qquad 4x - 2y = 0$$

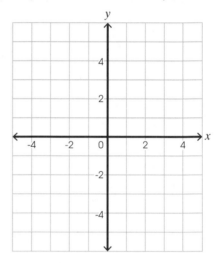

The solution is _____ .

Solve each system of equations by graphing.

① $y = 2x + 1 \qquad x - y = 0$

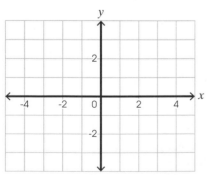

The solution is _____ .

② $2x - 3 = 0 \qquad y + 3 = 0$

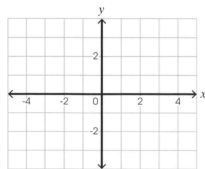

The solution is _____ .

ISBN: 978-1-77149-221-8

③ $y = x - 5$ $-2x - y + 1 = 0$ ④ $y = 4$ $5x + 3y - 2 = 0$

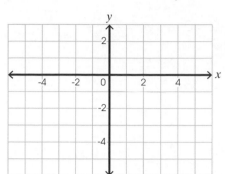   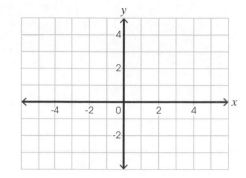

The solution is _____ .   The solution is _____ .

⑤ $4y + 1 = x$ $x + y + 4 = 0$ ⑥ $-2x - y + 7 = 0$ $y - 1 = -\dfrac{1}{3}(x - 3)$

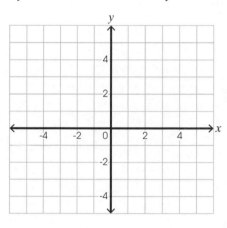   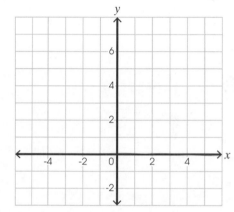

The solution is _____ .   The solution is _____ .

Determine if the given points are solutions to the systems of equations.

 HINT

⑦ $y = -2x$ **Point**
    $y = x + 3$ (-1,2)

⑧ $x + y - 8 = 0$ **Point**
    $2x - y = -1$ (3,5)

_____   _____

⑨ $y = -\dfrac{1}{2}x - 6$ **Point**
    $y = -\dfrac{1}{2}x$ (4,-8)

⑩ $y = -x$ **Point**
    $2x + 4y - 3 = 0$ $(-\dfrac{3}{2}, \dfrac{3}{2})$

_____   _____

> For a point to be a solution to a system of equations, it must satisfy all equations.
>
> e.g. $y = x + 1$ $-2y = 3x - 2$
>   Is (0,1) a solution?
>
> **Solution:** Substitute (0,1) into the equations.
>
> | $y = x + 1$ | | $-2y = 3x - 2$ | |
> |---|---|---|---|
> | LS | RS | LS | RS |
> | 1 | $0 + 1$ | $-2(1)$ | $3(0) - 2$ |
> | | $= 1$ ✔ | $= -2$ | $= -2$ ✔ |
>
> Since (0,1) satisfies both equations, it is a solution.

ISBN: 978-1-77149-221-8

Solve each system of equations by graphing. Then verify your answer.

⑪ $2y = x - 2$ $\frac{2}{3}x + y - \frac{4}{3} = 0$

⑫ $3x - 2y - 2 = 0$ $y = -\frac{1}{2}x + 5$

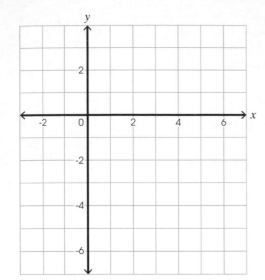

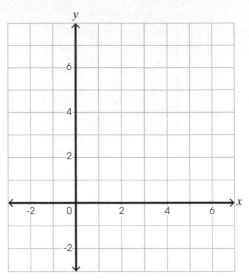

Verify

Verify

Answer the questions.

⑬

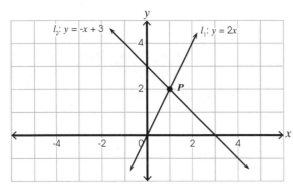

Point P is the intersection of l_1 and l_2. Another line, l_3, will share the same solution and is perpendicular to l_1.

a. Write an equation for l_3.

_____

b. Graph l_3.

⑭

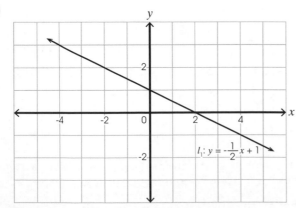

Two lines, l_2 and l_3, intersect l_1 at its y-intercept.

a. Write the equations for l_2 and l_3.

_____

b. Graph l_2 and l_3.

ISBN: 978-1-77149-221-8

Write a system of equations for each problem. Then solve it by graphing.

⑮ Christie types 50 words/min and Steven types 40 words/min. Steven starts typing 2 min sooner than Christie. After how many minutes will they type the same number of words?

Equations: _____

_____

_____

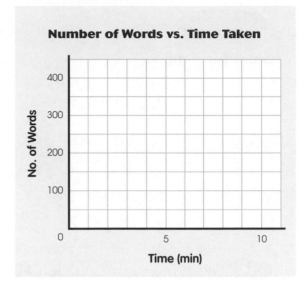

⑯ Sharon bought 3 DVDs and 3 books for $54. Jacob bought 7 DVDs and 10 books for $150. How much do each DVD and each book cost?

_____

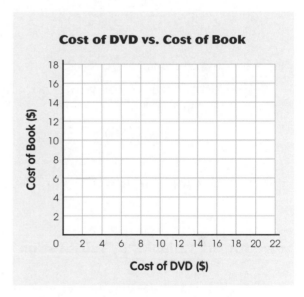

⑰ Bernice spent $13 on 6 bagels and 2 cups of coffee. Marc spent $11 on 2 bagels and 4 cups of coffee. How much do each bagel and each cup of coffee cost?

_____

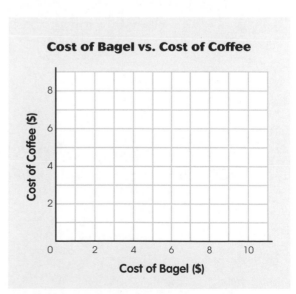

ISBN: 978-1-77149-221-8

2.2   Solving by Substitution

Example

TRY This

Solve for x and y.

$$x + 2y = 12$$
$$2x + 5y = 40$$

Solution:

$$x + 2y = 12 \quad ❶$$
$$2x + 5y = 40 \quad ❷$$

1st Isolate x in equation ❶.

$$x + 2y = 12$$
$$x = -2y + 12$$

2nd Substitute x into equation ❷. Solve for y.

$$2x + 5y = 40$$
$$2(-2y + 12) + 5y = 40$$
$$-4y + 24 + 5y = 40$$
$$y = 16$$

3rd Substitute 16 for y into equation ❶ or ❷ to find x.

$$x + 2(16) = 12$$
$$x = -20$$

The solution is $x = -20$ and $y = 16$.

Solve for x and y.

$$3x + y = 16$$
$$2x + 3y = 20$$

Solve for the variables by substitution.

① $m + 3n = 4$
   $m - 2n = -1$

② $2x + 3 = y$
   $4x - y = 1$

③ $3a + 2b = 24$
   $3a - 2b = -12$

④ $x + 3y = 19$
   $5x + 3y = 35$

⑤ $2p + 3q = 5$
   $8p + 6q = 0$

⑥ $t = 2s - 3$
   $s = t - 1$

⑦ $2x + 4y = 2$

$3x - 2y = 0$

⑧ $6x + 9y = 7$

$7x - 5y = 3$

⑨ $2(w + l) = 42$

$w = \frac{1}{2}l - 3$

⑩ $11x + 33y = 55$

$-7x + 21y = 28$

⑪ $8 - 5a = 3b$

$4a + 2b = -2$

⑫ $7x - 5y = 26$

$-6x + 7y = -6$

Solve for the point of intersection for each linear system. Then verify by graphing.

⑬ $2x + 3y - 3 = 0$

$4x - 6y + 2 = 0$

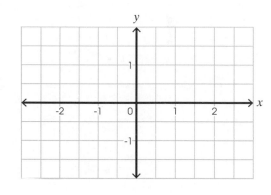

⑭ $y = \frac{1}{2}x + 4$

$y = -x + 1$

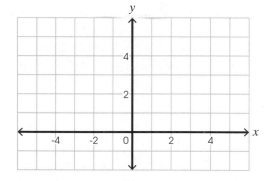

⑮ $x + 3y - 6 = 0$

$y = -\frac{1}{3}x - 1$

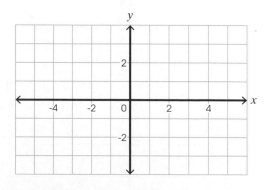

ISBN: 978-1-77149-221-8

Solve each linear system. Check your answers and show your work.

⑯ $m = 3n + 3$

 $2n - 7 = \frac{1}{2}m$

⑰ $x + y = 10\ 000$

 $0.03x + 0.012y = 282$

Your answers are correct if they satisfy all the equations in a system.

Check

Check

⑱ $0.4x + 0.15y = 72$

 $x + y = 240$

⑲ $2h + m = 25$

 $0.1h + 0.2m = 1.01$

⑳ $2.5i + 0.5j = 17$

 $10 - i - j = 0$

Check

Check

Check

Answer the questions.

㉑ Consider the equations given.

a. Does it matter which variable is solved first? Explain.

_____

_____

Equations

$3x + 2y = -1$ ❶

$4x + y = 12$ ❷

b. Do you have a preference for which variable to solve first? Explain.

_____

_____

c. Leo isolated y in equation ❷ and substituted the value of y back into equation ❷ to solve for x. Would he be able to solve for x? If not, how should he solve it?

_____

_____

Write a system of equations for each problem. Then solve by substitution.

㉒ Last year, the school math club spent $144 to buy T-shirts for $11 each and badges for $1 each. This year, for the same number of T-shirts and badges, they spent $165 on T-shirts for $12.50 each and badges for $1.25 each. How many T-shirts and badges did the club buy this year?

_____

㉓ The sum of an integer and twice the smaller integer is 17. The difference of the two integers is 5. What are the integers?

_____

㉔ Natalie walked at 2 km/h and ran at 6 km/h. She lives 3 km away from Kathy and arrived at her house in 45 min. How much of the distance did she walk and how much of it did she run?

_____

㉕ The perimeter of an isosceles triangle is 21 cm. One side is 3 cm less than another side. What are the side lengths of the triangle?

HINT

There are two possible sets of solutions.

_____

ISBN: 978-1-77149-221-8

2.3 Solving by Elimination

Example

Solve for x and y.

$$4x + 6y = 42$$
$$2x - y = -11$$

Solution: $4x + 6y = 42$ **①**

$2x - y = -11$ **②**

1st Multiply equation **②** by 2 to get $4x$.

$2(2x - y) = 2(-11)$ **②** × 2
$4x - 2y = -22$

2nd Subtract equation **①** by **②** × 2 to eliminate the x terms.

$4x + 6y = 42$ **①**

$-)$ $4x - 2y = -22$ **②** × 2
_____

$8y = 64$
$y = 8$

3rd Substitute 8 into y of equation **①** or **②** to get x.

$2x - 8 = -11$
$x = -1.5$

The solution is $x = -1.5$ and $y = 8$.

Try This

Solve for m and n.

$$m + 3n = 16$$
$$2m + 5n = 24$$

Solve for the variables by elimination.

① $a + 3b = 4$
$a - 4b = -3$

② $3x - y = 2$
$-x - y = 6$

③ $p + 4q = 2$
$3p + 5q = -1$

④
$2g + 7h = -46$
$5g - h = 33$

⑤
$7x + y = 33$
$9x - 2y = -20$

⑥
$4i + j = 81$
$3i + 3j = 81$

⑦
$3d - 4e = 5$
$2d - 8e = -34$

⑧
$7r - 2s = -1$
$3r + 4s = 53$

⑨
$2v + 3w = 5$
$3v - 2w = 14$

⑩
$4x + 3y = -1$
$6x - 5y = -87$

⑪
$8e + 9f = 7$
$10e - 6f = 3$

⑫
$-6a + 5b = -2$
$12a + 4b = 11$

ISBN: 978-1-77149-221-8

Solve each linear system by elimination. Verify your solution by graphing.

⑬ $3x + 6y + 3 = 0$
$y = -2x + 7$

⑭ $5x - 2y - 10 = 0$
$7x + 4y - 14 = 0$

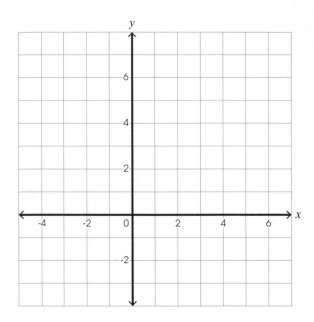

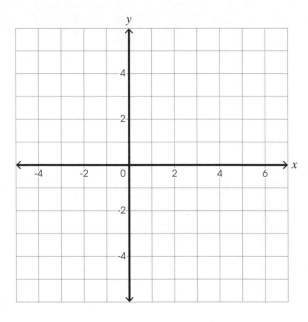

⑮ $-\dfrac{8}{5}x = y - 6$
$4x - y - 1 = 0$

⑯ $6x - y - 1 = 0$
$x - 6y - 48 = 0$

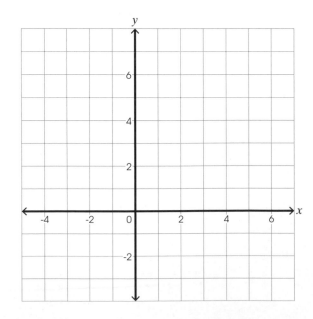

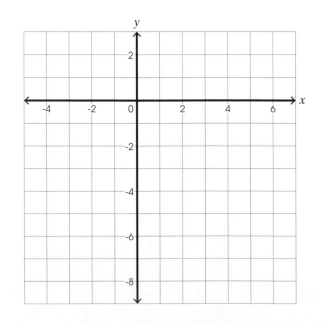

    ISBN: 978-1-77149-221-8

Solve each problem by elimination. Show your work.

⑰ The sum of an integer and three times one less than a second integer is 27. The second integer is 3 more than two times the first integer. What are the integers?

⑱ In 6 years, Brandon will be double the age of Debbie. 2 years ago, Brandon's age was 1 year more than triple of Debbie's age. How old are they now?

⑲ The sum of the perimeters of a square and an equilateral triangle is 45 cm. The perimeter of the square is 3 cm greater. Find the side lengths of each shape.

⑳ Jackson was in a 5-km marathon. He ran at 4 km/h for part of it and walked at 2 km/h for the rest. If it took him 1.5 h to complete the marathon, how long did he run and walk for?

㉑ A farmer's coop has chickens and rabbits. He says to his son, "There are a total of 38 heads and 118 legs." How many chickens and rabbits are there in the coop?

ISBN: 978-1-77149-221-8

Solve each problem by either substitution or elimination. Show your work.

㉒ The sum of two fractions with denominators of 8 and 6 is $\frac{13}{24}$. If the numerators of the fractions are switched, the sum is $\frac{5}{8}$. Find both of the original fractions.

㉓ David's piggy bank has 236 coins. 20 of them are nickels and the rest are dimes and quarters. If there is a total of $30.70, how many of his coins are quarters?

㉔ A 250-g brownie bar is made from a mix of dark and white chocolate. Using 120 g of dark and 130 g of white chocolate costs $3.70. Using 90 g of dark and 160 g of white chocolate costs $3.40. What are the costs of dark chocolate and white chocolate?

㉕ A ski resort is 240 km from Jeff's home. To get there, Jeff drove at 60 km/h to Simon's house, then Simon drove them both to the resort at 120 km/h. This took 2 h 20 min. What is the distance Jeff drove to Simon's house?

㉖ A science teacher is preparing for an experiment. She needs to make 6 L of 25% alcohol solution that is mixed from 60% and 10% alcohol solutions. How much of each solution does she need?

2.4 Possible Solutions

Graph the systems consisting $y = -x + 2$. Find the solutions. Then answer the questions.

①

System A

$y = -x + 2$
$2x + 2y = 4$

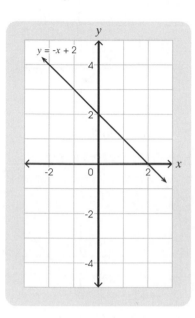

System B

$y = -x + 2$
$x + y + 1 = 0$

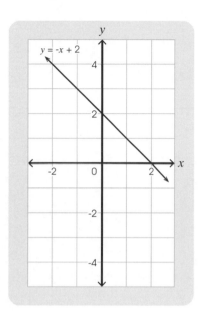

System C

$y = -x + 2$
$2x - y - 5 = 0$

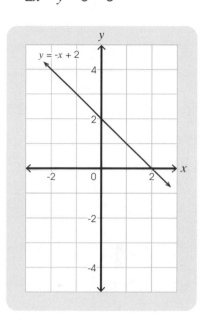

② Which linear system has an infinite number of solutions? Describe the relationship of the lines and compare their slopes.

_____

_____

③ Which linear system has no solutions? Describe the relationship of the lines and compare their slopes.

_____

_____

④ Which linear system has exactly one solution? Describe the relationship of the lines and compare their slopes.

_____

_____

⑤ The slopes of these two lines are the same but their y-intercepts are different. Which linear system is this?

_____

ISBN: 978-1-77149-221-8

Solve each linear system by substitution or by elimination. Then describe the relationship of the lines using the solutions.

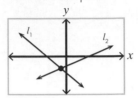
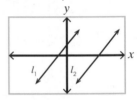
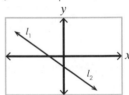

⑥ $2x + 5y = 12$

$\frac{1}{5}x + \frac{1}{2}y = -1$

_____

⑦ $0.7x + 1.4y = 2.1$

$-\frac{1}{2}x - y = -\frac{3}{2}$

_____

⑧ $-7x + 12y = 11$

$13x + 18y = 16\frac{1}{2}$

_____

⑨ $6y = -5x + 2$

$\frac{1}{3}x + \frac{2}{5}y = \frac{2}{15}$

⑩ $4x - 7y + 3\frac{1}{9} = 0$

$7y = 4x + 98$

_____   _____

_____   _____

 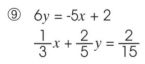 ISBN: 978-1-77149-221-8

Determine how many solutions each linear system has without solving them. Explain your reasoning.

⑪ $3x + 4y = 2$
$3x - 4y = 7$

No. of Solutions

_____

_____

_____

⑫ $x + 3y - 2 = 0$
$18x + 54y = 36$

No. of Solutions

_____

_____

_____

⑬ $2x - y - 7 = 0$
$0.5x - 0.25y - 0.3 = 0$

No. of Solutions

_____

_____

_____

Write equations with the given information.

⑭ Given that l_1 has the equation $3x - 2y + 7 = 0$, give another equation to make a system with

a. 1 solution.

_____

b. no solutions.

_____

c. an infinite number of solutions.

_____

⑮ Given that l_1 has the equation $7x + 6y - 12 = 0$,

a. write an equation of l_2 that has one point of intersection with l_1 and is perpendicular to it.

_____

b. write an equation of l_3 that will never intersect l_1.

_____

Answer the questions.

⑯ Given that l_1: $7x + 14y - 12 = 0$ and l_2: $kx - 5y + 3 = 0$ have no solutions, find the value of k.

_____

⑰ Given that l_1: $\frac{1}{2}x - \frac{1}{6}y + \frac{1}{3} = 0$ and l_2: $Ax + By + C = 0$, find a set of possible values for A, B, and C if

a. there is an infinite number of solutions.

_____

b. there are no solutions.

_____

⑱ Given the system of equations: $2x + 5y - 8 = 0$ and $2x + 5y + 4 = 0$,
a. find how many solutions it has.

_____

b. add a third equation to the system which does not affect the existing number of solutions.

_____

⑲ Given that l_1: $y = \frac{1}{3}x - 2$ and l_2: $3x - y + 2 = 0$, find the equation of a line that will intersect l_1 but not l_2.

_____

Set up the equations for each problem. Solve it if possible and show your work.

⑳ At a carnival, two clowns asked Jane to find their ages. Clown A said, "3 years ago, he was twice my age." Clown B said, "In 2 years, I'll be 5 less than twice his age." Can Jane find their ages based on the information? Explain.

_____

㉑ Mr. Li mixed 3 L of salt solution from the first jar with 2 L of salt solution from the second jar to form 5 L of 30% salt solution. Later, he mixed 6 L of the first jar and 4 L of the second jar to get 10 L of 30% salt solutions. What were the salt concentrations in the jars?

_____

㉒ Maxine ran 10 km on Sunday and 5 km/day afterwards. Natalie ran 6 km on Sunday and 5.5 km/day afterwards. After how many days would they have run the same total distance?

_____

㉓ 3 bags of chips and 3 bars of chocolate cost $12.15. 2 bags of chips and 2 bars of chocolate cost $8.10. How much does 1 bag of chips cost?

_____

㉔ Danny creates board games. He bought some dice for 50¢ each and blank cards for 80¢ each, for a total of $46. He later found another store that sells dice at 25¢ each and cards at 60¢ each, and spent a total of $27. He bought the same number of dice and cards at both stores. How many dice did he buy in all?

_____

3 Analytic Geometry

Words TO LEARN

Midpoint: a point that divides a line into two equal halves

Median: a line segment that joins a vertex of a triangle to the midpoint of its opposite side

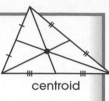
centroid

Altitude: a line segment that joins a vertex of a triangle and the perpendicular line of its opposite side

Centroid: the intersection of the three medians of a triangle

Circumcentre: the intersection of the perpendicular bisectors of the three sides of a triangle

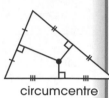
circumcentre

Orthocentre: the intersection of the three altitudes of a triangle

orthocentre

3.1 Length of a Line Segment

TRY THIS

Find the length of Line GH in the graph.

Example

Find the length of Line EF in the graph.

Solution: Use the Pythagorean theorem.

$$c^2 = a^2 + b^2$$

$$EF^2 = 3^2 + 4^2$$
$$EF^2 = 25$$
$$EF = 5$$

The length is 5 units.

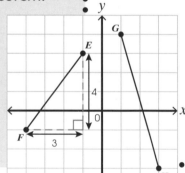

Find the length of each line segment.

① Line MN

② Line OP

③ Line QR

④ Line ST

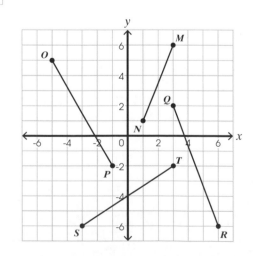

ISBN: 978-1-77149-221-8

Find the exact lengths of the lines with the given end points.

⑤
P(4,5)   Q(9,7)

⑥
S(2,-4)   T(4,3)

⑦
C(-1,5)   D(2,18)

⑧
J(2.5,7)   K(4,9)

⑨
M(0,-5)   N(9,$\frac{1}{2}$)

⑩
X(-3,-1)   Y(-$\frac{1}{2}$,0)

HINT

Distance Formula

The distance, d, of a line segment with end points, $A(x_1, y_1)$ and $B(x_2, y_2)$ is given as follows:

$$d = \sqrt{(x_2 - x_1)^2 + (y_2 - y_1)^2}$$

e.g. Find the length of a line segment with end points $A(1,1)$ and $B(3,4)$.

Solution:

$$d = \sqrt{(3-1)^2 + (4-1)^2}$$
$$= \sqrt{2^2 + 3^2}$$
$$= \sqrt{13}$$

The length is $\sqrt{13}$ units.

Answer the questions.

⑪
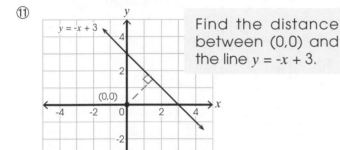

Find the distance between (0,0) and the line $y = -x + 3$.

1st Find the equation of the line that is perpendicular to $y = -x + 3$ and passes through the origin.

2nd Find the point of intersection of the two lines.

3rd Take (0,0) and the point of intersection as end points to find the distance.

⑫
Find the distance between (-2,-5) and the line $4x + y - 4 = 0$.

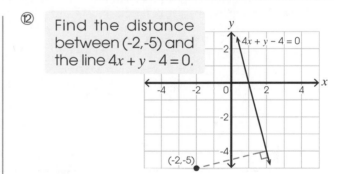

1st

2nd

3rd

Solve the problems. Show your work.

⑬ Ms. Ho is planning a scavenger hunt. She places Team A at (-4,17), Team B at (6,13), and the prize at (1,-2). Are Team A and Team B the same distance from the prize?

_____

⑭ A cable for a ski lift has stations at $A(-10,7)$, $B(-1,9)$, $C(8,-1)$, and $D(11,-4)$. How long is the cable?

_____

⑮ Wilson's home is at (2,18). There is a coffee shop at (3,15). A new tea store will open due north of Wilson and its distance from Wilson is the same as Wilson's distance from the coffee shop.

a. Where will the tea store be?

_____

b. Each unit on the grid represents 1 km. How far from the coffee shop will the tea store be?

_____

⑯ A path is modelled by the equation $y = 2x - 6$. Bailey is at (1,2.5) and he travels the shortest distance to get to the path. How far does he travel if each unit represents 10 m?

_____

   ISBN: 978-1-77149-221-8

Example

TRY THIS

Find the midpoint of Line AB.

Solution: Use the midpoint formula.

$$(x,y) = (\frac{x_1 + x_2}{2}, \frac{y_1 + y_2}{2})$$

Find the midpoint of a line with end points (4,5) and (-1,-3).

End points: $A(-3,-2)$ and $B(1,3)$

$$(x,y) = (\frac{-3 + 1}{2}, \frac{-2 + 3}{2})$$

$$= (-1, 0.5)$$

The midpoint is (-1,0.5).

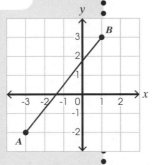

Find the midpoints of the lines in the graph and the lines with the given end points.

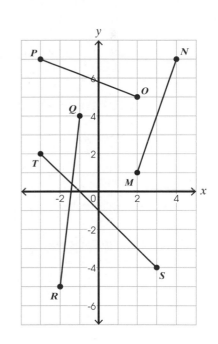

① Line MN

Line OP

Line QR

Line ST

② (-3,1) (4,-1)

③ (-2,-4) (5,0)

④ $(0, \frac{1}{2})$ (5,3)

⑤ $(a + 1, 0)$ $(0, a - 1)$

⑥ $(\frac{a}{2}, -1)$ (-2, a)

⑦ $(2a - 1, 1)$ $(a, 2a)$

Find the end points with the given points.

⑧
midpoint	end point
(-1,-4)	(2,-5)

x-coordinate: *y*-coordinate:

$-1 = \dfrac{x + 2}{2}$ $-4 = \dfrac{y + (-5)}{2}$

$x =$ _____ $y =$ _____

End point: (_____ , _____)

⑨
midpoint	end point
(3,7)	(6,-1)

⑩
midpoint	end point
$(6\frac{1}{2},15)$	(4,12)

⑪
midpoint	end point
$(0,-5\frac{1}{2})$	$(-\frac{3}{2},0)$

⑫
midpoint	end point
(0,0)	(-4,5)

⑬
midpoint	end point
(-2.5,0)	(1.5,4)

⑭
midpoint	end point
(a,-1)	(a − 1,a)

⑮
midpoint	end point
(-1,a)	(0,a + 1)

⑯
midpoint	end point
(a,a)	(a + 1,2a)

Answer the questions.

⑰ Point *A* is at (0,6) and Point *B* is at (4,0).

a. Point *M* is the midpoint of Line *AB*. What are the coordinates of Point *M*?

b. Point *B* is the midpoint of Line *AC*. What are the coordinates of Point *C*?

c. What is the length of Line *AC*?

d. Write an equation for Line *AC*.

ISBN: 978-1-77149-221-8

Draw the median as specified. Then find an equation of each median.

⑱ median from Vertex X

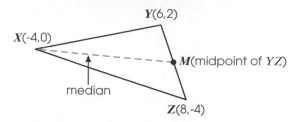

X(-4,0)
Y(6,2)
M(midpoint of YZ)
median
Z(8,-4)

1st Find the coordinates of the midpoint M of Line YZ.

2nd Find the slope of the median.

3rd Find an equation of the median.

⑲ median from Vertex D

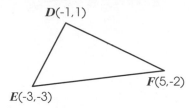

D(-1,1)
E(-3,-3)
F(5,-2)

⑳ median from Vertex K

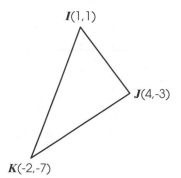

I(1,1)
J(4,-3)
K(-2,-7)

median from Vertex J

Solve the problems. Show your work.

㉑ A line segment has end points at $(k + 3, 2)$ and $(3, l + 2)$, and a midpoint at $(-1, -4)$. What are the values of k and l?

_____

㉒ A quadrilateral has vertices at $A(-7, 2)$, $B(-2, 3)$, $C(-6, 6)$, and $D(-1, 7)$. Determine if the diagonals have the same midpoint.

_____

㉓ The diameter of a circle is drawn from $(5, 3)$ to $(-1, -5)$. What are the coordinates of the centre of the circle? What is the diameter of the circle?

_____

㉔ Given the diagram shown,

a. what are the coordinates of R?

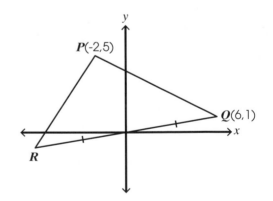

_____

b. what is the perimeter of $\triangle PQR$?

_____

Example

Find the equation of a circle with centre **(0,0)** and passes through **(3,8)**.

Solution: Find the radius first.

$$x^2 + y^2 = r^2$$
$$3^2 + 8^2 = r^2 \longleftarrow \text{substitute values}$$
$$r^2 = 73 \qquad \text{of } x \text{ and } y$$

The equation is $x^2 + y^2 = 73$.

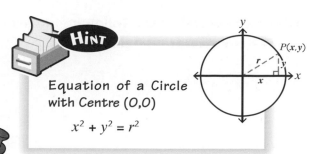

HINT

Equation of a Circle with Centre (0,0)

$$x^2 + y^2 = r^2$$

TRY This

Find the equation of a circle with centre **(0,0)** and passes through **(2,4)**.

Write the equations of the circles. Then match the equations with their graphs.

① a. radius of 1.5

_____ ◯

b. x-intercepts of 2 and -2

_____ ◯

c. passing through (0,6)

_____ ◯

d. diameter of 8

_____ ◯

e. y-intercepts of 1 and -1

_____ ◯

f. passing through (2.5,0)

_____ ◯

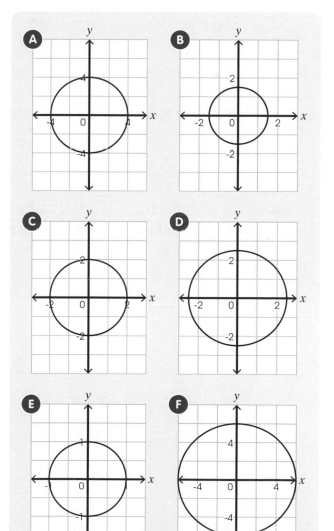

Determine whether the following points lie on, within, or outside the circles modelled by the given equations.

Consider a point at (x,y).
- It lies on the circle if
$$x^2 + y^2 = r^2$$
- It lies within the circle if
$$x^2 + y^2 < r^2$$
- It lies outside the circle if
$$x^2 + y^2 > r^2$$

② $x^2 + y^2 = 10$ (2,3)

③ $x^2 + y^2 = 50$ (-7,2)

④ $x^2 + y^2 = 29$ (2,-5)

⑤ $x^2 + y^2 = 9^2$ (-4,-6)

Solve the problems. Show your work.

⑥ Gavin drew a clock which is centred at (0,0) on a Cartesian coordinate plane. He shaded in the area the hour hand would cover from 1:00 to 3:00. If the area is 37.5π square units, what would the coordinates of the hour hand at 3:00 be?

⑦ A sailboat is sailing three laps around an island which is centred at the origin. The boat started sailing at (20,21). Find the total distance the sailboat will travel.

⑧ Mr. Ruffles wants to open a restaurant at (0,0). He expects that it will serve all residents within a 12.65-km radius. Write an equation to show the area the restaurant will serve. Ruffland is at (-4,11) and Kinfield is at (12,5). Are both locations within the restaurant's range?

3.4 Medians and Centroids

Example

Triangle ABC has its vertices as given in the diagram. Find the equation of the median from Vertex A.

Solution:

1st Find the midpoint, M, of BC.

$$(x,y) = (\frac{6 + (-4)}{2}, \frac{(-5) + 1}{2})$$
$$= (1,-2)$$

2nd Find the slope of the median.

$$m = \frac{7 - (-2)}{0 - 1}$$
$$= -9$$

3rd Find the equation.

$$y - (-2) = -9(x - 1)$$
$$y = -9x + 7$$

The equation is $y = -9x + 7$.

TRY This

Refer to Triangle ABC. Find the equation of the median from Vertex B.

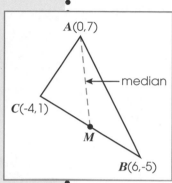

$A(0,7)$

median

$C(-4,1)$

M

$B(6,-5)$

Find the equations of the three medians of each triangle.

①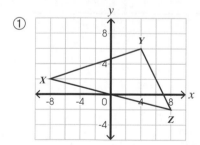

Median XM Median YM Median ZM

②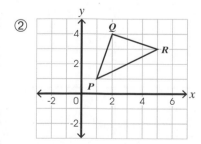

Median PM Median QM Median RM

ISBN: 978-1-77149-221-8

COMPLETE MATHSMART (GRADE 10)   **45**

Find the coordinates of the centroid of each triangle.

Steps to finding centroids

1st Find the equations of the medians.

2nd Solve for *x* and *y* with two of the equations.

3rd Check your answer by graphing.

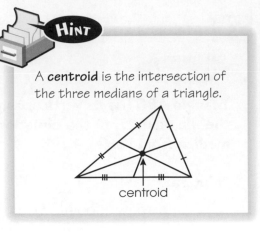

HINT

A **centroid** is the intersection of the three medians of a triangle.

centroid

③   *I*(1,2)   *J*(5,10)   *K*(6,3)

1st   **2nd**   **3rd**

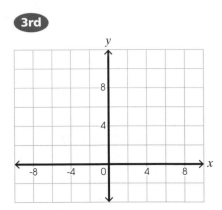

④   *D*(-3,-1)   *E*(2,7)   *F*(4,0)

1st   **2nd**   **3rd**

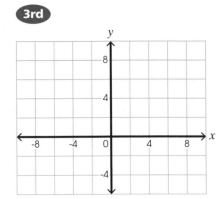

⑤   *X*(-2,1)   *Y*(1,2)   *Z*(2,-1)

1st   **2nd**   **3rd**

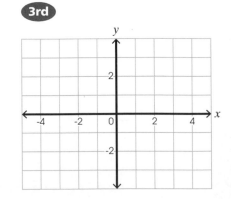

          ISBN: 978-1-77149-221-8

Solve the problems. Show your work.

⑥ Sidney was finding treasure. He left his home at (6,4) to seek the wise Yagua at (12,-2). He planned to go to Dragon's Lalr at (-1,-4) after the visit but he found the treasure exactly halfway between Yagua's home and Dragon's Lair. Then he went home. Find the equation of his route back home.

_____

⑦ Three bus stations are at $A(-1,-4)$, $B(5,4)$, and $C(6,-3)$ on a grid. Julia started at Station A and walked toward Station B. She stopped halfway to wait for her friend, Emma, who came from Station C. Write an equation to describe Emma's route.

_____

⑧ A triangular table top has its vertices at $P(0,0)$, $Q(7,16)$, and $R(13,8)$. Kelly wants to mark the centre of gravity of the table top for screwing in the supporting leg. What are the coordinates of the marking?

HINT

The centroid of a triangle is often referred to as the centre of gravity.

_____

⑨ Three wizards are standing at $A(-6,-4)$, $B(-1,3)$, and $C(7,1)$. They focus their magical powers on the altar that is positioned at the centroid. What are the coordinates of the altar?

_____

ISBN: 978-1-77149-221-8

3.5 Perpendicular Bisectors and Circumcentres

Example

Given the coordinates of the vertices of Triangle XYZ, find the equation of the perpendicular bisector of XZ.

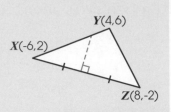

Solution:

1st Find the midpoint of XZ.

$$(x,y) = (\frac{-6 + 8}{2}, \frac{2 + (-2)}{2})$$

$$= (1,0)$$

2nd Find the slopes of XZ and its perpendicular bisector.

$$m_{xz} = \frac{-2 - 2}{8 - (-6)} = -\frac{2}{7}$$

$$\boxed{m_{\perp}} = \frac{7}{2} \leftarrow m_{\perp}:\text{ slope of the perpendicular bisector}$$

3rd Find the equation.

$$y - 0 = \frac{7}{2}(x - 1)$$

$$y = \frac{7}{2}x - \frac{7}{2}$$

The equation is $y = \frac{7}{2}x - \frac{7}{2}$.

Hint

The slope of a line and that of its perpendicular line are negative reciprocals of each other.

e.g. If the slope of Line AB is $\frac{2}{5}$, the slope of its perpendicular line is $-\frac{5}{2}$.

Try This

Refer to Triangle XYZ. Find the equation of the perpendicular bisector of XY.

Find the equation of the perpendicular bisector of each side of the triangle as specified.

①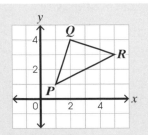

Vertices

$P(\underline{\hspace{1cm}} , \underline{\hspace{1cm}})$

$Q(\underline{\hspace{1cm}} , \underline{\hspace{1cm}})$

$R(\underline{\hspace{1cm}} , \underline{\hspace{1cm}})$

PQ	PR	QR

ISBN: 978-1-77149-221-8

Find the equations of the perpendicular bisectors.
Then find the circumcentre of the triangle.

A **circumcentre** is the intersection of the perpendicular bisectors (or right bisectors) of the three sides of a triangle.

circumcentre

②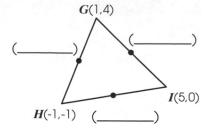

m_{GH} = _____ $m_\perp$ = _____

m_{GI} = _____ $m_\perp$ = _____

m_{HI} = _____ $m_\perp$ = _____

perpendicular bisector of GH:

_____

perpendicular bisector of GI: circumcentre of $\triangle GHI$:

_____

perpendicular bisector of HI:

_____

③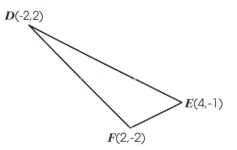

perpendicular bisectors:

circumcentre of $\triangle DEF$:

④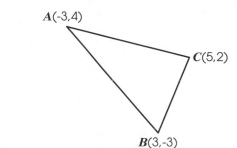

perpendicular bisectors:

circumcentre of $\triangle ABC$:

Find the circumcentre of each triangle with the given vertices. Use a compass to verify your answer by graphing.

⑤ △*ABC*

   A(-1,3)

   B(-4,-6)

   C(3,-5)

   _____

   △*PQR*

   P(-10,6)

   Q(-8,0)

   R(-2,2)

   _____

   △*HIJ*

   H(9,5)

   I(13,1)

   J(7,-1)

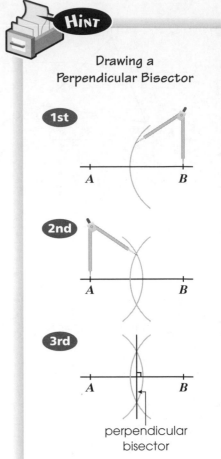

HINT

Drawing a
Perpendicular Bisector

1st

2nd

3rd

perpendicular
bisector

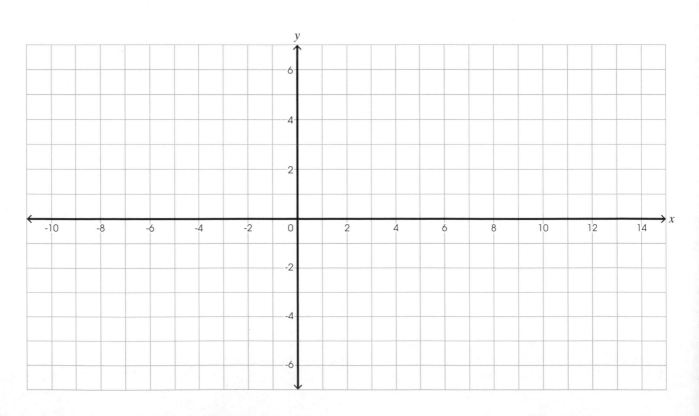

ISBN: 978-1-77149-221-8

Solve the problems. Show your work.

⑥ King Leo wants to divide his triangular land by bisecting each side of his land perpendicularly. The vertices of his land are at $A(0,0)$, $B(3,12)$, and $C(9,3)$.

   a. Find the equations of the dividers.

_____

   b. King Leo resides at the point where the three dividers meet. What are the coordinates of the King's residence?

_____

⑦ The equation of a circle is $x^2 + y^2 = 50$. Tori draws a triangle with its vertices on the circle at $(5,5)$, $(-5,-5)$, and $(5,-5)$.

   a. What is the circumcentre of the triangle?

_____

   b. Pick another set of three points of a triangle that lie on the circle. Does the triangle have the same circumcentre as Tori's?

_____

ISBN: 978-1-77149-221-8

3.6 Altitudes and Orthocentres

Example

Find the equation of the altitude, CG, in the given triangle.

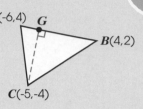

Solution:

1st Find the slope of CG.

$$m_{AB} = \frac{2-4}{4-(-6)} = -\frac{1}{5}$$

$$m_{CG} = 5 \longleftarrow \text{negative reciprocal of } -\frac{1}{5}$$

2nd Find the equation.

$$y - (-4) = 5(x - (-5))$$
$$y = 5x + 21$$

The equation is $y = 5x + 21$.

Try This

Refer to Triangle ABC. Find the equation of the altitude from Vertex A.

Draw the altitudes in each triangle. Then find the equations of the altitudes.

①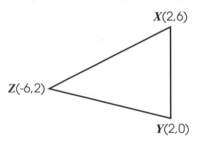

$X(2,6)$

$Z(-6,2)$

$Y(2,0)$

②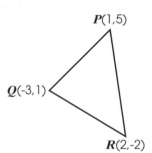

$P(1,5)$

$Q(-3,1)$

$R(2,-2)$

Find the equations of the altitudes and the orthocentre of each triangle.

③

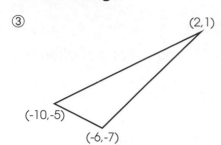

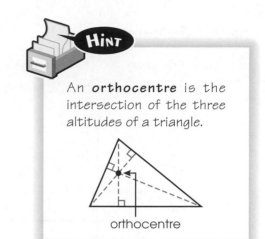

Equations of Altitudes

_____ _____ _____

Orthocentre

_____

④

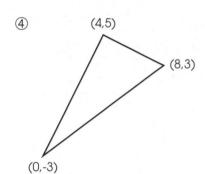

Equations of Altitudes

_____ _____ _____

Orthocentre

_____

⑤

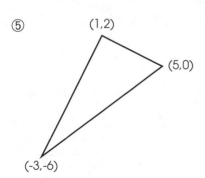

Equations of Altitudes

_____ _____ _____

Orthocentre

_____

ISBN: 978-1-77149-221-8

Answer the questions.

⑥ Two triangles are given as shown.

a. Match the equations of the altitudes with the correct triangles.

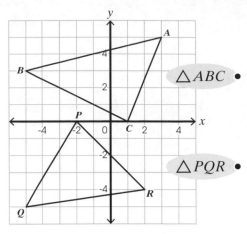

△ABC •

△PQR •

equations of altitudes

- $y = -\dfrac{2}{5}x + 1$
- $y = -4x + 4$
- $y = x$
- $y = -\dfrac{3}{5}x - 2\dfrac{4}{5}$
- $y = -7x - 14$
- $y = 2x - 1$

b. Find the coordinates of the orthocentres.

△ABC

△PQR

⑦ A triangle has its vertices at $A(5,4)$, $B(-1,-4)$, and $C(6,-3)$. Sketch the triangle and show that AC is an altitude of the triangle.

_____

⑧ Identify and draw the orthocentres of the right triangles shown. Find the relationship between the vertex at the right angle and the orthocentre of a right triangle.

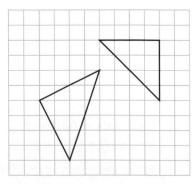

_____

ISBN: 978-1-77149-221-8

Solve the problems. Show your work.

⑨ Jackie traces the front face of a roof. The roof forms a triangle with two vertices at (-6,12) and (2,12) and the tip of the roof at (1,16). Find the equation of the altitude from the base of the roof to its tip.

Make a sketch here.

⑩ A line has end points at $P(-8,-3)$ and the origin. The area of the triangle formed between P, Q, and the origin is 20 square units. What are the coordinates of Q if Q lies below the origin on the y-axis? Find the equation of the altitude of (0,0) and Q.

Make a sketch here.

⑪ Find the equation of the altitude of AC and the area of the shaded region.

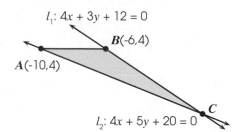

l_1: $4x + 3y + 12 = 0$

$B(-6,4)$

$A(-10,4)$

C

l_2: $4x + 5y + 20 = 0$

⑫ The orthocentre of the triangle shown is at (-2,-1). Find a.

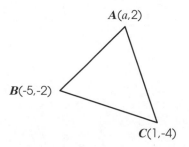

$A(a,2)$

$B(-5,-2)$

$C(1,-4)$

ISBN: 978-1-77149-221-8

3.7   Classifying Shapes

Example

The points $A(-1,-1)$, $B(1,5)$, and $C(5,1)$ form a triangle. Classify the triangle by its sides.

Solution: Find the side lengths.

l_{AB}: $\sqrt{(1-(-1))^2+(5-(-1))^2} = \sqrt{40}$

l_{AC}: $\sqrt{(5-(-1))^2+(1-(-1))^2} = \sqrt{40}$

l_{BC}: $\sqrt{(5-1)^2+(1-5)^2} = \sqrt{32}$

Two sides have the same length. It is an isosceles triangle.

TRY THIS

Classify the triangle with vertices at $P(-6,2)$, $Q(-3,-4)$, and $R(7,1)$ by its sides.

HINT

$d = \sqrt{(x_2-x_1)^2+(y_2-y_1)^2}$

Classify each triangle by its sides. Then determine whether or not it is a right triangle.

① $X(0,7)$ $Y(-6,-11)$ $Z(6,-5)$

side lengths

slopes

② $D(-1,3)$ $E(-4,-6)$ $F(5,1)$

side lengths

slopes

③ $A(2,1)$ $B(4,4)$ $C(4,-2)$

side lengths

slopes

④ $P(-8,3)$ $Q(0,7)$ $R(2,3)$

side lengths

slopes

ISBN: 978-1-77149-221-8

Sketch each quadrilateral with the given vertices. Then find its side lengths and the slopes of the sides to determine the type of quadrilateral it is.

⑤

W(1,4) X(5,8)
Y(14,5) Z(10,1)

_____

⑥

A(2,1) B(1,3)
C(5,5) D(6,3)

_____

⑦

I(-1,4) J(6,1)
K(3,-6) L(-4,-3)

_____

⑧

P(-1,6) Q(1,1)
R(-1,-4) S(-3,1)

_____

Solve the problems.

⑨ Two points, $A(-4,3)$ and $B(5,0)$, both lie on the circle $x^2 + y^2 = 5^2$.

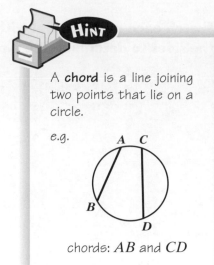

   a. What is the equation of the perpendicular bisector of chord AB?

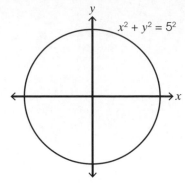

   b. Does the perpendicular bisector of chord AB pass through the centre of the circle?

⑩ $S(9,25)$ and $T(-5,-23)$ both lie on a circle that is centred at $(2,1)$. Is ST a diameter of the circle?

⑪ Milo needs to cut a wooden circle in half. He marked $X(10,0)$ and $Y(-8,-6)$ on the edge of the circle. Explain how Milo can make use of the points X and Y to find the equation of the line that cuts the circle in half. Then find the equation of the line.

Explanation:

Equation of the line:

Answer the questions.

⑫ A square has the vertices shown. The midpoints of the sides join to form another shape.

    a. Without graphing, identify and name the new shape by finding the lengths and slopes of the lines.

    b. Find the area of the new shape.

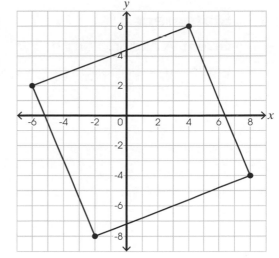

⑬ A and B are the midpoints of PQ and QR respectively.

    a. What type of triangle is $\triangle PQR$?

    b. Without finding the actual areas, show that the area of $\triangle AQB = \dfrac{1}{4}\triangle PQR$.

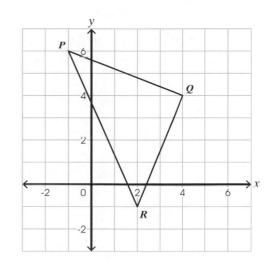

⑭ The vertices of the triangle lie on a circle as shown and AC is the diameter of the circle. If the area of the triangle is 120 square units, what are the coordinates of the centre of the circle?

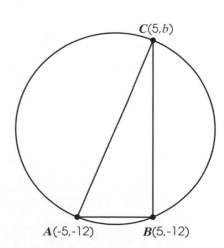

ISBN: 978-1-77149-221-8

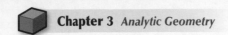

Prove the following statements. Explain your reasoning.

⑮ **Statement 1**

Given: A quadrilateral has vertices at $J(1,4)$, $K(6,4)$, $L(3,0)$, and $M(-2,0)$.

Prove: The diagonals of the quadrilateral are right bisectors of each other.

Statement 2

Given: A triangle has vertices at $A(-2,3)$, $B(6,-1)$, and $C(4,5)$. M and N are the midpoints of AB and BC respectively.

Prove: MN is parallel to AC. The length of MN is half of AC.

Statement 3

Given: A triangle has vertices at $A(-3,1)$, $B(1,5)$, and $C(2,4)$.

Prove: The distances from the vertices to the circumcentre are the same.

 ISBN: 978-1-77149-221-8

Solve the problems. Show your work.

⑯   A group of scouts is setting up a tent. They lay out the tent by stationing the corners at (1,-1), (7,3), (3,5), and (-3,1). At what coordinates should they set up the centre pole if it needs to be where the diagonals intersect?

⑰   Kaylee made a kite. She placed two rods, one from (-1,1) to (5,3) and the other one from (1,5) to (4,-4).

a. Do the rods bisect each other perpendicularly?

b. Does the kite have the proper "kite" shape?

⑱   An engineer is studying the floor plan of a building. The vertices of the base are at (-25,-25), (-65,45), (-5,75), and (35,15). Is the floor plan in the shape of a square?

⑲   Lynn made a map that shows her home at (10,70), a park at (30,50), and a forest. If the midpoint between her home and the forest is (-5,50) and the midpoint between the park and the forest is (5,40), where is the forest? Where is the centroid of the three locations?

4 Polynomials

Words TO LEARN

Like terms: terms that have the same variables raised to the same power

e.g. $2x^2$, $-x^2$, $0.5x^2$

Trinomial: a polynomial that consists of three terms

e.g. $x^2 + 3x + 8$

4.1 Expanding and Factoring

TRY This

Example

Expand $(a + 2)(a - 3)$ and simplify.

$$(a + 2)(a - 3)$$

$$= a^2 - 3a + 2a - 6 \longleftarrow \begin{array}{l} a \times a + a \times (\text{-}3) \\ 2 \times a + 2 \times (\text{-}3) \end{array}$$

$$= a^2 - a - 6 \longleftarrow \text{simplify}$$

$$(x + 1)(x - 5)$$

$$= \boxed{} + \boxed{}$$

$$= \boxed{}$$

$$(x - 4)(x + 2)$$

$$= \boxed{} + \boxed{}$$

$$= \boxed{}$$

Expand and simplify.

① $(x + 1)(x + 3)$

② $(n - 1)(n - 2)$

③ $(k - 2)(k + 3)$

④ $(b + 6)(b - 6)$

⑤ $(a + 2)(a - 7)$

⑥ $(d - 4)(d + 2)$

⑦ $(3x - 1)(x + 1)$

⑧ $(2y + 4)(y - 2)$

⑨ $(t - 1)(2t + 3)$

⑩ $(s + 3)(3s + 1)$

⑪ $(6h + 1)(h - 2)$

⑫ $(k - 2)(4k - 1)$

      ISBN: 978-1-77149-221-8

⑬ $(x + y)^2$ ⑭ $(a - b)^2$ ⑮ $(3y + 1)(2y - 2)$

⑯ $(5k - 1)(2k + 3)$ ⑰ $(4j - 1)(3j + 2)$ ⑱ $(c - d)(3c + d)$

⑲ $(x + y)(2x - 3y)$ ⑳ $3(m - n)(2m + n)$ ㉑ $5(2x + y)^2$

Try This

$$2x^2 - 6x + 8$$

$$8x^3 + 2x^2 - 4x$$

Example

Factor the polynomials.

$$4a^2 + 2$$
$$= 2(2a^2 + 1) \longleftarrow \text{factor out 2}$$

$$3ab + a^2b - 5ab^2$$
$$= a(3b + ab - 5b^2) \longleftarrow \text{factor out } a$$
$$= ab(3 + a - 5b) \longleftarrow \text{factor out } b$$

Find the GCF of the terms in each polynomial. Then factor it.

㉒ $3m^2 + 9mn \longleftarrow$ GCF: $3m$ ㉓ $2x^3y + x^2y$ **GCF**

     $= 3m(\underline{\quad\quad} + \underline{\quad\quad})$

㉔ $2x^3y + x^2y + 3xy^2$ **GCF**   ㉕ $3a^2b + 15ab - 12ab^2$ **GCF**

㉖ $6x^2yz^2 - 18x^3y^2z^3$ **GCF**   ㉗ $18abc - 12ac^2 + 54bc$ **GCF**

㉘ $4xy + 6yz + 8xz$ **GCF**   ㉙ $13m^3n^2 - 39m^2n^2 + 91mn$ **GCF**

ISBN: 978-1-77149-221-8

Circle the common factor in each polynomial. Then factor it.

③⓪ $x(x - 2) + 3(x - 2)$

③① $a(b - 6) + 2(b - 6)$

Distributive Property

$ab + ac = a(b + c)$

$= (x - 2)(\underline{\quad} + \underline{\quad})$

③② $-2a(a - 1) + (a - 1)$

③③ $3m(n + 1) - (n + 1)$

③④ $(x - 1)^2 + 4(x - 1)$

③⑤ $6p^2q + (5 - x)p^2q$

③⑥ $x^2(x + y) - 2(x + y)^2$

③⑦ $mn(m - n)^2 - 2(m - n)$

Factor each polynomial.

③⑧ $\boxed{ax - ay}$ + $\boxed{2x - 2y}$ ← common factor of $ax - ay$: a
common factor of $2x - 2y$: 2

You may need to rearrange to group the like terms before factoring.

$= a(\underline{\quad} - \underline{\quad}) + 2(\underline{\quad} - \underline{\quad})$

e.g. $ay + bz + az + by$

$= (a + 2)(\underline{\quad} - \underline{\quad})$

$= \boxed{ay + az}$ + $\boxed{by + bz}$

③⑨ $3y - xy + 3z - xz$

④⓪ $ay + bz + az + by$

common factor: a common factor: b

④① $6x - 12y + x(x - 2y)$

④② $-2a^2 - 2ab - 4a - 4b$

④③ $x^3y^2 - x^2y^3 + x^2 - xy$

④④ $-3mn^2 + n - 2m + 6m^2n$

④⑤ $-4p + 2 + pq^2 - 2p^2q^2$

④⑥ $i^3 - j^3 + i^2j - ij^2$

ISBN: 978-1-77149-221-8

Determine whether or not the expressions in each pair are the same.

47. $(a + b)^3$ $(a^3 + b^3)$

48. $(x + y)^2$ $x^2 + 2xy + y^2$

49. $4x + 1$ $\dfrac{4x^3y^2 + xy^2}{xy^2}$

50. $\dfrac{c^2d^2 + cd^3 + cd^2}{c + d + 1}$ c^2d

Solve the problems. Show your work.

51. Theo has a rectangular cardboard as shown. Its area is $x^3 + x^2y + xy + y^2$.

   a. What is its width?

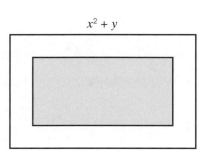

$x^2 + y$

   b. The shaded area that will be cut out is x^3. What will the area of the remaining border be? Write the answer in factored form.

52. A triangle has an area of $a^3 - a^2b + ab - b^2$. What are its possible base and height?

Area of Triangle

$A = \dfrac{bh}{2}$

$2A = bh$

4.2 Factorization of Trinomials (1)

TRY THIS

Example

Factor each trinomial.

$x^2 + 7x + 10$ ← coefficient of x: **7**
constant: **10**

$= (x + \boxed{2})(x + \boxed{5})$ ← $2 + 5 = $ **7**
$2 \times 5 = $ **10**

$x^2 - x - 6$ ← coefficient of x: **-1**
constant: **-6**

$= (x - 3)(x + 2)$ ← $-3 + 2 = $ **-1**
$-3 \times 2 = $ **-6**

Factor.

$x^2 + 4x + 3$

Think

Which two integers give a sum of 4 and a product of 3?

$x^2 - 4x - 5$

Think

Which two integers give a sum of -4 and a product of -5?

Fill in the blanks and factor each trinomial.

① $x^2 - 5x + 6$

_____ + _____ = -5

_____ × _____ = 6

② $x^2 + 6x + 8$

_____ + _____ = 6

_____ × _____ = 8

③ $x^2 + 5x + 6$

_____ + _____ = 5

_____ × _____ = 6

④ $x^2 + 5x + 4$

_____ + _____ = 5

_____ × _____ = 4

⑤ $x^2 - x - 2$

_____ + _____ = -1

_____ × _____ = -2

⑥ $x^2 + x - 2$

_____ + _____ = 1

_____ × _____ = -2

⑦ $x^2 + 2x - 15$

_____ + _____ = 2

_____ × _____ = -15

⑧ $x^2 + 3x + 2$

_____ + _____ = 3

_____ × _____ = 2

⑨ $x^2 - x - 12$

_____ + _____ = -1

_____ × _____ = -12

⑩ $x^2 - 2x - 8$

_____ + _____ = -2

_____ × _____ = -8

ISBN: 978-1-77149-221-8

Factor the trinomials.

⑪ $x^2 + 3x - 4$ ⑫ $x^2 + 7x + 12$

⑬ $x^2 - 9x + 8$ ⑭ $x^2 + 3x - 10$

⑮ $x^2 - x - 20$ ⑯ $x^2 + 9x + 18$

⑰ $x^2 + 2x + 1$ ⑱ $x^2 + 4x + 4$

⑲ $x^2 + 9x + 8$ ⑳ $x^2 - 9x + 20$

㉑ $x^2 + 10x + 24$ ㉒ $x^2 + 10x + 25$

㉓ $x^2 + 14x + 49$ ㉔ $x^2 + 20x + 100$

㉕ $-32 + 4x + x^2$ ㉖ $-5x + x^2 - 36$

㉗ $x^2 + 3xy + 2y^2$

$= (x + \boxed{} y)(x + \boxed{} y) \longleftarrow$ $\blacksquare + \blacksquare = 3$
                                       $\blacksquare \times \blacksquare = 2$

㉘ $x^2 + xy - 2y^2$

㉙ $x^2 - xy - 2y^2$

㉚ $x^2 - 3xy + 2y^2$

㉛ $x^2 - 2xy - 3y^2$

㉜ $x^2 + 4xy + 3y^2$

㉝ $x^2 - xy - 6y^2$

㉞ $x^2 - 6xy + 9y^2$

ISBN: 978-1-77149-221-8

Factor and simplify.

㉟ $\dfrac{x^2 - 14x + 24}{x - 2}$

㊱ $\dfrac{x^2 - 11x + 24}{x - 8}$

㊲ $\dfrac{x^2 + x - 20}{(x + 5)(x + 1)}$

㊳ $\dfrac{x^2 - 8x - 48}{2(x + 4)}$

㊴ $\dfrac{x^2 + 21x - 100}{(x + 25)^2}$

㊵ $\dfrac{x^2 - 7x + 6}{(x - 1)^3}$

Answer the questions.

㊶ Anna thinks that the polynomial below cannot be factored. Is she correct? Explain.

$$x^2 - 2x + 13$$

㊷ Ken factored a polynomial as shown.

$$-x^2 - 2x - 24$$
$$= -(x^2 - 2x - 24)$$
$$= -(x - 6)(x + 4)$$

Was it done correctly? If not, find the correct answer.

㊸ Gordon and Linda factored the same polynomial as shown.

Gordon: $x^2 + 6 + 5x$
$\qquad = (x + 5)(x + 1)$

Linda: $\qquad x^2 + 6 + 5x$
$\qquad = x^2 + 5x + 6$
$\qquad = (x + 2)(x + 3)$

Whose solution is correct? Explain.

Solve the problems. Show your work.

㊹ A rectangle has an area of $x^2 + 4x - 21$. What are its possible dimensions?

_____

㊺ The area of a trapezoid is $x^2 + 2xy + y^2$. What is its possible height?

_____

㊻ The total number of eggs is $x^2 + xy - 2y^2$.

  a. Given that the cartons each have the same number of eggs, what is the possible number of cartons?

_____

  b. Can $x < y$? Explain.

_____

  c. Find the number of eggs in each carton and the number of cartons if $y = 0$.

_____

4.3 Factorization of Trinomials (2)

Example

Factor $3x^2 + 7x + 2$.

Solution:

Think The coefficient of x^2 is not 1.

Expand $3x^2 + 7x + 2$ into $3x^2 + \blacksquare x + \blacksquare x + 2$ for factorization (as introduced in 4.1).

$\blacksquare + \blacksquare = 7$ ← coefficient of x

$\blacksquare \times \blacksquare = 6$ ← product of coefficient of x^2 and the constant ($3 \times 2 = 6$)

The integers must be 1 and 6.

$3x^2 + 7x + 2$
$= 3x^2 + x + 6x + 2$ ←——— expand
$= (3x^2 + x) + (6x + 2)$ ←——— group into two expressions
$= x(3x + 1) + 2(3x + 1)$ ← factorize
$= (3x + 1)(x + 2)$

Try This

Factor.

$2x^2 + 3x + 1$

$= 2x^2 + \boxed{}\, x + \boxed{}\, x + 1$

$2x^2 + x - 3$

$= 2x^2 + \boxed{}\, x + \boxed{}\, x - 3$

Factor each trinomial.

① $3x^2 + 5x + 2$

② $2x^2 - 9x + 9$

③ $5x^2 + 11x + 2$

④ $4x^2 - 4x + 1$

⑤ $7x^2 - 26x - 8$

⑥ $2x^2 + 7x - 114$

⑦ $3x^2 + 4x - 4$

⑧ $2x^2 + x - 10$

⑨ $4x^2 + 7x - 2$

ISBN: 978-1-77149-221-8

⑩ $4x^2 - 4x - 3$

⑪ $6x^2 - 5x + 1$

⑫ $8x^2 + 10x - 3$

⑬ $9x^2 - 3x - 20$

⑭ $4x^2 + 4x - 15$

⑮ $8x^2 + 10x + 3$

⑯ $6x^2 - 5x - 6$

⑰ $2x^2 + 37x - 19$

⑱ $6x^2 - 17x + 12$

Answer the questions.

⑲ Ivan factored a polynomial as shown.

$$6x^2 - 7x - 5$$
$$= 6x^2 - 3x + 10x - 5$$
$$= 3x(2x - 1) + 5(2x - 1)$$
$$= (3x + 5)(2x - 1)$$

However, it was done incorrectly. Explain what was done wrong. Find the correct answer.

⑳ Lowry wanted to factor $4x^2 - 4x - 3$. He expanded it correctly into $4x^2 - 6x + 2x - 3$. However, he was unsure of which way to regroup them before factoring them.

$(4x^2 - 6x) + (2x - 3)$ or $(4x^2 + 2x) - (6x + 3)$

Which way is correct? Show your work.

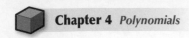

Solve the problems. Show your work.

㉑ The product of two integers is $12x^2 - x - 1$. Find the integers.

_____

㉒ The area of a parallelogram is $10x^2 - 27x + 5$. Find its possible base and height.

_____

㉓ The area of a shape is $9x^2 - 9x + 2$. Factor it to find its possible side lengths. Is it possible that they are the side lengths of a square? Explain.

_____

㉔ Joseph factored a polynomial into $x + 1$ and $6x^2 - 13x + 6$. Did Joseph fully factor the polynomial? If not, factor it further.

_____

㉕ Katy thinks that $2x + 1$ and $2x - 1$ are factors of $4x^2 - 1$. Is she correct? Explain.

_____

4.4 Perfect-square Trinomials and Differences of Squares

Example

Factor each perfect-square trinomial.

$x^2 + 6x + 9$ ◄—— $a^2 = x^2$, so $a = x$
$b^2 = 9$, so $b = 3$

$= (x + 3)^2$ ◄—— $(a + b)^2$

$4x^2 - 4x + 1$ ◄—— $a^2 = 4x^2$, so $a = 2x$
$b^2 = 1$, so $b = -1$

$= (2x - 1)^2$ ◄—— $(a - b)^2$

HINT

Perfect-square Trinomials

$a^2 + 2ab + b^2 = (a + b)^2$
$a^2 - 2ab + b^2 = (a - b)^2$

Try This

$x^2 + 4x + 4$

$a^2 = $ _____ $b^2 = $ _____

$a = $ _____ $b = $ _____

Find a and b for each perfect-square trinomial. Then factor it.

① $x^2 - 2x + 1$

$a = $ _____

$b = $ _____

② $x^2 - 8x + 16$

$a = $ _____

$b = $ _____

③ $x^2 - 6x + 9$

$a = $ _____

$b = $ _____

④ $x^2 + 10x + 25$

$a = $ _____

$b = $ _____

⑤ $x^2 + 14x + 49$

$a = $ _____

$b = $ _____

⑥ $x^2 - 12x + 36$

$a = $ _____

$b = $ _____

⑦ $64 - 16x + x^2$

$a = $ _____

$b = $ _____

⑧ $x^2 + 12x + 36$

$a = $ _____

$b = $ _____

⑨ $81 + 18x + x^2$

$a = $ _____

$b = $ _____

⑩ $x^2 - 24x + 144$

$a = $ _____

$b = $ _____

⑪ $x^2 + 2xy + y^2$

$a = $ _____

$b = $ _____

⑫ $x^2 - 4xy + 4y^2$

$a = $ _____

$b = $ _____

⑬ $16x^2 + 24x + 9$

$a = $ _____

$b = $ _____

⑭ $9x^2 - 6x + 1$

$a = $ _____

$b = $ _____

⑮ $4x^2 - 20x + 25$

$a = $ _____

$b = $ _____

⑯ $9x^2 + 12x + 4$

$a = $ _____

$b = $ _____

⑰ $4x^2 - 12x + 9$

$a = $ _____

$b = $ _____

⑱ $16x^2 - 8xy + y^2$

$a = $ _____

$b = $ _____

ISBN: 978-1-77149-221-8

Identify the perfect-square trinomials. Check and factor them.

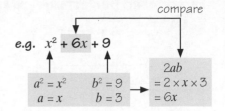

⑲ $x^2 + 3x + 4$ ◯

⑳ $x^2 - 14x + 49$ ◯

Identifying Perfect-square Trinomials

compare

e.g. $x^2 + 6x + 9$

$a^2 = x^2$	$b^2 = 9$	$2ab$
$a = x$	$b = 3$	$= 2 \times x \times 3$
		$= 6x$

Since $2ab = 2(x)(3) = 6x$, it is a perfect-square trinomial. On the other hand, $x^2 + \mathbf{5x} + 9$ is not a perfect-square trinomial.

㉑ $4x^2 + 9x + 25$ ◯

㉒ $x^2 + 2x + 1$ ◯

㉓ $x^2 + 16x + 64$ ◯

㉔ $16x^2 + 8x + 1$ ◯

㉕ $16x^2 + 4x + 9$ ◯

㉖ $25x^2 - 10x + 1$ ◯

㉗ $x^2 - 2x + 1$ ◯

㉘ $9x^2 - 30x + 25$ ◯

㉙ $4x^2 + 6x + 25$ ◯

㉚ $16x^2 + 24x + 9$ ◯

Check the correct answers about perfect-square trinomials. Give an example to explain your choice.

㉛ In a perfect-square trinomial, the signs of both perfect squares, a^2 and b^2,

Ⓐ must be the same.

Ⓑ must be different.

Ⓒ can be the same or different.

㉜ In a perfect-square trinomial, can a and b be the same?

Ⓐ Yes

Ⓑ No

ISBN: 978-1-77149-221-8

Find a and b for each difference of squares. Then factor it.

Difference of Squares

$a^2 - b^2 = (a + b)(a - b)$

e.g. Factor $x^2 - 9$.

$x^2 - 9$ ⟵ $a^2 = x^2$, so $a = x$
$b^2 = 9$, so $b = 3$

$= (x + 3)(x - 3)$ ⟵ $(a + b)(a - b)$

㉝ $x^2 - 4$ $a =$ ____ $b =$ ____

㉞ $x^2 - 36$ $a =$ ____ $b =$ ____

㉟ $x^2 - 1$ $a =$ ____ $b =$ ____

㊱ $4x^2 - 1$ $a =$ ____ $b =$ ____

㊲ $9x^2 - 4$ $a =$ ____ $b =$ ____

㊳ $25x^2 - 1$ $a =$ ____ $b =$ ____

㊴ $16x^2 - 9$ $a =$ ____ $b =$ ____

㊵ $x^4 - y^2$ $a =$ ____ $b =$ ____

㊶ $4x^4 - 9y^2$ $a =$ ____ $b =$ ____

Factor the binomials that are differences of squares.

㊷ $x^2 + 1$

㊸ $x^2 - 16$

㊹ $4x^2 - 16y^2$

㊺ $x^2 - 12$

㊻ $16x^2 - 1$

㊼ $9x^2 - y^4$

㊽ $x^3 - 1$

㊾ $4x^2 + 9$

㊿ $x^2y^2 - 1$

(51) $25x^4 - 9y^2$

(52) $x^2 + y^2$

(53) $x^2 - 4y^4$

ISBN: 978-1-77149-221-8

Answer the questions.

54 John states that any difference of squares will be positive because the numbers involve squares. Is he correct? Explain.

55 Given $x^2 + kx + 6$, what values of k will make the trinomial factorable?

56 Use the concept of difference of squares to evaluate $152^2 - 148^2$ without using a calculator.

57 Sally says, "If you multiply two consecutive odd numbers and add 1, you'll get a perfect square." Prove that Sally is correct.

Solve the problems. Show your work.

58 The border of a frame is shaded as shown. Find its area in factored form.

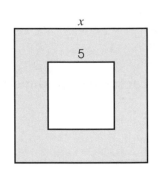

59 A puzzle piece is as shown. Find its area in factored form.

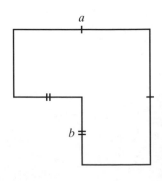

Example

Factor the polynomial.

$4a^2 - 16$ ← 4 is the GCF.

$= 4(a^2 - 4)$ ← $a^2 - 4$ is a difference of squares.

$= 4(a + 2)(a - 2)$

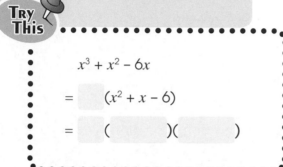

Try This

$x^3 + x^2 - 6x$

$= \boxed{}(x^2 + x - 6)$

$= \boxed{}()()$

HINT

Ask yourself the questions below for factoring a polynomial:

Is there a GCF?

If yes, simplify the polynomial by factoring out the GCF.

How many terms are there?

• 2 terms: determine whether they make a difference of squares

• 3 terms: factor them into two binomials

• 4 terms: group them before factoring

Factor the polynomials.

① $y^2 - 6y$

② $2x^3 - 18x$

③ $12ac^2 - 75c$

④ $16a^4 - 81$

⑤ $-12x + 4x^2$

⑥ $x^4 - y^4$

⑦ $6z^2 + 3z - 30$

⑧ $2b^2 - 12b + 18$

⑨ $6x^3 - 9x^2 - 6x$

⑩ $3d^3 - 5d^2 - 2d$

⑪ $2x^3 + 4x^2 - 6x$

⑫ $36q - 12q^2 + q^3$

⑬ $a^3 - 4a^2 + 2a - 8$

⑭ $x^2 - y^2 + 7x + 7y$

⑮ $2p^2 + 2pq - 2p - 2q$

⑯ $i^3 - 3i^2 + 9i - 27$

⑰ $x^3 - 7x + 2x^2 - 14$

⑱ $-7y + xy + 3x - 21$

⑲ $c^2 + 2c - d^2 - 2d$

⑳ $2q + 15p + 6pq + 5$

㉑ $6xy - 15x + 4y - 10$

㉒ $x^2 - 2xy + y^2 - x + y$

㉓ $9a^2 + 6a + 1 - 6b - 18ab$

㉔ $x^2 - 3xy + 4 + 4x - 6y$

Factor each polynomial fully.

㉕ $x^4 - y^4$

㉖ $64a^4 - 1$

㉗ $\dfrac{x^4}{81} - \dfrac{16}{625}$

㉘ $2m^3n + 4m^2n^2 + 2mn^3 - 2mnp^2$

Check whether each expression is factored correctly. If not, point out the mistake.

㉙ $a^3 - 2a^2b + ab^2 - 2b^3$

$= a^2(a - 2b) + b^2(a - 2b)$

$= (a^2 + b^2)(a - 2b)$

$= (a + b)(a - b)(a - 2b)$

㉚ $-12x^2 - 10x - 12$

$= -2(6x^2 + 5x + 6)$

$= -2(2x + 3)(3x + 2)$

Solve the problems. Show your work.

㉛   The figure shown has an area of $x^2 + 4\frac{1}{2}x + 4\frac{1}{2}$. What is the height of the figure in terms of x?

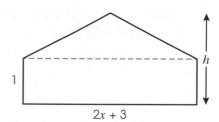

1

$2x + 3$

h

㉜   The area of a square is $121a^2 + 44a + 4$.

a. What is its perimeter?

b. What is the possible value of a?

ISBN: 978-1-77149-221-8

Graphs of Quadratic Relations

Words TO LEARN

Parabola: a graph of a quadratic relation that is shaped like the letter "U"

Axis of symmetry: a line that divides a parabola into two equal halves

Vertex: the highest or lowest point of a parabola

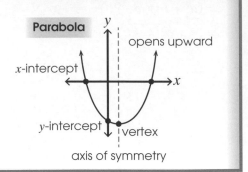

Parabola

opens upward

x-intercept

y-intercept

vertex

axis of symmetry

5.1 Properties of Quadratic Relations

TRY THIS

Example

Identify and check the representations of quadratic relations.

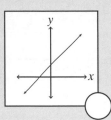

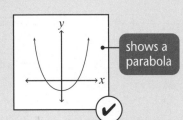

shows a parabola

second differences are constant but not 0

x	y		
-2	8	>-4	
-1	4	>-4	>0
0	0	>4	>8
1	4	>4	>0
2	8		>4

○

x	y		
-2	-3	>3	
-1	0	>5	>2
0	5	>7	>2
1	12	>9	>2
2	21		>2

✔

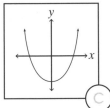 A

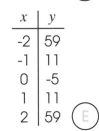 B

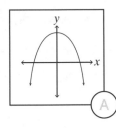 C

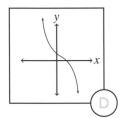 D

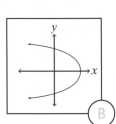

x	y
-2	59
-1	11
0	-5
1	11
2	59

E

x	y
-2	-2
-1	1
0	-2
1	1
2	4

F

Graph the quadratic relations.

① $y = x^2$

x	y
-2	
-1	
0	
1	
2	

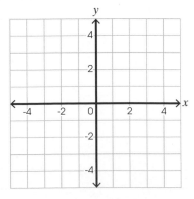

② $y = -2x^2 + 4$

x	y
-2	
-1	
0	
1	
2	

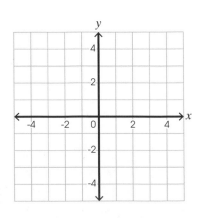

ISBN: 978-1-77149-221-8

Graph the quadratic relations. Write the key characteristics of each in the table.

③ $y = x^2 - 4$

x	y
-2	
-1	
0	
1	
2	

④ $y = -x^2 + x + 2$

x	y
-2	
-1	
0	
1	
2	

⑤ $y = -\dfrac{1}{2}(x - 1)^2$

x	y
-2	
-1	
0	
1	
2	

⑥ $y = 2(x + 1)^2 + 2$

x	y
-2	
-1	
0	
1	
2	

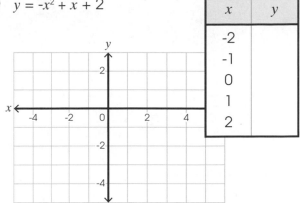

	$y = x^2 - 4$	$y = -x^2 + x + 2$	$y = -\dfrac{1}{2}(x - 1)^2$	$y = 2(x + 1)^2 + 2$
x-intercept(s)	(——,——)(——,——)			
y-intercept	(——,——)			
Direction of Opening	—————			
Axis of Symmetry	x = ———			
Vertex	(——,——)			
Max./Min. Value	y = ———			

ISBN: 978-1-77149-221-8

Sketch the parabolas with the given characteristics.

⑦

A vertex: (-3,0)
y-intercept: (0,1)

B x-intercept: (1.5,0)
y-intercept: (0,-6)

C no x-intercepts
opens upward

D x-intercepts: (2,0), (-2,0)
max. value: 3

A   **B**

C   **D**

Answer the questions without graphing.

⑧ $y = x^2 + 7$

a. What is the direction of opening?

_____

b. What is the y-intercept?

_____

⑨ $y = x^2 - 16x + 63$

a. What is the direction of opening?

_____

b. Will there be a maximum value or a minimum value?

_____

⑩ $y = -2(x - 1)^2$ ◄── Expand and rewrite in the form: $y = ax^2 + bx + c$.

a. What is the direction of opening?   _____

b. What is the y-intercept?   _____

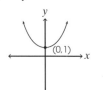

HINT

Standard Form of Quadratic Relations

$$y = \boxed{a}x^2 + bx + \boxed{c}$$

direction of opening   y-intercept
• a > 0, upward
• a < 0, downward

e.g. $y = x^2 + 1$ $y = -x^2 + 1$

ISBN: 978-1-77149-221-8

Circle T for true and F for false.

⑪ The axis of symmetry is always the y-axis.   **T / F**

⑫ The vertex always lies on the axis of symmetry.   **T / F**

⑬ A parabola with no x-intercepts and with a positive y-intercept always opens upward.   **T / F**

⑭ All parabolas have y-intercepts.   **T / F**

⑮ Consider $y = ax^2 + bx + c$.

    a. If it is an equation of a parabola, then a cannot be 0.   **T / F**

    b. If a is negative, the parabola will open downward.   **T / F**

    c. c is the y-intercept.   **T / F**

Study each scenario and answer the questions.

⑯
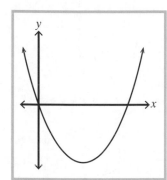

The graph shows the path made by Steven's dive.

a. Check the equation that represents the graph where x represents the horizontal distance and y represents the water depth.

   (A) $y = 0.1x^2 + 8$ (B) $y = 0.1x^2 - 2x$ (C) $y = -0.2x^2 - x$

b. What was the maximum water depth Steven reached?

⑰
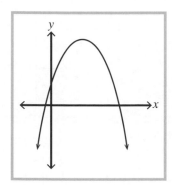

The graph shows the water arch Karen's garden hose made while she watered her plants.

a. Check the equation that represents the graph where x represents the horizontal distance and y represents the height.

   (A) $y = 2x^2 + 5$ (B) $y = -0.5x^2 - 1$ (C) $y = -0.6x^2 + 2.7x + 1.5$

b. How far away was Karen from the plants?

5.2 Finding Zeros

Example

Find the zeros of the relation and make a sketch of its graph.

$$y = (x + 1)(x - 2)$$

Solution: To find the zeros, set $y = 0$.

$y = 0$ when $x + 1 = 0$ or $x - 2 = 0$.

$x + 1 = 0$
$x = -1$

$x - 2 = 0$
$x = 2$

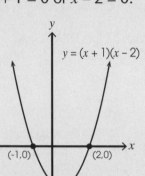

$y = (x + 1)(x - 2)$

$(-1,0)$ $(2,0)$

The zeros occur at $(-1,0)$ and $(2,0)$.

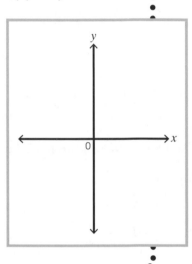

HINT

Finding the zeros of a relation is the same as finding its x-intercepts.

TRY This

Find the zeros and make a sketch of the graph.

$$y = (x + 2)(x - 1)$$

Find the zeros of the relations. Match each relation with its graph.

① **A** $y = (x - 1)(x + 3)$ **B** $y = (x + 4)(x - 4)$

C $y = (x + 2)(3 - x)$ **D** $y = (4 - x)(x + 1)$

E $y = (x - 2)^2$ **F** $y = (x + 3)^2$

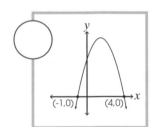

$(-4,0)$ $(4,0)$

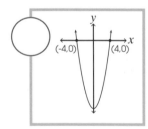

$(-1,0)$ $(4,0)$

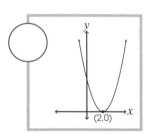

$(2,0)$

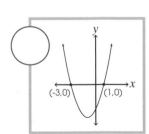

$(-3,0)$ $(1,0)$

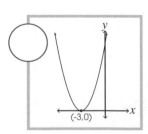

$(-3,0)$

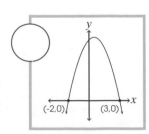

$(-2,0)$ $(3,0)$

Find the *y*-intercept, zeros, axis of symmetry, and vertex of each relation. Then sketch its graph.

② $y = (x - 2)(x + 2)$

y-intercept	**zeros**
$y = (0 - 2)(0 + 2)$ ←— set $x = 0$	$x - 2 = 0$ $\vert$ $x + 2 = 0$
$y = ($_____$)($_____$)$	$x =$ _____ $\vert$ $x =$ _____
$y =$ _____	$($_____$, 0)$ $\vert$ $($_____$, 0)$
$(0,$ _____$)$	

The axis of symmetry can be found by taking the mean of the zeros.

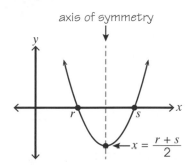

axis of symmetry

$x = \dfrac{r + s}{2}$

To find the vertex, substitute the axis of symmetry into the relation.

axis of symmetry	**vertex**
$x = \dfrac{\quad + \quad}{2}$ ←— mean of the zeros	$y = ($_____ $- 2)($_____ $+ 2)$
$x =$ _____	$y = ($_____$)($_____$)$
	$y =$ _____
	$($_____ , _____$)$

③ $y = (x + 1)(2 - x)$

y-intercept	**zeros**	**axis of symmetry**	**vertex**

④ $y = (x - 1)^2$

y-intercept	**zeros**	**axis of symmetry**	**vertex**

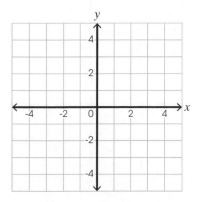

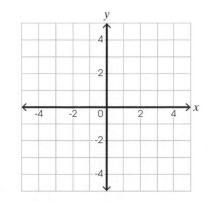

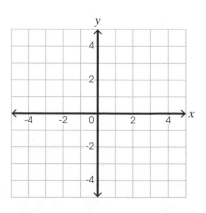

ISBN: 978-1-77149-221-8

Factor the equation of each relation and write it in factored form. Find the features of the relation. Then sketch the graph.

⑤ $y = 2x^2 - 2x$

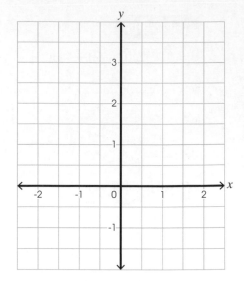

y-intercept: _____   zeros: _____

axis of symmetry: _____   vertex: _____

⑥ $y = -x^2 + 3x - 2$

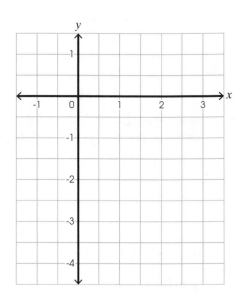

y-intercept: _____   zeros: _____

axis of symmetry: _____   vertex: _____

⑦ $y = -3x^2 + 6x + 9$

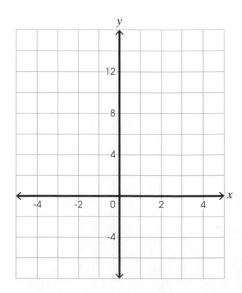

y-intercept: _____   zeros: _____

axis of symmetry: _____   vertex: _____

    ISBN: 978-1-77149-221-8

Determine an equation for a relation with the given graph.

Solution:

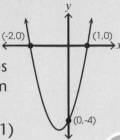

1st Substitute the zeros into the factored form of the relation.

$$y = a(x - (-2))(x - 1)$$
$$y = a(x + 2)(x - 1)$$

2nd Substitute the *y*-intercept into the relation to find *a*.

$$-4 = a(0 + 2)(0 - 1)$$
$$-4 = -2a$$
$$a = 2$$

3rd Substitute the value of *a* into the relation.

$$y = 2(x + 2)(x - 1)$$

The equation is $y = 2(x + 2)(x - 1)$.

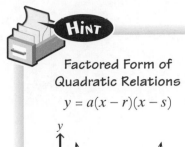

HINT

Factored Form of Quadratic Relations

$$y = a(x - r)(x - s)$$

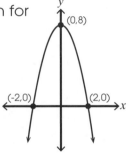

TRY THIS

Determine an equation for the parabola.

Determine the equation of each parabola sketched in the graph.

⑧

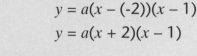

_____

⑨

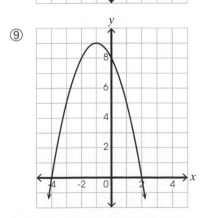

_____

Make a sketch of the parabola with the features described. Then write an equation for the relation.

⑩

zeros	vertex
(2,0) (-2,0)	(0,-8)

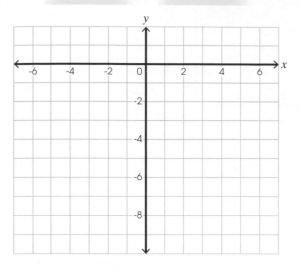

⑪

zeros	y-intercept
(3,0)	(0,-9)

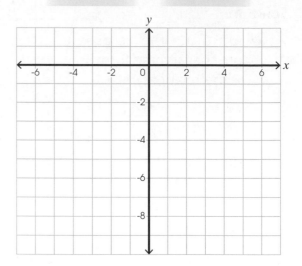

Plot the points and draw the curve of good fit. Then find an equation for the relation represented by the curve.

 HINT

A **curve of good fit** is a curve that has a good estimation to a set of points.

e.g.

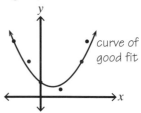

curve of good fit

⑫

x	y
0	-2
0.5	-1
-3	4
2	4
-1	-2
1.5	1.5
-2	0

Equation:

_____

⑬

x	y
2	0
6	3.5
-1	-0.5
4	1
0	-0.5
-6	2.5
-4	1

Equation:

_____

ISBN: 978-1-77149-221-8

Solve the problems. Show your work.

⑭ A tennis ball is thrown. Its height, h, in metres, with respect to time, t, in seconds, can be modelled by $h = -\frac{3}{4}(t - 2)(t + 1)$. When does the ball hit the ground?

⑮ Princess Linda drops a rose from her balcony 3 m above the ground to a knight. The knight picks up the rose 3 m away from the base of her castle. If the rose's path resembles half of a parabola as shown, what is the equation that models its path?

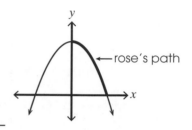

rose's path

⑯ Mr. Jones has made the table below to show the cost of each sweater he sells and the profit he makes from selling them.

Cost ($)	20	38	4	30	50	75	12
Profit ($)	24	31	6	30	30	8	16

a. Plot the points and find the curve of good fit.

b. Find an equation for the curve.

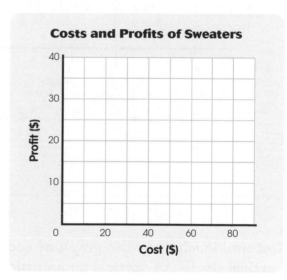

Costs and Profits of Sweaters

c. At what cost of each sweater would Mr. Jones make no profit? At what cost would he make the maximum profit? Use the equation to find the answers.

ISBN: 978-1-77149-221-8

5.3 Transformations of Quadratic Relations (1)

Complete the tables of values. Graph the relations and answer the questions.

① $y = x^2$

x	y
-2	
-1	
0	
1	
2	

$y = 2x^2$

x	y
-2	
-1	
0	
1	
2	

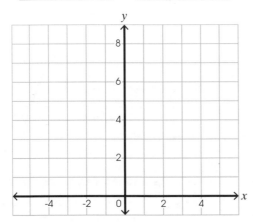

Compare the coefficients of x^2. Is $y = 2x^2$ a vertical stretch or vertical compression of $y = x^2$?

_____

② $y = x^2$

x	y
-2	
-1	
0	
1	
2	

$y = \frac{1}{2}x^2$

x	y
-2	
-1	
0	
1	
2	

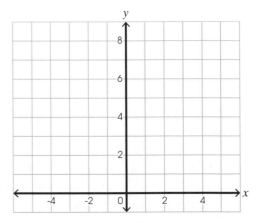

Compare the coefficients of x^2. Is $y = \frac{1}{2}x^2$ a vertical stretch or vertical compression of $y = x^2$?

_____

Determine whether the graph of each relation is a vertical stretch or vertical compression of $y = x^2$.

③ $y = \frac{1}{4}x^2$ •

$y = 1\frac{1}{2}x^2$ •

$y = 0.1x^2$ •

$y = 5x^2$ •

$y = 2.7x^2$ •

$y = \sqrt{5}x^2$ •

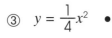

• vertical stretch

• vertical compression

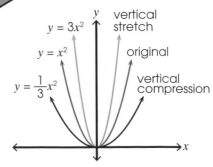

HINT

$y = 3x^2$ vertical stretch

$y = x^2$ original

$y = \frac{1}{3}x^2$ vertical compression

Transform $y = x^2$ to $y = ax^2$:

• for $a > 1$, vertical stretch

• for $0 < a < 1$, vertical compression

ISBN: 978-1-77149-221-8

Answer the questions.

④ a. Match the relations with their graphs by considering their values of a. Label them.

$$y = 1.5x^2 \qquad y = 4x^2 \qquad y = 0.4x^2$$

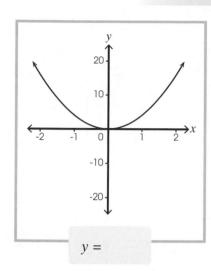
$y =$

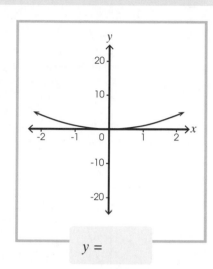
$y =$

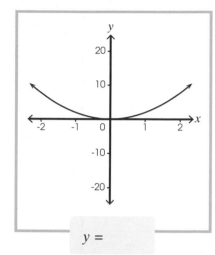
$y =$

b. Describe how you matched the relation with its graph.

_____

_____

_____

⑤ a. Use the answers from Question 4 to make a sketch of each relation.

$y = -4x^2$

$y = -0.4x^2$

$y = -1.5x^2$

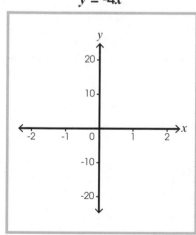

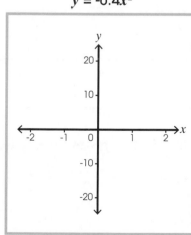

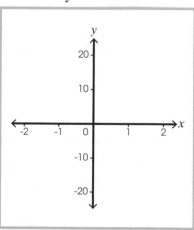

b. Describe the difference between the graphs of the relations $y = ax^2$ and $y = -ax^2$. How are they related to the x-axis?

_____

_____

ISBN: 978-1-77149-221-8

Make a sketch of each relation and describe the transformations applied to $y = x^2$.

⑥ a. $y = -2x^2$ $\qquad$ $y = -\dfrac{1}{2}x^2$

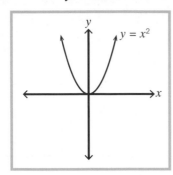 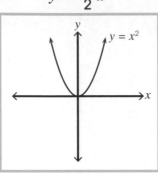

$y = -\dfrac{3}{2}x^2$ $\qquad\qquad$ $y = -4x^2$

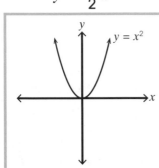 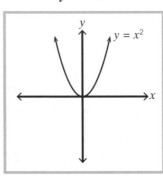

HINT

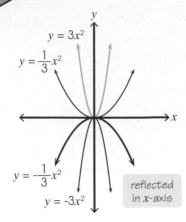

$y = 3x^2$

$y = \dfrac{1}{3}x^2$

$y = -\dfrac{1}{3}x^2$

$y = -3x^2$

reflected in x-axis

Transform $y = x^2$ to $y = ax^2$:

- for $a < -1$,
  vertical stretch and reflection in the x-axis
- for $-1 < a < 0$,
  vertical compression and reflection in the x-axis

b. Transformations applied to $y = x^2$:

$y = -2x^2$ _____

$y = -\dfrac{1}{2}x^2$ _____

$y = -\dfrac{3}{2}x^2$ _____

$y = -4x^2$ _____

Write an equation for a parabola with the given descriptions.

⑦ • vertically stretched by a factor of 5
  • opens downward

⑧ • vertically compressed by a factor of $\dfrac{1}{4}$
  • opens upward

⑨ • vertically compressed by a factor of $\dfrac{2}{3}$
  • opens upward

⑩ • vertically stretched by a factor of $8\dfrac{3}{4}$
  • opens downward

Complete the table of values of each relation. Make a sketch of its graph and answer the questions.

①

$y = x^2 + 2$		$y = x^2 - 2$	
x	y	x	y
-2		-2	
-1		-1	
0		0	
1		1	
2		2	

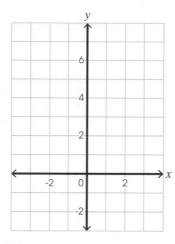

Describe the transformations applied to $y = x^2$ to get the transformed function $y = x^2 + k$ when

a. $k > 0$:

_____

_____

b. $k < 0$:

_____

_____

Match each relation with its graph in each group.

② **A** $y = x^2 + 1$

   B $y = x^2 - 1$

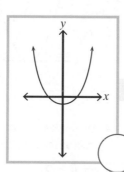

HINT

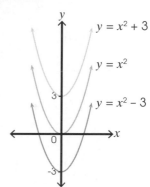

$y = x^2 + 3$

$y = x^2$

$y = x^2 - 3$

Transform $y = x^2$ to $y = x^2 + k$:

• for $k > 0$, translated up

• for $k < 0$, translated down

③ **A** $y = -x^2 - 2$

   B $y = -x^2 + 2$

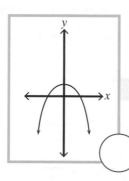

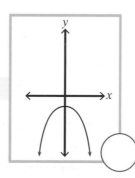

④ **A** $y = -x^2 + 3$

   B $y = x^2 + 3$

   C $y = -x^2 - 3$

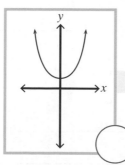

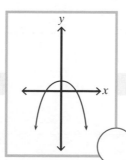

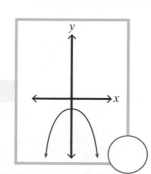

Complete the table of values for each relation. Then make a sketch of its graph and answer the questions.

⑤

$y = (x - 1)^2$		$y = (x + 1)^2$	
x	y	x	y
-1		-3	
0		-2	
1		-1	
2		0	
3		1	

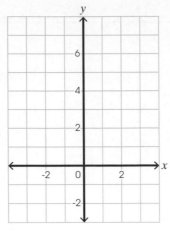

Describe the transformation applied to $y = x^2$ to get the transformed function $y = (x - h)^2$ when

a. $h > 0$:

_____

_____

b. $h < 0$:

_____

_____

Match each graph with its relation. Describe the transformation each relation applied to $y = x^2$. Then answer the question.

⑥

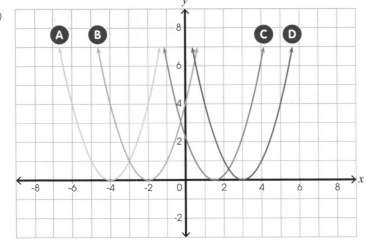

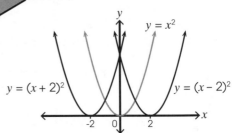

Transform $y = x^2$ to $y = (x - h)^2$:

• for $h > 0$,
  translated to the right

• for $h < 0$,
  translated to the left

◯ $y = (x - 3)^2$ _____

◯ $y = (x - 1.5)^2$ _____

◯ $y = (x + 4)^2$ _____

◯ $y = (x + 2)^2$ _____

⑦ Identify the vertices of the relations. What do you notice about the vertex and the value of h for $y = (x - h)^2$?

_____

_____

ISBN: 978-1-77149-221-8

Make a sketch of the graph of each relation. Then answer the question.

⑧

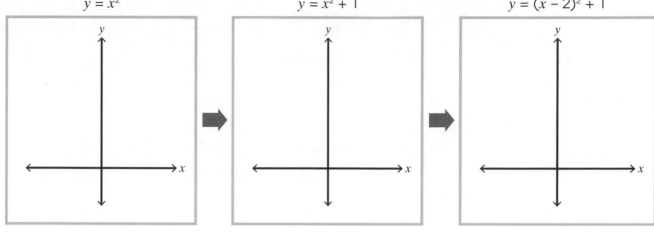

$y = x^2$ $y = x^2 + 1$ $y = (x - 2)^2 + 1$

Describe the transformation from $y = x^2$ to $y = (x - 2)^2 + 1$.

_____

Complete the table of the relations. Then match the relations with their graphs.

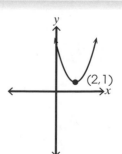

⑨

	upward or downward	stretched or compressed	vertex
$y = 2(x - 1)^2 + 2$			
$y = -\dfrac{1}{2}(x - 2)^2 + 1$			
$y = -2(x + 1)^2 - 1$			
$y = (x - 2)^2 + 1$			

HINT

Vertex Form of Quadratic Relations

$$y = a(x - h)^2 + k$$

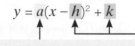

- direction of opening
  + value: opens upward
  − value: opens downward

    vertex at (h,k)

- vertical stretch:
  $a > 1$ or $a < -1$
- vertical compression:
  $0 < a < 1$ or $0 > a > -1$

e.g.

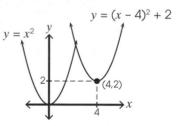

$y = x^2$ $y = (x - 4)^2 + 2$

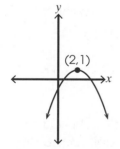
(2,1)

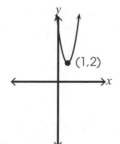
(1,2)

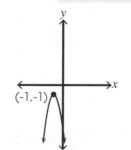
(-1,-1)

(2,1)

$y = $ _____   _____   _____   _____

Describe the roles of the parameters a, h, and k in the vertex form of quadratic relations.

$$y = a(x - h)^2 + k$$

⑩ **Parameter a**

- a is positive:

  opens _____

- a is negative:

  opens _____

- $a > 1$ or $a < -1$:

  vertically _____
  by a factor of a

- $0 < a < 1$ or $0 > a > -1$:

  vertically _____
  by a factor of a

Parameter h

- $h > 0$:

  translated h units to the _____

- $h < 0$:

  translated h units to the _____

vertex: (_____ , _____)

Parameter k

- $k > 0$:

  translated k units _____

- $k < 0$:

  translated k units _____

Match the relations with the correct descriptions for each group.

⑪

$y = 2(x + 1)^2$ •

$y = (x + 1)^2 - 1$ •

$y = (x - 1)^2 + 1$ •

$y = 2(x - 1)^2 + 2$ •

- • translated 1 unit to the left and 1 unit down

- • vertically stretched by a factor of 2 and translated 2 units up

- • vertically stretched by a factor of 2 and translated 1 unit to the left

- • vertex at (1,1)

⑫

$y = -3(x - 1)^2 + 2$ •

$y = -\frac{1}{2}(x - 1)^2 + 1$ •

$y = 3(x + 1)^2 + 2$ •

$y = \frac{1}{2}(x + 1)^2$ •

- • vertically compressed by a factor of $\frac{1}{2}$ and reflected in the x-axis

- • vertically stretched by a factor of 3 and translated 1 unit to the left

- • vertically compressed by a factor of $\frac{1}{2}$ and translated 1 unit to the left

- • vertex at (1,2)

ISBN: 978-1-77149-221-8

Sketch the graph of each relation. Label the vertex with its coordinates.

⑬ $y = (x - 2)^2 + 1$ $y = (x + 3)^2 - 4$ $y = (x - 1)^2 - 2$

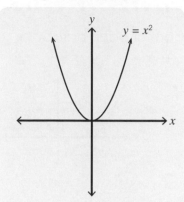 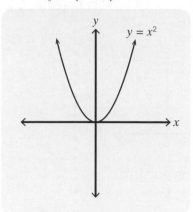 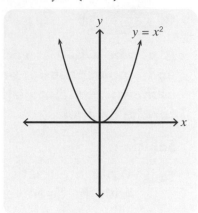

      $y = 2(x + 1)^2 - 3$ $y = \dfrac{1}{3}(x - 3)^2$ $y = \dfrac{1}{2}(x + 1)^2 - 1$

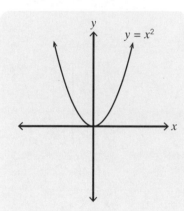 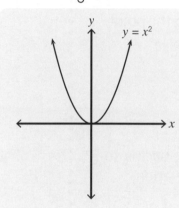 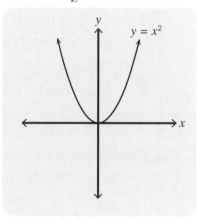

Find an equation for each parabola as described.

⑭
- vertex at (-8,1)
- opens upward
- vertically stretched by a factor of 2

_____

⑮
- opens downward
- vertically compressed by a factor of $\dfrac{1}{3}$
- vertex at (-4,2)

_____

⑯
- vertex at (2,-5)
- opens downward
- vertically stretched by a factor of 5

_____

⑰
- translated 3 units up
- vertex lies on the y-axis
- vertically compressed by a factor of $\dfrac{1}{4}$
- reflected in the x-axis

_____

⑱
- vertex at (0,0)
- reflected in the x-axis
- vertically compressed by a factor of 0.5

_____

⑲
- translated 4 units to the left
- vertex lies on the x-axis
- not vertically stretched or compressed

_____

5.5 Modelling Quadratic Relations

Example

A parabola has its vertex and a point that lies on it as shown. Find an equation for the parabola.

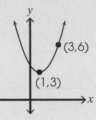

Solution:

1st Write the relation in vertex form with the given vertex, (1,3).

$$y = a(x - \mathbf{1})^2 + \mathbf{3}$$
$$\,\underset{h}{\uparrow}\,\underset{k}{\uparrow}$$

2nd Solve for a by substituting the point, (3,6), into the relation.

$$\mathbf{6} = a(\mathbf{3} - 1)^2 + 3$$
$$6 = 4a + 3$$
$$a = \frac{3}{4}$$

3rd Substitute the value of a back into the vertex form of the relation.

$$y = \frac{\mathbf{3}}{\mathbf{4}}(x - 1)^2 + 3$$

The equation is $y = \frac{3}{4}(x - 1)^2 + 3$.

Find an equation for each parabola.

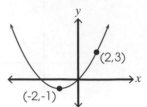

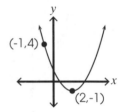

Find an equation for each parabola using the indicated vertex and point.

①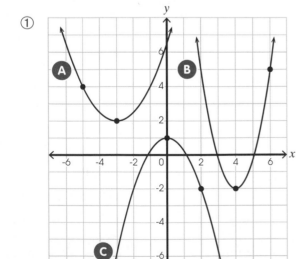

Ⓐ vertex: (_____ , _____)   point: (_____ , _____)

Ⓑ vertex: (_____ , _____)   point: (_____ , _____)

Ⓒ vertex: (_____ , _____)   point: (_____ , _____)

ISBN: 978-1-77149-221-8

Match each relation with the correct vertex and a point that lies on its parabola.

② **A** $y = 2(x + 1)^2 - 3$

    B $y = \frac{2}{3}(x - 6)^2 - 1$

    C $y = -(x - 2)^2 + 4$

    D $y = \frac{3}{2}(x - 6)^2 - 1$

    E $y = 3(x - 2)^2 + 4$

    F $y = -(x + 1)^2 - 3$

vertex: (2,4)   vertex: (-1,-3)   vertex: (6,-1)
point: (4,0)   point: (-3,5)   point: (3,5)

vertex: (-1,-3)   vertex: (2,4)   vertex: (6,-1)
point: (-3,-7)   point: (4,16)   point: (8,5)

Plot the points on the grid to make a sketch of a parabola. Then find an equation that represents it.

③

x	y
-2	3.5
-1	1
0	-0.5
1	-1
2	-0.5

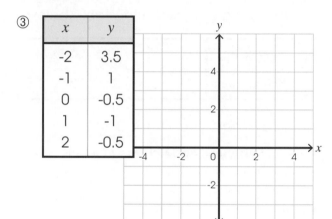

_____

④

x	y
-3	6
-2	3
-1	2
0	3
1	6

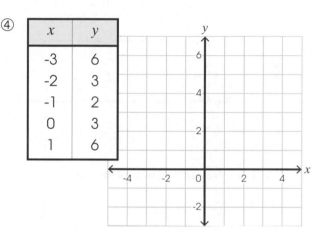

_____

⑤

x	y
-3	-5
-2	1
-1	3
0	1
1	-5

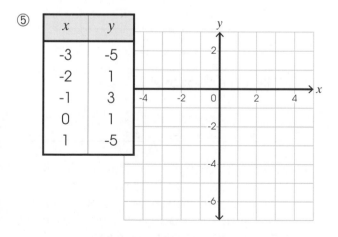

_____

⑥

x	y
-5	-1
-3	2
-1	3
1	2
3	-1

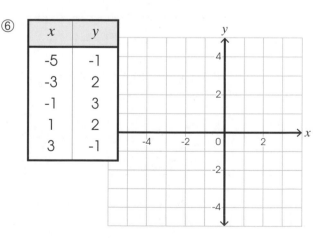

_____

ISBN: 978-1-77149-221-8

Determine whether each statement is true or false.

⑦ Consider a quadratic relation in the form of $y = -(x + p)^2 - q$ for $p > 0$ and $q < 0$.

a. The parabola has a minimum value of q.
T / F

b. The vertex of the parabola cannot be at (0,0).
T / F

c. The parabola is a translation of $y = x^2$ to the left.
T / F

d. The parabola is an upward translation of $y = x^2$.
T / F

Study each word problem. Then answer the questions.

⑧ Emma formed rectangles with a piece of string and recorded the lengths and areas of the rectangles in the table below.

Length (cm)	2	3	5	7	10
Area (cm²)	18	24	30	28	10

a. Plot the points. Draw to show the curve of good fit.

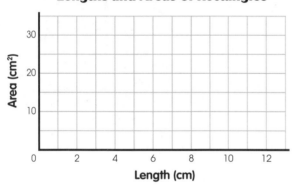

Lengths and Areas of Rectangles

b. Write an equation in vertex form to model the graph.

_____

c. Use the equation to find the area when the length is 6.5 cm.

_____

⑨ Jason threw a ball. The horizontal distances between him and the ball, and the heights of the ball are shown in the table below.

Distance (m)	0	2	3	6	7
Height (m)	2	3.5	3.8	3	2.5

a. Draw the curve of good fit.

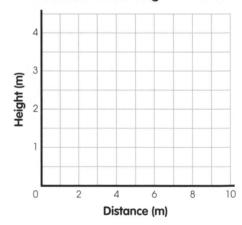

Distances and Heights of a Ball

b. Write an equation.

_____

c. Find the height of the ball when the distance is 5.75 m. Compare the answers from the graph and the equation. Is your equation a good approximation of the graph?

_____

ISBN: 978-1-77149-221-8

Solve the problems. Show your work.

⑩ A bridge is being built over a canal. It must span 50 m and its centre must be 4 m above the water.

  a. Sketch a diagram to illustrate the scenario and label the key points.

  b. Write an equation to model the scenario.

⑪ Elva and Belinda are playing a game of catch. They stand 10 m apart and throw the ball over a 2-m high net between them.

  a. Make a sketch of the graph that illustrates the scenario and label the key points. Then write an equation to model the path of the ball.

  b. If the girls each move 1 m closer toward each other, what will the equation of the path of the ball be?

⑫ Andrew dived into the water from the edge of a swimming pool. He reached a maximum depth of 2 m when he was 4 m away from the edge horizontally. He reached the surface of the water when he was 8 m away from the edge.

  a. Sketch a diagram and label the key points. Then write an equation.

  b. If he reached a maximum depth of 3.5 m instead, what would the equation be?

ISBN: 978-1-77149-221-8

6 Solving Quadratic Equations

Words TO LEARN

Root: a solution to an equation

  e.g. $x^2 - 2x + 1 = 0$ ←— root: $x = 1$

Partial factoring: a method which is used to partially factor a polynomial when it cannot be fully factored

  e.g. $x^2 - 4x + 1$ ←— cannot be fully factored
  $= x(x - 4) + 1$ ←— partially factored

Quadratic equation: an equation that has a highest degree of 2 for one of its terms

  e.g. $y = x^2 - 2x + 1$ ←— a quadratic equation
  $y = x^3 - 2x^2 + 1$ ←— not a quadratic equation

6.1   Standard Form to Factored Form

Example

Find the roots of the quadratic equation.

$$x^2 + x - 20 = 0$$

Solution:

1st Factor the quadratic equation.
  $x^2 + x - 20 = 0$
  $(x + 5)(x - 4) = 0$

2nd Find the values of x. For the equation to hold true, either $(x + 5)$ or $(x - 4)$ must be 0.

  $x + 5 = 0$ $x - 4 = 0$
  $x = -5$ or $x = 4$

The roots are $x = -5$ and $x = 4$.

Try This

Find the roots.

$$x^2 - 7x + 12 = 0$$

Find the roots of the quadratic equations.

① $x^2 - x - 6 = 0$

② $x^2 - 4x - 21 = 0$

③ $x^2 + 7x + 6 = 0$

④ $2x^2 - 11x + 5 = 0$ ⑤ $x^2 + 4x = 12$

HINT

Bring all values to one side to set the equation to 0 before solving.

e.g. $x^2 + x = 20$
             $x^2 + x - 20 = 0$

⑥ $x^2 - 16 = 6x$ ⑦ $3x^2 - 12 = -16x$ ⑧ $7x + 5 = 6x^2$

⑨ $4x^2 = 4x + 3$ ⑩ $4x^2 - 3x = 5x + 21$ ⑪ $6x^2 - 5 = -25x + 4$

Solve each equation. Then verify your solutions by substitution.

⑫ $x(4x + 12) = 27$ ⑬ $3x(x + 5) = -4x + 14$

⑭ $2(x^2 - 1) = -x(8x + 1)$ ⑮ $x(5x + 1) = -7x^2 + 1$

ISBN: 978-1-77149-221-8

Find the points of intersection.

⑯ $y = 3x + 10$
    $y = 4x^2 - x - 25$

1st Solve for x.

2nd Find the coordinates of the points by substituting the values of x.

⑰ $y = 2x^2 + 3x - 1$
    $y = -8x^2 - 30x + 6$

⑱ $y = 2x^2 - 4x + 1$
    $y = -x^2 - 3x + 15$

Find the roots and vertex of each quadratic equation. Then make a sketch of its graph with the key points labelled.

HINT

Refer to p. 85 for how to find the vertex of a quadratic equation with its roots.

⑲ $y = -2x(x + 2) + 6$

⑳ $y = -(x + 3)^2 + 4$

㉑ $y = 8x^2 - 22x + 5$

Roots	Vertex

Roots	Vertex

Roots	Vertex

ISBN: 978-1-77149-221-8

Solve the problems. Show your work.

㉒ A positive number plus itself squared is 240. What is the number?

_____

㉓ The sum of a series of positive numbers (e.g. 1, 2, 3, 4, 5) is given by $S = \frac{n(n + 1)}{2}$, where S represents the sum and n represents the last number in the series. If the sum is 153, what is n?

_____

㉔ The sum of the squares of two consecutive even numbers is 52. What are the numbers?

_____

㉕ The length and width of a rectangle are $(x + 2)$ and $(x - 3)$. If its area is 24 cm², what are its dimensions?

_____

㉖ A rectangle has an area of 133 cm². The length is 2 cm less than triple the width. Find the dimensions of the rectangle.

_____

㉗ The dimensions of a photo frame are as shown. If its area is 200 cm², what is its thickness, w?

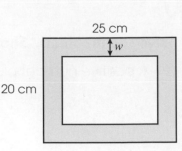

㉘ A right triangle has a height that is 2 cm greater than twice its base and the longest side is 1 cm longer than its height. What is the length of the base?

㉙ A ball was thrown and its height in metres is modelled by $h = -(t - 2)^2 + 6$, where t is the time in number of seconds the ball was in the air. When was the ball 6 m above the ground?

Make a sketch of the graph.

㉚ A clothing store sells 120 T-shirts each week at $15 each. For every $0.50 decrease in price, 12 more T-shirts would be sold each week. If they want to maximize revenue, how much should each T-shirt be sold at?

Make a sketch of the graph.

ISBN: 978-1-77149-221-8

Example

Factor each relation. If it cannot be factored fully, use partial factoring.

$y = x^2 + 2x - 15$ ← can be factored fully

$y = (x + 5)(x - 3)$

$y = x^2 + 2x - 14$ ← cannot be factored fully; use partial factoring

$y = x(x + 2) - 14$ ← factor out x from $x^2 + 2x$ and leave -14 as is

Try This

Factor the relations using partial factoring.

$y = x^2 + 4x - 3$

$y = x^2 - x + 8$

Factor the relations. For those that cannot be fully factored, use partial factoring.

① $y = x^2 + 3x - 16$

② $y = x^2 + 5x - 14$

③ $y = x^2 + 5x - 12$

④ $y = x^2 - 9x - 10$

⑤ $y = x^2 - x + 6$

⑥ $y = -(x^2 - 2x + 9)$

⑦ $y = -x^2 + 6x + 27$

⑧ $y = 2x^2 - 4x - 7$

⑨ $y = 2x^2 + x + 1$

⑩ $y = 2x^2 - 5x + 9$

⑪ $y = 2x^2 + 13x + 21$

⑫ $y = -(2x^2 - x + 7)$

⑬ $y = 3x^2 - 4x + 11$

⑭ $y = -2x^2 + 7x + 15$

⑮ $y = 3x^2 + 5x + 1$

⑯ $y = x^2 + 6x + 7$

⑰ $y = 2x^2 - 15x + 25$

⑱ $y = 3x^2 - x + 5$

Example

Write the quadratic relation in vertex form.

$$y = 2x^2 + 4x - 5$$

1st Factor the relation using partial factoring if it cannot be factored fully.

$$y = 2x^2 + 4x - 5$$
$$y = 2x(x + 2) - 5$$

2nd Find the axis of symmetry.

$y = 2x(x + 2) - 5$ is simply a translation of 5 units down of $y = 2x(x + 2)$. So, they must have the same axis of symmetry.

$$y = 2x(x + 2)$$
$$0 = 2x(x + 2) \leftarrow \text{Set } y = 0 \text{ to solve for } x.$$

$$\begin{array}{ccc} 2x = 0 & & x + 2 = 0 \\ x = 0 & \text{or} & x = \text{-}2 \end{array}$$

Axis of symmetry: $x = \dfrac{0 + (\text{-}2)}{2} = \text{-}1$

3rd Substitute the value of x into $y = 2x^2 + 4x - 5$ to find the vertex.

$$y = 2(\text{-}1)^2 + 4(\text{-}1) - 5$$
$$y = \text{-}7$$

Vertex: (-1,-7)

4th Write the equation in vertex form.

$$y = 2(x + 1)^2 - 7$$

same as the value of   vertex
a in its standard form

The equation in vertex form is $y = 2(x + 1)^2 - 7$.

 **HINT**

The value of a is the same in all three forms of a quadratic relation.

TRY THIS

$$y = 2x^2 + 3x + 7$$

1st Factor.

2nd Find the axis of symmetry.

3rd Substitute to find the vertex.

4th Write the equation in vertex form.

$$y = 3x^2 - x + 2$$

 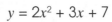

Write each quadratic relation in vertex form.

⑲ $y = 3x^2 + 12x - 2$

⑳ $y = 2x^2 + 8x + 2$

㉑ $y = x^2 + 4x - 2$

Equation

Equation

Equation

㉒ $y = 2x^2 - 3x + 7$

㉓ $y = -x^2 + 6x - 1$

㉔ $y = -2x^2 + 2x - 3$

Equation

Equation

Equation

Find each quadratic relation in vertex form. Then sketch its graph and label the key points.

㉕ $y = x^2 - 6x - 1$

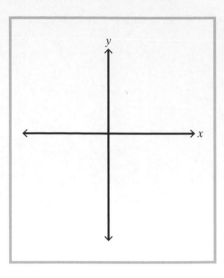

㉖ $y = 2x^2 + 2x - 5$

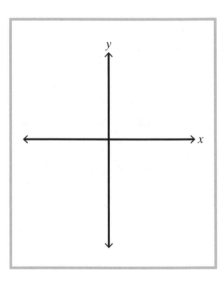

Answer the questions.

㉗ Consider $y = x^2 + kx + l$. Show that the axis of symmetry is $x = \frac{-k}{2}$.

㉘ A parabola has roots at -2 and 5. Its equation is $y = x^2 + kx + l$. Find k and l.

ISBN: 978-1-77149-221-8

Solve the problems. Show your work.

㉙ Jason threw a rock from a bridge into the river below. The rock's path can be modelled by $h = -8t^2 + 16t + 11$, where h is the height of the rock above the water level in metres and t is the time in seconds.

a. How high is the bridge above water?

_____

b. When did the rock reach its maximum height?

_____

c. What was the maximum height of the rock?

_____

㉚ A farmer has a grazing pen. He wants to build another one with fencing. The pens are not connected and the total area of the pens is modelled by $A = -2l^2 + 60l + 40$, where A is the area in square metres and l is the length in metres.

a. What is the maximum total area of the pens?

_____

b. Sketch the graph. What does "40" represent in the equation?

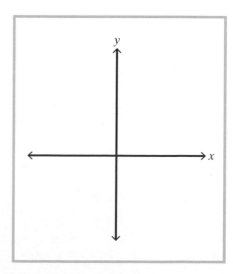

_____

6.3 Completing the Square

Try This

$x^2 - 4x + c$

$$c = (\frac{\boxed{}}{2})^2$$

$$c = \boxed{}$$

$x^2 + 6x + c$

$$c = (\frac{\boxed{}}{2})^2$$

$$c = \boxed{}$$

Example

Find the value of c that will make the expression factorable. Then factor it.

$$x^2 + 8x + c$$

Solution:

The goal is to find the value of c that makes the expression a perfect-square trinomial. To do so, square half of the coefficient of x.

Think: $(\frac{\mathbf{8}}{2})^2 = 4^2 = \mathbf{16}$

$x^2 + \boxed{8}x + c$

$x^2 + 8x + \mathbf{16}$

$= (x + 4)^2$

Fill in each box to make each expression a perfect-square trinomial. Then factor it.

① $x^2 - 2x + \boxed{}$

② $x^2 - 6x + \boxed{}$

Hint

The constant term in a perfect-square trinomial is always half of the coefficient of the x term squared.

$$x^2 + bx + \mathbf{c} = x^2 + bx + (\frac{\mathbf{b}}{\mathbf{2}})^2$$

③ $x^2 - 10x + \boxed{}$

④ $x^2 - 12x + \boxed{}$

⑤ $x^2 - x + \boxed{}$

⑥ $x^2 - 3x + \boxed{}$

⑦ $3(x^2 - 2x + \boxed{})$

⑧ $2(x^2 - 8x + \boxed{})$

⑨ $-(x^2 + 3x + \boxed{})$

⑩ $2x^2 - 4x + ?$
$\downarrow$
$2(x^2 - 2x + \boxed{})$

⑪ $4x^2 + 12x + ?$
$\downarrow$
$4(x^2 + 3x + \boxed{})$

⑫ $-2x^2 - 10x + ?$
$\downarrow$
$-2(x^2 + 5x + \boxed{})$

ISBN: 978-1-77149-221-8

ISBN: 978-1-77149-221-8

Example

Write $y = x^2 - 10x - 6$ in vertex form.

Solution:

$y = x^2 - 10x - 6$

$y = (x^2 - 10x) - 6$ ⟵ complete the square on $x^2 - 10x$

$y = (x^2 - 10x + \mathbf{25 - 25}) - 6$ ⟵ adding 25 and subtracting it results in no change to the relation

$y = (x^2 - 10x + 25) - 25 - 6$

$y = (x - 5)^2 - 31$ ⟵ factor and simplify

The vertex form is $y = (x - 5)^2 - 31$.

HINT

The vertex form of quadratic relations is $y = a(x - h)^2 + k$.

TRY THIS

Write $y = x^2 - 2x + 7$ in vertex form.

Write each quadratic relation in vertex form.

⑬ $y = x^2 - 4x - 1$

⑭ $y = x^2 - x$

⑮ $y = x^2 - 8x - 2$

⑯ $y = x^2 + 10x + 10$

⑰ $y = x^2 - 3x + 8$

⑱ $y = x^2 + 4x + 7$

⑲ $y = x^2 - 10x + 8$

⑳ $y = x^2 - 5x + 1$

㉑ $y = 3x^2 - 6x$

㉒ $y = 2x^2 + 12x - 15$

㉓ $y = -x^2 + 6x - 1$

㉔ $y = 3x^2 - 30x + 27$

㉕ $y = 5x^2 - 10x + 25$

㉖ $y = -2x^2 + 14x - 2$

Write each relation in vertex form and find its vertex. Match each relation with its graph. Then answer the question.

㉗ **A** $y = -x^2 + 6x - 17$

B $y = 2x^2 + 20x + 51$

Vertex: _____

Vertex: _____

C $y = 3x^2 + 6x - 6$

D $y = 2x^2 - 12x + 10$

Vertex: _____

Vertex: _____

E $y = -3x^2 - 30x - 74$

F $y = -x^2 - 2x - 10$

Vertex: _____

Vertex: _____

㉘ For the relations above that have the same vertices, how did you determine which graph is the correct one? Explain your reasoning.

_____

_____

_____

_____

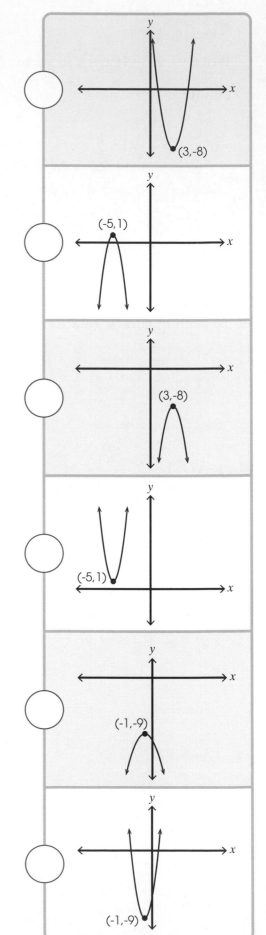

ISBN: 978-1-77149-221-8

Write each relation in vertex form. Describe the transformations applied to the graph of $y = x^2$ for each relation. Then sketch its graph.

㉙ $y = -x^2 + 4x - 8$

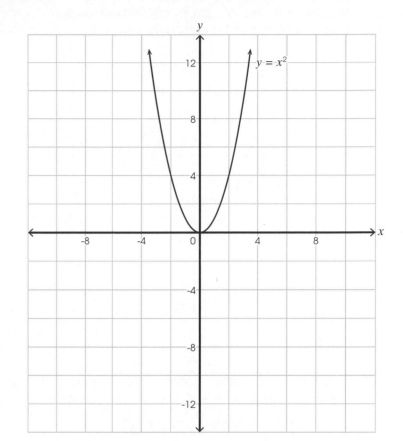

Transformations:

_____

_____

_____

㉚ $y = 3x^2 - 6x + 1$

Transformations:

_____

_____

_____

㉛ $y = -2x^2 - 24x - 73$

Transformations:

_____

_____

_____

Solve the problems. Show your work.

㉜ A toy catapult launched a ball. The height of the ball could be modelled by $h = -3t^2 + 15t$, where h is the height in centimetres and t is the time elapsed in seconds. What was the maximum height the ball reached?

_____

㉝ A swimmer jumped off a diving board into a pool. Her height relative to the water surface in metres can be modelled by $h = x^2 - 5x + 3$, where x is the horizontal distance from the board in metres. What was the greatest depth the swimmer reached?

_____

㉞ A factory's monthly profit in thousands of dollars can be modelled by $P = -\frac{1}{3}x^2 + \frac{10}{3}x - \frac{7}{3}$, where x is the number of units produced in thousands.

a. What is the maximum profit?

_____

b. How many units must be sold to obtain the maximum profit?

_____

㉟ Betty is given 40 Popsicle sticks to build a fence for her toy house. What is the maximum area she can fence in? What are the length and width in Popsicle sticks?

_____

ISBN: 978-1-77149-221-8

Quadratic Formula

$$x = \frac{-b \pm \sqrt{b^2 - 4ac}}{2a}$$

The quadratic formula is used to determine the solutions of an equation without factoring or graphing.

Example

Solve the equations using the quadratic formula. Round the answers to 2 decimal places.

$$3x^2 + 9x - 1 = 0$$

Solution:

1st Determine the values of a, b, and c.
$$a = 3, \ b = 9, \ c = -1$$

2nd Substitute the values into the quadratic formula. Then solve.

$$x = \frac{-b \pm \sqrt{b^2 - 4ac}}{2a}$$

$$x = \frac{-9 \pm \sqrt{9^2 - 4(3)(-1)}}{2(3)}$$

$$x = \frac{-9 \pm \sqrt{93}}{6}$$

$$x \doteq 0.11 \text{ and } x \doteq -3.11$$

TRY This

Solve $2x^2 - 4x + 1 = 0$ using the quadratic formula. Round the answers to 2 decimal places.

Solve each equation using the quadratic formula. Round the answers to 2 decimal places.

① $2x^2 + 3x + 1 = 0$

$a = \underline{\quad}$

$b = \underline{\quad}$

$c = \underline{\quad}$

② $x^2 - 3x + 1 = 0$

$a = \underline{\quad}$

$b = \underline{\quad}$

$c = \underline{\quad}$

③ $-2x^2 + 8x - 1$

$a = \underline{\quad}$

$b = \underline{\quad}$

$c = \underline{\quad}$

④ $-x^2 + 5x - 2 = 0$

$a = \underline{\quad}$

$b = \underline{\quad}$

$c = \underline{\quad}$

⑤ $5x^2 - 7x + 1 = 0$ ⑥ $-2x^2 + 6x - 3 = 0$ ⑦ $-x^2 - 3x - 1 = 0$

⑧ $4x^2 + 6x + 1 = 0$ ⑨ $-x^2 + 5x - 3 = 0$ ⑩ $6x^2 + 8x - 1 = 0$

⑪ $-3x^2 + 9x = -2$ ⑫ $3x^2 - 10x = 4$

HINT

Simplify an equation as much as possible before solving it.

⑬ $2x(x - 1) + 3 = 5x - 1$ ⑭ $2x^2 - 5(x + 1) = -6(x - 1)^2$

⑮ $4x(x + 2) = -7(x^2 - 2) - 12$ ⑯ $2(x - 1)^2 = (5x + 1)(x + 1)$

Find the roots of each relation using the quadratic formula. Match each relation with its graph.

⑰ **A** $y = 3x^2 + 8x - 5$ **B** $y = -2x^2 - 7x - 6$ **C** $y = -10x^2 + 13x + 2$

D $y = -0.5x^2 + 5x + 4$ **E** $y = -1.6x^2 + 0.8x + 5$ **F** $y = -2.75x^2 + 1.6x + 2$

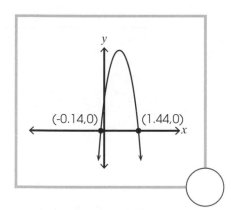

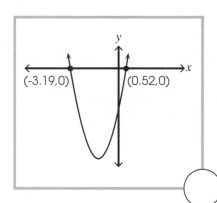

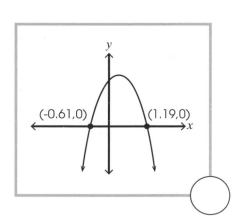

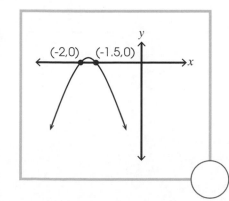

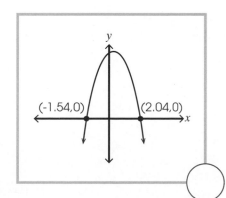

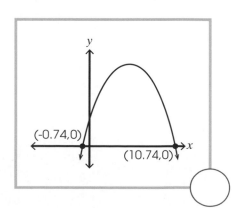

ISBN: 978-1-77149-221-8

Find the points of intersection of each pair of parabolas. Round the answers to 2 decimal places.

⑱ $y = -x^2 + 7x$
    $y = -6x^2 - x + 3$

Points of Intersection

_____ _____

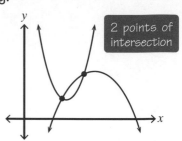

HINT

For two relations to intersect, their points of intersection must lie on the relations.

e.g.

2 points of intersection

1st Equate the relations and then solve for x.

2nd Substitute the values of x to find the corresponding values of y.

⑲ $y = 3x^2 - 7x - 1$
    $y = -x^2 + 2x + 3.25$

Points of Intersection

_____ _____

⑳ $y = x^2 - 5x + 3$
    $y = -2(0.6x^2 - x + 1)$

Points of Intersection

_____ _____

㉑ $y = x^2 + 3x + 1$
    $y = 3x^2 - 4x - 2$

Points of Intersection

_____ _____

㉒ $y = 3(x^2 - x - 1)$
    $y = -x(x - 6)$

Points of Intersection

_____ _____

ISBN: 978-1-77149-221-8

Solve each equation using the strategy specified. Then answer the questions.

㉓ $x^2 - 10x + 25 = 0$

by quadratic formula

by factoring

Which strategy do you prefer? Explain.

_____

_____

_____

㉔ $6x^2 + 29x - 42 = 0$

by quadratic formula

by factoring

Which strategy do you prefer? Explain.

_____

_____

_____

㉕ In your opinion, what are the advantages and disadvantages of using the quadratic formula to solve quadratic equations?

_____

_____

㉖ For each equation below, write **F** if you would solve it by factoring and **Q** if you would solve it using the quadratic formula.

a. ◯ $x^2 - 2x - 8 = 0$

b. ◯ $x^2 + 8x - 1 = 0$

c. ◯ $-3x^2 + 10x - 4 = 0$

d. ◯ $\frac{1}{2}x^2 + \frac{1}{2}x - 12 = 0$

e. ◯ $2x^2 + 8x - 10 = 0$

f. ◯ $-4x^2 + 7x - 1 = 0$

g. ◯ $0.8x^2 + 9x + 5 = 0$

h. ◯ $0.5x^2 - x + 0.5 = 0$

Solve the problems. Show your work.

㉗ The sum of two numbers is -1 and their product is -306. Find the numbers.

_____

㉘ The sum of the squares of three consecutive integers is 677. If the integers are negative, find the integers.

_____

㉙ Andrew covered a pit with a net. The length of the net is 9 m longer than its width and it covers 52 m². What are the dimensions of the net?

_____

㉚ A right triangle has a base that is 2 cm shorter than its height. Its hypotenuse is 16 cm longer than its height. What are the side lengths?

_____

㉛ A section of a trail can be modelled by $y = -x^2 + 4x + 1$, where x and y are the coordinates on a map. If a path $y = x - 12$ runs across the map, at which points will the trail and the path intersect?

_____

ISBN: 978-1-77149-221-8

6.5 Nature of Roots

HINT

The **discriminant** is the expression $b^2 - 4ac$ in the quadratic formula.

$$x = \frac{-b \pm \sqrt{b^2 - 4ac}}{2a} \longleftarrow \text{discriminant}$$

Example

Find the discriminant of the quadratic equation.

$$x^2 + 3x - 4$$

Solution:

Substitute the values of a, b, and c into the discriminant.

$$b^2 - 4ac = 3^2 - 4(1)(-4) \longleftarrow \begin{array}{l} a = 1 \\ b = 3 \\ c = -4 \end{array}$$
$$= 9 + 16$$
$$= 25$$

The discriminant is 25.

Try This

Find the discriminant.

$$x^2 + 2x + 1$$

Find the discriminant and roots of each equation. Then complete the table and answer the question.

① **A** $x^2 - 12x + 35 = 0$ **B** $x^2 - 6x + 9 = 0$

C $-6x^2 + 5x + 6 = 0$ **D** $x^2 - 2x + 5 = 0$

E $x^2 + 5x - 36 = 0$ **F** $x^2 + 10x + 25 = 0$

	No. of Roots	Discriminant > / < / =
A		0
B		0
C		0
D		0
E		0
F		0

Compare the numbers of roots of the equations and the values of their discriminants. Do you notice a pattern? If so, describe it.

_____

_____

Example

Find the number of roots the relation has using the discriminant.

$$y = 2x^2 + 2x - 1$$

Solution:

$$b^2 - 4ac = 2^2 - 4(2)(-1)$$
$$= 4 + 8$$
$$= 12 > 0$$

The relation has 2 real roots.

 Try This

$$y = -x^2 - 8x + 2$$

 **HINT**

The discriminant of a quadratic relation tells you the number of real roots it has.

- $b^2 - 4ac > 0$
  two real roots

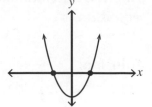

- $b^2 - 4ac = 0$
  one real root

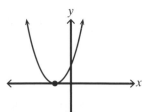

- $b^2 - 4ac < 0$
  no real roots

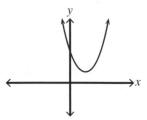

Determine the number of real roots each relation has using the discriminant.

② $y = x^2 + 10x + 64$

0 / 1 / 2 real root(s)

③ $y = 2x^2 - x - 3$

_____

④ $y = 3x^2 - x + 1$

_____

⑤ $y = 4x^2 - 12x + 9$

_____

⑥ $y = -x^2 - 8x + 17$

_____

⑦ $y = -8x^2 - 6x - 1$

_____

ISBN: 978-1-77149-221-8

Determine if each equation has solutions using the discriminant. Check the ones that do and write the number of solutions they have.

⑧

A _____ $2x^2 + 1 = -9x$

B _____ $5x(x + 2) = -5$

C _____ $-1 = 3x(x - 2)$

D _____ $4x^2 - x = 2x - 17$

E _____ $3(4x - 3) = 4x^2$

F _____ $x^2 + 3x = x - 6$

Ⓐ   Ⓑ

Ⓒ   Ⓓ

Ⓔ   Ⓕ

Determine the number of x-intercepts each parabola has using the discriminant. Match the graphs.

⑨ $y = 2(x - 3)^2$

⑩ $y = -(10 - x)^2$

⑪ $y = -3(x - 1)^2 + 1$

⑫ $y = (4x - 1)(x + 1) - 5$

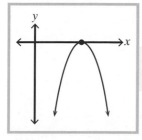 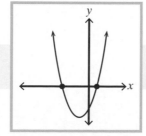 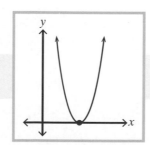 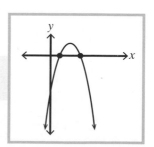

$y =$ _____   _____   _____   _____

Answer the questions.

⑬

$$x^2 + bx + 36 = 0$$

For what values of b will the equations have

a. no real roots?

b. 2 real roots?

⑭

$$y = 2x^2 + 6x + k$$

The parabola touches the x-axis at only one point.

a. What is the value of k?

b. What is the x-intercept?

⑮

$$y = -x^2 + 2x + 3 \qquad y = kx + 3$$

The parabola intersects the line at one point.

a. What is the value of k?

b. What is the point of intersection?

⑯

$$y = x^2 + 4x - 12 \qquad y = 3x - 14$$

a. Use the discriminant to find the number of points of intersection between the parabola and the line.

b. Verify your answer by sketching its graph.

ISBN: 978-1-77149-221-8

Solve the problems. Show your work.

⑰ Ryan determines the profit his bakery shop makes from selling cupcakes using the model $P = -75c(c - 6)$, where c is the price of each cupcake in dollars. Is it possible that he can make a $700 profit from selling cupcakes?

⑱ A ball is thrown. The path of the ball is modelled by $h = -0.3(t + 1)(t - 5)$, where h is the height of the ball in metres and t is the time after which it has been thrown in seconds. How many times does the ball reach a height of 2.7 m?

⑲ Cleo is asked to find two numbers that multiply to 18 and add to 8. However, Cleo knows that it is impossible. Use the discriminant to show that she is right.

⑳ The square of Denny's age is equal to 6 more than 5 times his age. The square of Belinda's age is the same as 24 less than 10 times her age.

a. Use the discriminant to find out how many solutions there are for each person.

b. Find the solutions. Which solutions are not applicable? Explain.

7 Triangles and Trigonometry

Words TO LEARN

Congruent triangles: a set of triangles that have corresponding angles with equal measures and corresponding sides with equal lengths

Similar triangles: a set of triangles that have corresponding angles with equal measures and corresponding sides in the same ratio

Scale factor: the ratio of the corresponding sides in geometry

Trigonometry: a branch of mathematics dealing with relations between the angles and sides of triangles

---

7.1 Congruent and Similar Triangles

Show that the triangles in each pair are congruent.

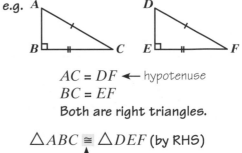

HINT

Properties of Congruent Triangles

- side-side-side (SSS)
- side-angle-side (SAS)
- angle-side-angle (ASA)
- angle-angle-side (AAS)
- right angle-hypotenuse-side (RHS)

e.g.

$AC = DF$ ← hypotenuse
$BC = EF$
Both are right triangles.

$\triangle ABC \cong \triangle DEF$ (by RHS)

↑
congruent to

①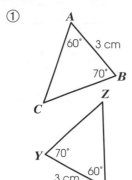

②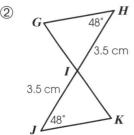

③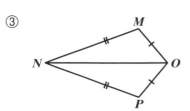

④

⑤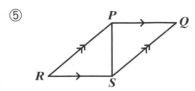

ISBN: 978-1-77149-221-8

Identify the pairs of congruent triangles. Prove that they are congruent.

⑥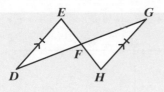

△DEF ◯ △GHF

(by _____)

⑦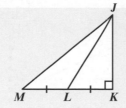

⑧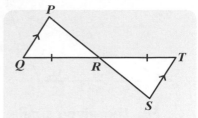

⑨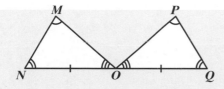

⑩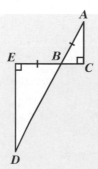

Show that the triangles in each pair are similar.
Then find the ratios of the corresponding sides.

⑪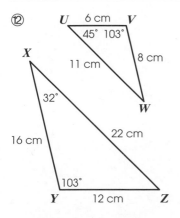

---

⑫

Example

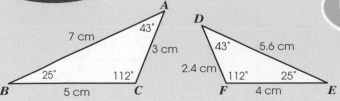

Try This

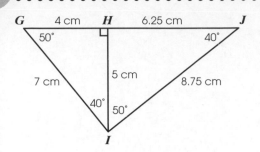

For the given similar triangles, state their corresponding angles and find the scale factor.

Solution:

$\angle A = \angle D$, $\angle B = \angle E$, $\angle C = \angle F$

$\dfrac{AB}{DE} = \dfrac{7}{5.6} = 1.25$

$\dfrac{BC}{EF} = \dfrac{5}{4} = 1.25$ ← scale factor

$\dfrac{AC}{DF} = \dfrac{3}{2.4} = 1.25$

The scale factor is 1.25.

Identify the triangles that are similar. Then state the corresponding angles and find their scale factors.

⑬

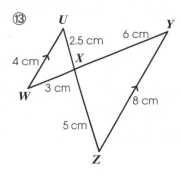

⑭

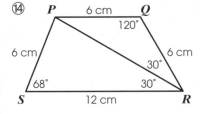

⑮

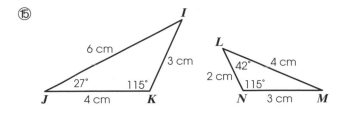

⑯

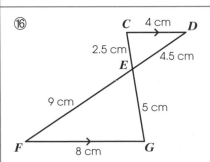

ISBN: 978-1-77149-221-8

Identify whether the triangles in each pair are congruent, similar, or neither. For the triangles that are congruent or similar, find their scale factors. Then answer the questions.

⑰
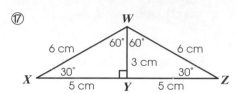

scale factor

congruent / similar / neither

⑱
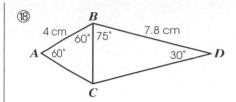

scale factor

congruent / similar / neither

⑲
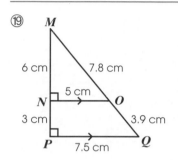

scale factor

congruent / similar / neither

⑳
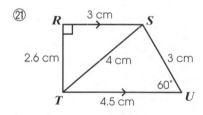

scale factor

congruent / similar / neither

㉑
R ─── 3 cm ─── S
2.6 cm   4 cm   3 cm
               60°
T   4.5 cm   U

scale factor

congruent / similar / neither

㉒
P
1.8 cm   56°   1 cm
Q   34°
56° 1.5 cm   R
2.7 cm   2.25 cm
34°
S

scale factor

congruent / similar / neither

㉓ What is the relationship between congruency and scale factor?

_____

㉔ Are all congruent triangles also similar triangles? Explain.

_____

_____

ISBN: 978-1-77149-221-8

Chapter 7 *Triangles and Trigonometry*

Find the unknowns for each pair of triangles.

㉕ $\triangle ABC \cong \triangle A'B'C'$

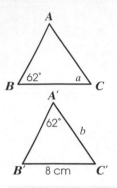

a = _____

b = _____

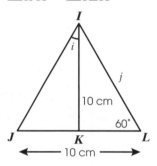

Pythagorean Theorem

$a^2 + b^2 = c^2$

㉖ $\triangle DEF \sim \triangle GHF$

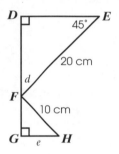

d = _____

e = _____

㉗ $\triangle IJK \cong \triangle ILK$

i = _____

j = _____

㉘ $\triangle LMN \sim \triangle PON$

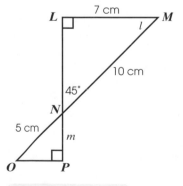

l = _____

m = _____

㉙ $\triangle PQR \sim \triangle QSR$

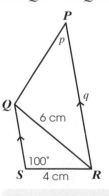

p = _____

q = _____

ISBN: 978-1-77149-221-8

Answer the questions.

③⓪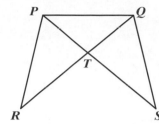

Given
$\triangle PQR \cong \triangle QPS$

a. Prove that $\triangle PQT$ is an isosceles triangle.

b. Prove that $\triangle PRT \cong \triangle QST$.

③①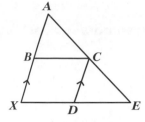

Given
$\triangle ABC \cong \triangle CDE$

a. Prove that $\triangle ABC \sim \triangle AXE$.

b. Prove that $\triangle AXE$ is an enlargement of $\triangle ABC$ by a scale factor of 2.

③②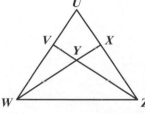

Given
$\triangle VYW \cong \triangle XYZ$

a. Prove that $\triangle WYZ$ is an isosceles triangle.

b. Prove that $\triangle UWX \cong \triangle UZV$.

③③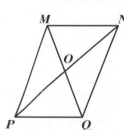

Given
$\triangle MNO \cong \triangle QPO$

a. Prove that $\triangle MOP \sim \triangle QON$.

b. Prove that $\triangle MNP \cong \triangle QPN$.

ISBN: 978-1-77149-221-8

7.2   Solving Problems on Similar Triangles

Find the missing measurements for each pair of similar triangles.

① △LMN ~ △LOP

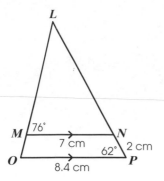

∠MLN = _____   LN = _____

② △ABC ~ △DEC

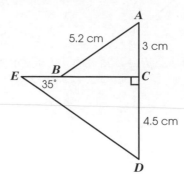

∠CAB = _____   DE = _____

③ △DEF ~ △GHF

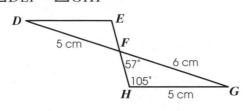

∠EDF = _____   DE = _____

④ △IJK ~ △ILM

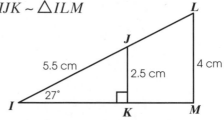

∠ILM = _____   JL = _____

⑤ △PQR ~ △PST

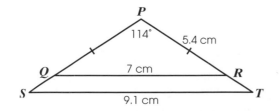

∠QST = _____   RT = _____

∠QRT = _____   PS = _____

⑥ △MNO ~ △PMO

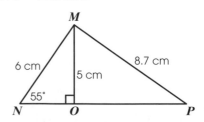

∠PMO = _____   OP = _____

∠MPO = _____   NO = _____

ISBN: 978-1-77149-221-8

Solve the problems with the given diagrams.

⑦ The distances between Cities X, Y, and Z are as shown.
Louise drew a diagram to represent the distances.
What are the missing lengths, a and b?

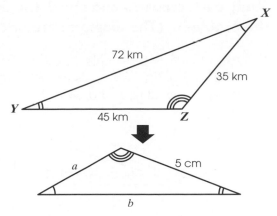

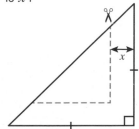

_____

⑧ To make a corner of a frame, Sally cut out an isosceles triangle along the dotted lines as
shown. The cut-out and the original triangle are similar triangles. The hypotenuses of the
original triangle and the cut-out are 5 cm and 2 cm respectively. What is x?

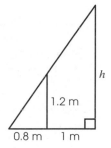

_____

⑨ A 1.2-m tall girl is standing 1 m away from a street light. Her shadow is 0.8 m long.

  a. What is the height of the street light, h?

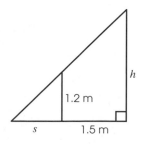

_____

  b. How long is her shadow, s, if she is 1.5 m away from the street light?

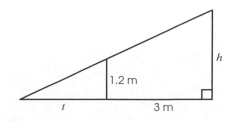

_____

  c. How long is her shadow, t, if she moves 2 m further away from the street light instead?

_____

ISBN: 978-1-77149-221-8

Study each scenario and check the diagram that represents the scenario correctly. Then solve the problem. (The diagrams are not drawn to scale.)

⑩ A ramp has a length of 3.6 m for a rise of every 0.3 m. What is the length of the ramp, *l*, for a rise of 0.54 m?

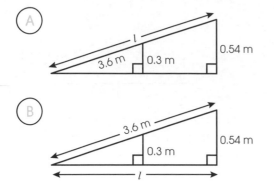

⑪ Annie casts a shadow that is 1.36 m long and a 4-m-tall tree casts a shadow that is 4.76 m long. What is the height, *h*, of Annie?

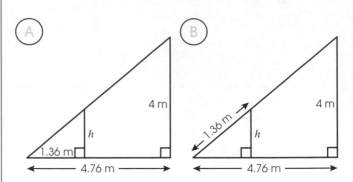

⑫ Every step of a set of stairs has a height that is half of its length. Kyle ran 30 steps and Ian reached a height of 4 times that of Kyle. How many steps, *s*, did Ian climb?

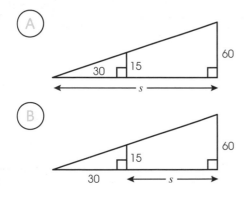

⑬ Jordan and his brother, who are 1.6 m and 1.2 m tall respectively, are looking at a picture on a wall at the same angle of elevation. The picture is hung at 2 m from the ground on the wall. If Jordan is 0.86 m away from the wall, how far apart are the brothers?

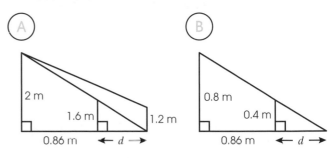

Make a sketch to illustrate each scenario. Then solve the problem.

⑭ **A** The shadows that a pencil casts by a flashlight in 2 different angles are as shown. How long is the pencil?

_____

B A board is leaning against a wall and a cube box that has a side length of 50 cm. The foot of one end of the board is 1 m away from the box horizontally. What is the length of the board?

_____

C Students A, B, C, and D are pulling a rope across a stream as shown. Use the measurements to approximate the width of the river.

_____

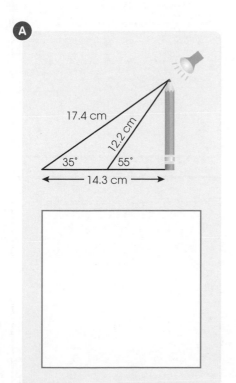

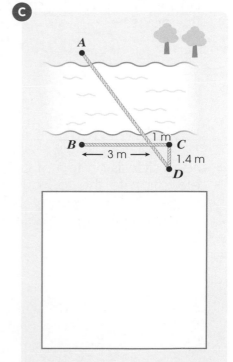

Draw to illustrate each scenario. Then solve the problem.

⑮ Sally was in the yard. She found that her shadow was 1 m long and a tree beside her cast a shadow that was 4 m long. Sally was 1.4 m tall. How tall was the tree?

_____

⑯ The pole of a circus's tent is supported by two wires. One wire connects the top of the pole to the ground and is anchored 8.5 m away from the pole, forming a 67° angle with the ground. The other wire also forms a 67° angle but it is anchored 6.8 m away from the pole and 4 m down from the top of the pole. How tall is the pole?

_____

⑰ Two poles that are 2 m and 3 m tall have their tops tethered by ropes and secured by an anchor in the ground between them. The angles at which the poles are tethered by the ropes are the same. If the anchor and the shorter pole are 3.5 m apart, how far apart are the poles?

_____

⑱ Jack stands on top of a 9-m-tall building. The angle of elevation to the top of another building is 35° and the angle of depression to the base of that building is 55°. The two buildings are 6.3 m apart. How tall is the other building?

_____

Example

Label the opposite side, the adjacent side, and the hypotenuse of the triangle in relation to θ.

hypotenuse
• the longest side

opposite
• the side that is across θ

adjacent
• the side that is an arm of θ but not the hypotenuse

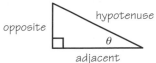 **HINT**

In any right triangle, the three sides are named as shown in relation to the acute angle θ.

hypotenuse
opposite
θ
adjacent

"θ" is commonly used to denote an angle.

TRY THIS

Label the sides of the triangle in relation to θ.

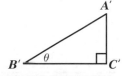
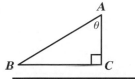

Complete the tables in relation to θ.

① a.

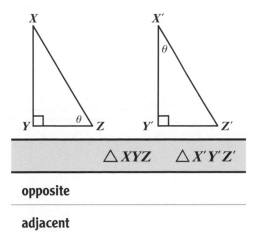

	△ABC	△A′B′C′
opposite		
adjacent		
hypotenuse		

b.

	△XYZ	△X′Y′Z′
opposite		
adjacent		
hypotenuse		

② Circle the two triangles which have opposite sides, adjacent sides, and hypotenuses in relation to θ.

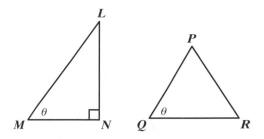
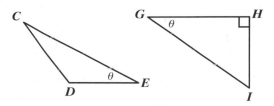

	△_____	△_____
opposite		
adjacent		
hypotenuse		

For each pair of similar triangles, find the ratios of the sides in relation to θ. Then answer the question.

③ $\triangle DEF \sim \triangle D'E'F'$

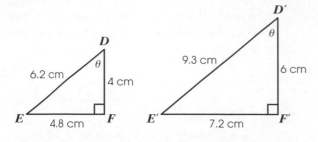

	$\triangle DEF$	$\triangle D'E'F'$
$\dfrac{\text{opposite}}{\text{hypotenuse}}$		
$\dfrac{\text{adjacent}}{\text{hypotenuse}}$		
$\dfrac{\text{opposite}}{\text{adjacent}}$		

④ $\triangle PQR \sim \triangle STR$

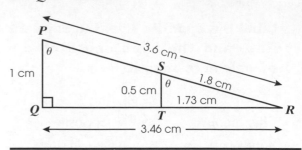

	$\triangle PQR$	$\triangle STR$
$\dfrac{\text{opposite}}{\text{hypotenuse}}$		
$\dfrac{\text{adjacent}}{\text{hypotenuse}}$		
$\dfrac{\text{opposite}}{\text{adjacent}}$		

⑤ From the two pairs of similar triangles above, what do you notice about the ratios: $\dfrac{\text{opposite}}{\text{hypotenuse}}$, $\dfrac{\text{adjacent}}{\text{hypotenuse}}$, and $\dfrac{\text{opposite}}{\text{adjacent}}$?

_____

_____

Find the unknowns of each pair of similar triangles with the given information in relation to θ.

⑥

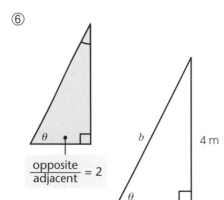

$\dfrac{\text{opposite}}{\text{adjacent}} = 2$

⑦

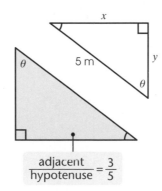

$\dfrac{\text{adjacent}}{\text{hypotenuse}} = \dfrac{3}{5}$

⑧

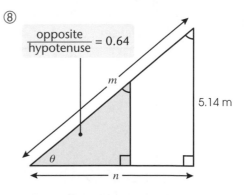

$\dfrac{\text{opposite}}{\text{hypotenuse}} = 0.64$

$a = $ _____ $b = $ _____ $x = $ _____ $y = $ _____ $m = $ _____ $n = $ _____

 ISBN: 978-1-77149-221-8

Determine whether each statement is true or false.

⑨ The adjacent side of a right triangle is always the same regardless of which angle it is in relation to.   T / F

⑩ The hypotenuse of a right triangle is always the same regardless of which angle it is in relation to.   T / F

⑪ It is impossible for an isosceles triangle to have a hypotenuse.   T / F

⑫ A triangle that has a hypotenuse cannot be an equilateral triangle.   T / F

⑬ The hypotenuse is not necessarily the longest side in a right triangle; it depends on which angle it is in relation to.   T / F

Solve the problems. Show your work.

⑭ In a model, an 8-cm ramp is built to cover a distance of 6 cm.

a. If the actual ramp covers a distance of 3 m, how long is the ramp?

_____

b. If the ramp has a rise of 2.65 m, what is the rise of the ramp in the model? Do they have the same slope? Explain.

_____

⑮ The frame of a staircase is as shown. For every run of 1 m, there is a rise of 0.15 m. What is s?

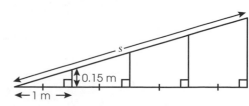

7.4   The Primary Trigonometric Ratios (2)

Example

Identify the sine, cosine, and tangent ratios for θ.

$$\sin \theta = \frac{YZ}{XY} \longleftarrow \frac{\text{opposite}}{\text{hypotenuse}}$$

$$\cos \theta = \frac{XZ}{XY} \longleftarrow \frac{\text{adjacent}}{\text{hypotenuse}}$$

$$\tan \theta = \frac{YZ}{XZ} \longleftarrow \frac{\text{opposite}}{\text{adjacent}}$$

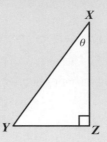

**Primary Trigonometric Ratios:
Sine, Cosine, and Tangent**

Consider any right triangle and one of its acute angles.

- sine (abbrev.: sin)
$$\sin \theta = \frac{\text{opposite}}{\text{hypotenuse}} = \frac{AB}{AC}$$

- cosine (abbrev.: cos)
$$\cos \theta = \frac{\text{adjacent}}{\text{hypotenuse}} = \frac{BC}{AC}$$

- tangent (abbrev.: tan)
$$\tan \theta = \frac{\text{opposite}}{\text{adjacent}} = \frac{AB}{BC}$$

Try This

Identify the primary trigonometric ratios for θ.

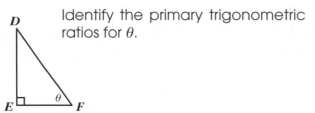

Find the ratios. Round the answers to 2 decimal places.

①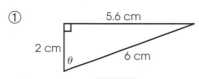

$$\sin \theta = \underline{\quad\quad} \doteq \underline{\quad\quad}$$

$$\cos \theta = \underline{\quad\quad} \doteq \underline{\quad\quad}$$

$$\tan \theta = \underline{\quad\quad} \doteq \underline{\quad\quad}$$

②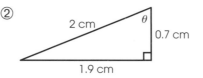

③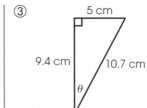

④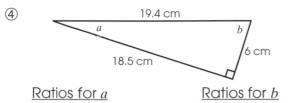

Ratios for *a*   Ratios for *b*

⑤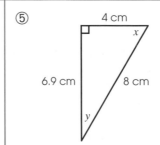

Ratios for *x*

Ratios for *y*

Evaluate each ratio using a calculator. Round your answers to 2 decimal places.

⑥   Sine   Cosine

sin 30° _____   cos 60° _____

sin 45° _____   cos 81° _____

sin 54° _____   cos 75° _____

sin 90° _____   cos 42° _____

sin 15° _____   cos 28° _____

HINT

Before evaluating, make sure that your calculator is in degree mode.

Tangent

tan 30° _____   tan 40° _____

lan 78° _____   tan 75° _____

tan 54° _____   tan 45° _____

⑦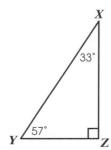

$\sin X$ _____

$\cos Y$ _____

$\sin Y$ _____

$\tan X$ _____

$\cos Z$ _____

Find the ratios in relation to the highlighted angles. Then answer the questions.

⑧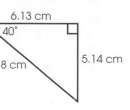

⑨

⑩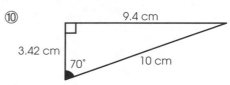

sin 40° ≐ _____

$\dfrac{\text{opposite}}{\text{hypotenuse}}$ ≐ _____

cos 40° ≐ _____

$\dfrac{\text{adjacent}}{\text{hypotenuse}}$ ≐ _____

tan 40° ≐ _____

$\dfrac{\text{opposite}}{\text{adjacent}}$ ≐ _____

⑪ What do you notice about each pair of trigonometric ratio and the specified ratio?

_____

⑫ If the tangent ratio of an angle in a right triangle is 1, what can you infer about the sides of the triangle?

_____

_____

ISBN: 978-1-77149-221-8

Label the angles in each triangle with the given ratios.

⑬
sin $a \doteq 0.83$
tan $b \doteq 0.67$

4 cm
7.21 cm
6 cm

⑭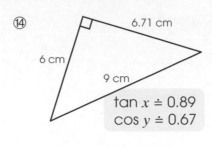
6.71 cm
6 cm
9 cm
tan $x \doteq 0.89$
cos $y \doteq 0.67$

⑮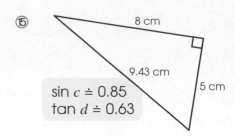
8 cm
9.43 cm
5 cm
sin $c \doteq 0.85$
tan $d \doteq 0.63$

⑯
sin $m = 0.92$
sin $n = 0.4$
4 cm
10 cm
9.2 cm

⑰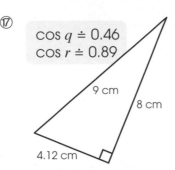
cos $q \doteq 0.46$
cos $r \doteq 0.89$
9 cm
8 cm
4.12 cm

⑱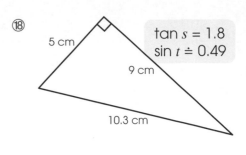
5 cm
9 cm
10.3 cm
tan $s = 1.8$
sin $t \doteq 0.49$

Solve for the unknowns.

⑲ $\sin 25° = \dfrac{x}{5}$

$0.42 \doteq \dfrac{x}{5}$

$x \doteq$ _____

⑳ $\tan 75° = \dfrac{a}{3}$

_____ $\doteq \dfrac{a}{3}$

$a \doteq$ _____

㉑ $\cos 35° = \dfrac{m}{10}$

_____ $\doteq \dfrac{m}{10}$

$m \doteq$ _____

㉒ $\cos 42° = \dfrac{4}{y}$

㉓ $\tan 72° = \dfrac{9}{k}$

㉔ $\sin 82° = \dfrac{b}{10}$

㉕ $\tan 10° = \dfrac{j}{15}$

㉖ $\cos 88° = \dfrac{12}{y}$

㉗ $\sin 38° = \dfrac{n}{7}$

㉘ $\sin 26° = \dfrac{i}{9}$

㉙ $\tan 21° \doteq \dfrac{6}{d}$

㉚ $\cos 63° = \dfrac{g}{20}$

ISBN: 978-1-77149-221-8

Example

Find the value of x.

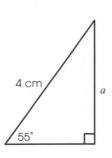

5 cm

28°

x

Solution:

Think In relation to the given measure of the angle, 28°, x is the adjacent side and the hypotenuse is 5 cm. Use the cosine ratio to solve for x.

$$\cos 28° = \frac{x}{5}$$

$$0.88 \doteq \frac{x}{5}$$

$$x \doteq 4.4$$

TRY THIS

Find the value of a.

4 cm

a

55°

Find the lengths of the missing sides.

③①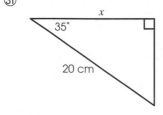

x

35°

20 cm

③②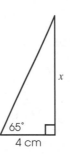

x

65°

4 cm

③③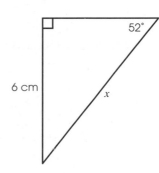

52°

6 cm

x

③④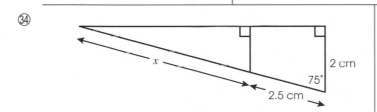

x

2 cm

75°

2.5 cm

③⑤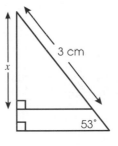

3 cm

x

53°

Find the measures of θ. Round your answers to the nearest degree.

③⑥ $\theta = \sin^{-1}(0.8)$

③⑦ $\theta = \cos^{-1}(0.5)$

③⑧ $\sin \theta = 0.5$

③⑨ $\tan \theta = \frac{5}{4}$

④⓪ $\cos \theta = 0.3$

④① $\sin \theta = \frac{0.4}{1.3}$

④② $\cos \theta = \frac{8}{9}$

④③ $\tan \theta = \frac{12}{5}$

④④ $\sin \theta = \frac{1.54}{2.07}$

HINT

Inverses of Primary Trigonometric Ratios

$\sin \theta = x$
$\theta = \sin^{-1}x$

$\cos \theta = x$
$\theta = \cos^{-1}x$

$\tan \theta = x$
$\theta = \tan^{-1}x$

Example

Find the measure of θ.

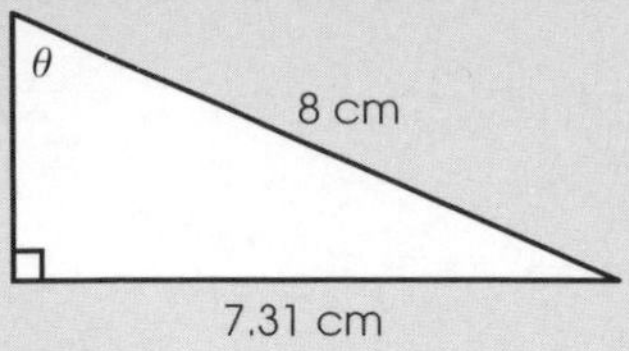

Solution:

Think In relation to θ, the opposite side and the hypotenuse are given. So, use the sine ratio to find θ.

$$\sin\theta = \frac{7.31}{8}$$

$$\theta = \sin^{-1}\left(\frac{7.31}{8}\right)$$

$$\theta \doteq 66^\circ$$

Try This

Find the measures of θ.

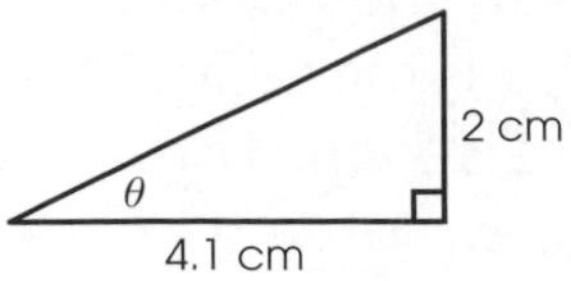

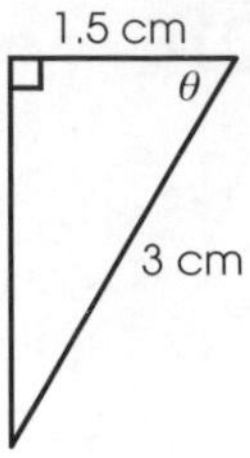

Check the correct ratio that solves for θ. Then find the measure of θ.

45

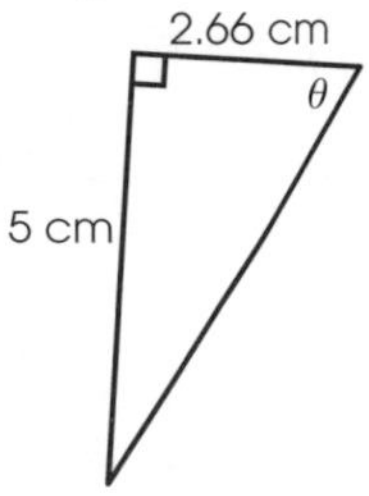

(A) $\tan\theta = \frac{5}{2.66}$

(B) $\tan\theta = \frac{2.66}{5}$

46

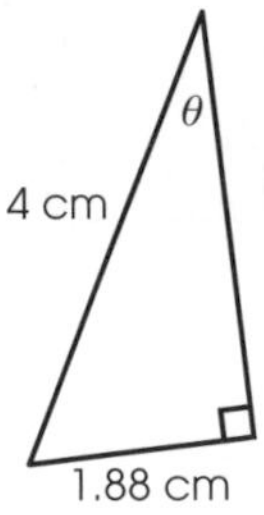

(A) $\sin\theta = \frac{1.88}{4}$

(B) $\cos\theta = \frac{1.88}{4}$

47

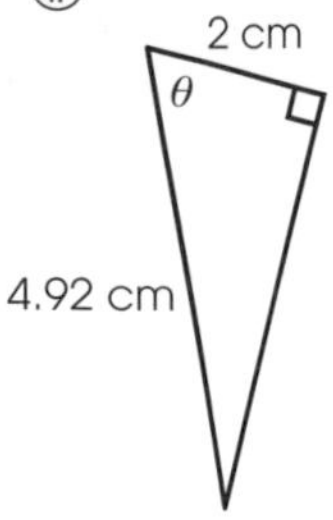

(A) $\cos\theta = \frac{2}{4.92}$

(B) $\cos\theta = \frac{4.92}{2}$

48

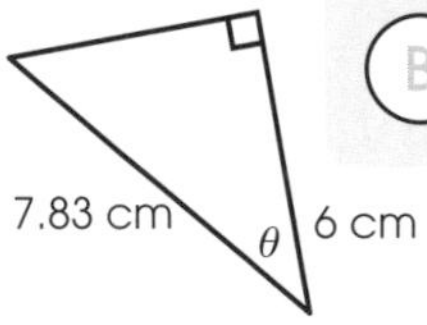

(A) $\sin\theta = \frac{6}{7.83}$

(B) $\cos\theta = \frac{6}{7.83}$

49

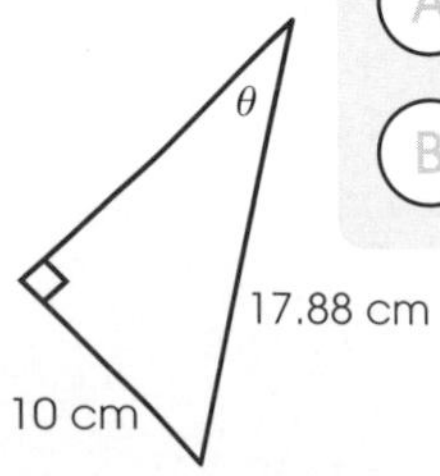

(A) $\sin\theta = \frac{10}{17.88}$

(B) $\tan\theta = \frac{17.88}{10}$

50

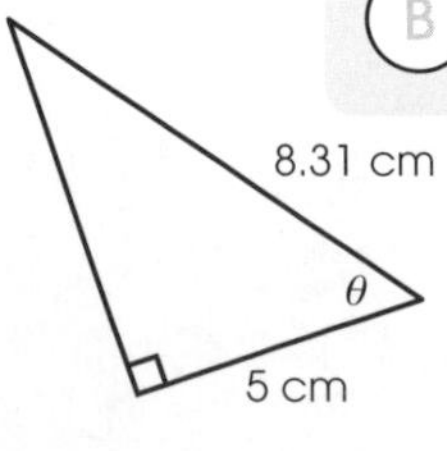

(A) $\sin\theta = \frac{5}{8.31}$

(B) $\cos\theta = \frac{5}{8.31}$

(51)

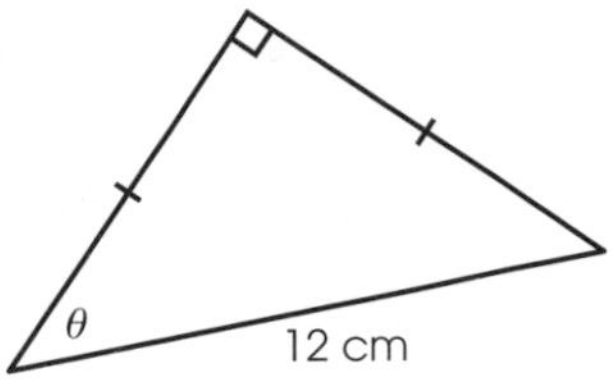

(52)

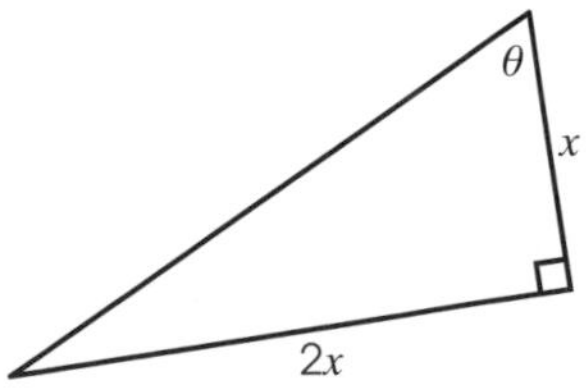

ISBN: 978-1-77149-221-8

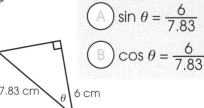

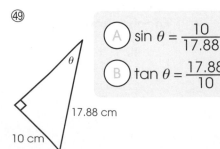

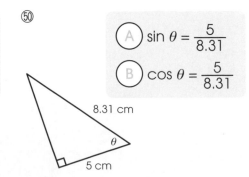

Solve for the unknowns using trigonometric ratios.

(53)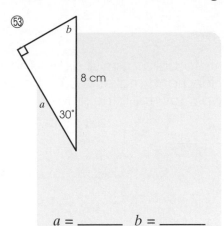

8 cm
30°

$a =$ _____ $b =$ _____

(54)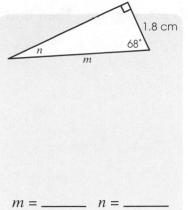

1.8 cm
68°
n
m

$m =$ _____ $n =$ _____

(55)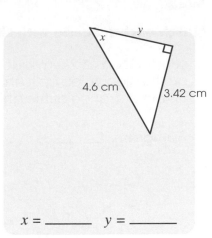

x
y
4.6 cm
3.42 cm

$x =$ _____ $y =$ _____

(56)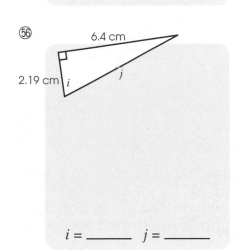

6.4 cm
2.19 cm
i
j

$i =$ _____ $j =$ _____

(57)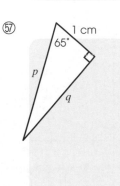

1 cm
65°
p
q

$p =$ _____ $q =$ _____

(58)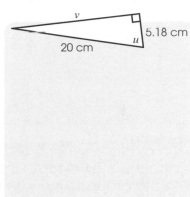

v
20 cm
u
5.18 cm

$u =$ _____ $v =$ _____

(59)

a
h
62°
20 cm
32 cm
38°

$a =$ _____ $h =$ _____

HINT

Keep in mind that the trigonometric ratios that you have learned can only be applied to right triangles.

(60)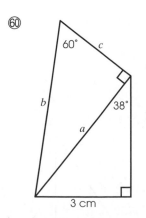

60°
c
b
38°
a
3 cm

$a =$ _____ $b =$ _____ $c =$ _____

(61)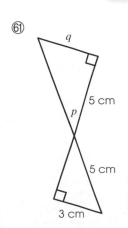

q
5 cm
p
5 cm
3 cm

$p =$ _____ $q =$ _____

ISBN: 978-1-77149-221-8

7.5 Solving Problems Modelled by Right Triangles

Match each scenario with the correct diagram. Then find the answer.

① Justin leans a 2.5-m ladder at a 57° angle to the floor to go up to the attic. How high is the entrance of the attic from the floor?

Diagram: _____

② Agnes wants to build a small slide. The slide is 2 m long and makes a 30° angle with the lawn. How tall is the slide?

Diagram: _____

③ An old tree is supported by a wire that is attached to the top of the tree and nailed to the ground. The wire is 13 m long and makes a 65° angle with the ground. How tall is the tree?

Diagram: _____

④ A squirrel stands 2 m away from a tree. It is looking at a pinecone and the angle of elevation is 40°. How high does the squirrel have to climb to reach the pinecone?

Diagram: _____

A
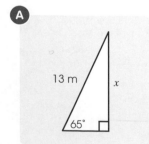

B
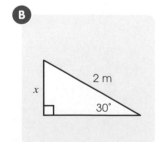

C
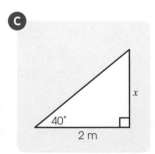

D
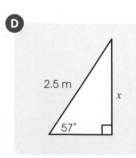

ISBN: 978-1-77149-221-8

Label each triangle with the information given in each problem. Then find the answer.

⑤ Alex looks up at a flagpole with an angle of elevation of 36.9°. Alex is 1.2 m tall and is standing 7.6 m from the flagpole. Find the height of the flagpole.

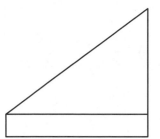

⑥ Candice has a treehouse. She stands 5 m from the base of the tree and the angle of elevation to the tree house is measured to be 23.75°. If Candice is 1.4 m tall, how high up is the treehouse from the ground?

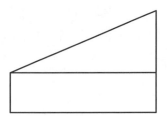

⑦ Julius's basketball is caught between the rafters on the ceiling. The angle of elevation to the ball is 41° and the angle of depression to the ground directly below the ball is 30°. Julius is 2.6 m off the ground on a stage. How high is the ceiling?

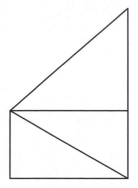

⑧ A park is 40° northwest of Jane's house and 50° northeast of Kate's house. If Kate's house is 40 km due west of Jane's house, whose house is closer to the park? By how much?

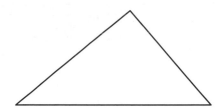

ISBN: 978-1-77149-221-8

For each problem, draw to illustrate the scenario. Then solve the problem.

⑨ Barney stares at a beehive that is in a tree with an estimated angle of elevation of 48°. He is 2.7 m away from the tree. What is the vertical distance between Barney and the beehive?

⑩ Sandra stands 15 m away from a tower. She looks up at the Canadian flag at the top of the 60-m tall tower. Sandra is 1.4 m tall. What is the angle of elevation?

⑪ Lisa and Ella are 1.2 m apart. Lisa is 1.48 m tall and her angle of elevation to the top of Ella's head is 3°. How tall is Ella?

⑫ Paul biked 3 km east and 2 km south from his home to a library. What is the bearing* from the library to Paul's house?
*bearing = a clockwise angle from the north

ISBN: 978-1-77149-221-8

For each problem, draw to illustrate the scenario. Then solve the problem.

⑬ Max stands on top of a house and looks at the neighbouring building that is 20 m away. The angle of elevation to the top of the building is 56° and the angle of depression to its base is 21.8°.

a. What is the height of the house?

b. What is the height of the building?

⑭ A firefighter is standing 6 m away from a building and 2.4 m off the ground on a ladder. When he looks up, he sees a cat at an angle of elevation of 66° and a dog on the roof of the building at an angle of 82.4°.

a. How high above the ground is the dog?

b. How high above the ground is the cat?

8 Acute Triangle Trigonometry

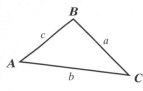

Sine law

In any acute triangle,

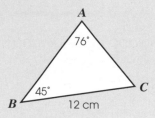

$$\frac{a}{\sin A} = \frac{b}{\sin B} = \frac{c}{\sin C}$$

Cosine law

In any acute triangle,

$$c^2 = a^2 + b^2 - 2ab \cos C$$

8.1 The Sine Law

Example

Find the length of AC.

A
76°
45°
B   12 cm   C

$$\frac{a}{\sin A} = \frac{b}{\sin B}$$

$$\frac{12}{\sin 76°} = \frac{b}{\sin 45°}$$

$$\frac{12}{0.97} \doteq \frac{b}{0.71}$$

$$b \doteq 8.78$$

$a = 12$
$b = AC$
$A = 76°$
$B = 45°$

The length of AC is about 8.78 cm.

Try This

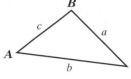

Find the length of AB.

A
15.4 cm
B 38°   64°
C

$$\frac{b}{\sin B} = \frac{c}{\sin C}$$

The length of AB is about _____ .

Find the length of BC.

①
A
80°
14 cm
B 55°   C

BC: _____

②
B
72°
A 47°   C
10.8 cm

BC: _____

③
A
58°
2.84 cm
B 60°   C

BC: _____

Find the measures of ∠B to the nearest degree.

④
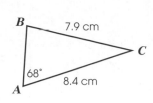

∠B: _____

⑤
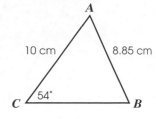

∠B: _____

⑥
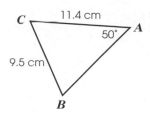

∠B: _____

Find the length of each unknown side. Round your answers to 2 decimal places.

⑦
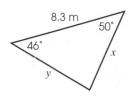

x: _____

y: _____

⑧
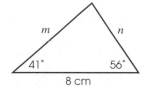

m: _____

n: _____

⑨
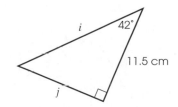

p: _____

q: _____

⑩
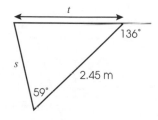

s: _____

t: _____

⑪
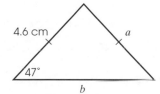

a: _____

b: _____

⑫
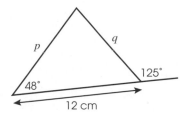

i: _____

j: _____

⑬
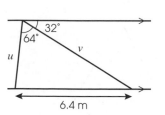

u: _____

v: _____

⑭
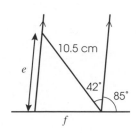

e: _____

f: _____

⑮
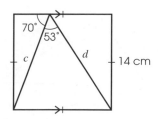

c: _____

d: _____

ISBN: 978-1-77149-221-8

Find the measure of each unknown angle to the nearest degree.

⑯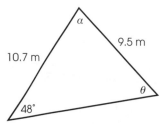

α: _____

θ: _____

⑰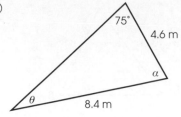

α: _____

θ: _____

⑱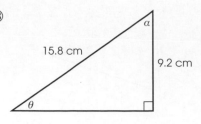

α: _____

θ: _____

⑲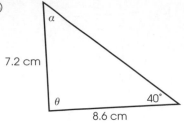

α: _____

θ: _____

⑳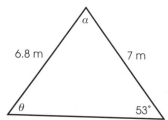

α: _____

θ: _____

㉑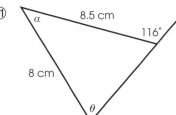

α: _____

θ: _____

㉒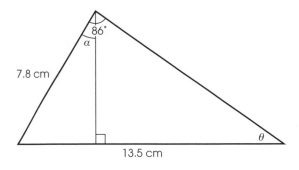

α: _____   θ: _____

㉓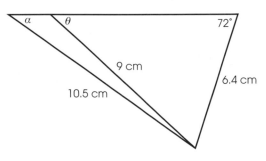

α: _____   θ: _____

㉔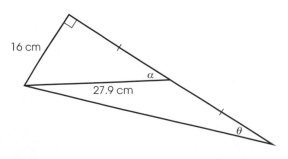

α: _____   θ: _____

㉕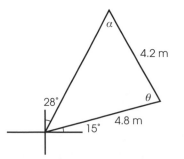

α: _____   θ: _____

ISBN: 978-1-77149-221-8

Find the measure of each unknown angle and the length of each unknown side.

㉖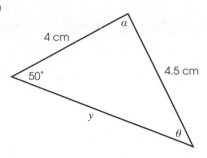

α: _____

θ: _____

y: _____

㉗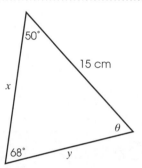

θ: _____

x: _____

y: _____

㉘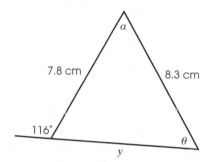

α: _____

θ: _____

y: _____

㉙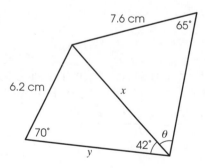

θ: _____

x: _____

y: _____

㉚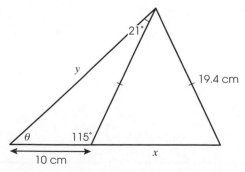

θ: _____

x: _____

y: _____

ISBN: 978-1-77149-221-8

8.2   Solving Problems Using the Sine Law

Draw a labelled triangle. Then find the measure of each unknown angle and the length of each unknown side.

① In $\triangle ABC$, $\angle A = 70°$, $\angle B = 65°$, and $a = 15$ cm.

② In $\triangle PQR$, $\angle Q = 42°$, $\angle R = 67°$ and $q = 8.4$ cm.

③ In $\triangle ABC$, $\angle B = 47°$, $\angle C = 82°$, and $a = 5$ cm.

④ In $\triangle PQR$, $\angle Q = 76°$, $r = 10$ cm and $q = 12$ cm.

Answer the questions.

⑤ Sue claims that if a and b are adjacent sides in an acute triangle, then $a \sin B = b \sin A$. Is she correct? Show your reasoning.

⑥ Why does it make sense that the sine law can also be written in the form below?

$$\frac{\sin A}{a} = \frac{\sin B}{b} = \frac{\sin C}{c}$$

⑦ If Katie wants to calculate an unknown side length or angle measure in an acute triangle, what minimum information does she need?

_____

⑧ With the given triangle, show that the sine law is true for all acute triangles.

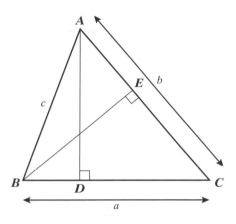

_____

⑨ Which quadrilateral has the shortest diagonal?

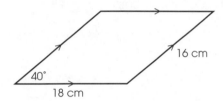 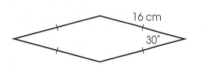 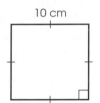

_____

⑩ Find the unknown lengths and angles to the nearest whole numbers.

a.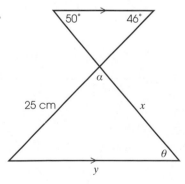

b.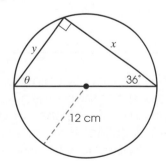

c.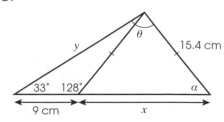

α: _____ x: _____ θ: _____ x: _____ α: _____ x: _____

θ: _____ y: _____ y: _____ θ: _____ y: _____

Solve the problems. Show your work.

⑪ The area of △ABC is 48.75 cm². What is the perimeter of △ABC?

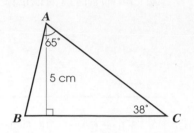

_____

⑫ Two swimmers are 18 m apart. There is a starfish below them. The angles of depression from Swimmer A and Swimmer B to the starfish are 47° and 58° respectively. Who is closer to the starfish?

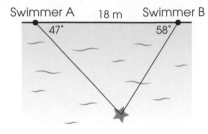

_____

⑬ Joe and Sue are standing at a seashore 150 m apart. The coastline is a straight line between them. Joe can see a ship at an angle of 72° and Sue can see it at an angle of 38°. How far are they from the ship?

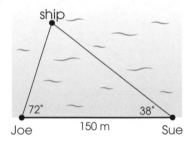

_____

⑭ Airplane A is flying toward an airport which is 125 km away. Pilot A can see Airplane B 45° to his right. Airplane B is also flying toward the airport. Pilot B can see Airplane A 50° to his left. How far is Airplane B from the airport?

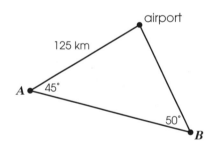

_____

⑮ Airplane A and Airplane B are both approaching an airport from directions directly opposite one another. When Airplane A is 12 km away from the airport, Pilot A reports an angle of depression of 67.5° to the tower and Pilot B reports an angle of depression of 52° to the same tower. How far apart are the airplanes?

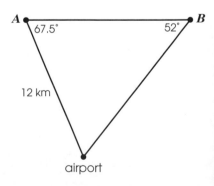

_____

 ISBN: 978-1-77149-221-8

⑯ The compass bearing of Ship A from the port is S62°E and from the lighthouse is N75°E. The compass bearing of Ship B from the port is S25°W and from the lighthouse is N70°W. If Ship A is 12 km from the port, how far is Ship B from the port?

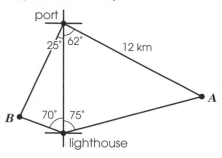

Compass Bearing

- directions measured either from the north or from the south

- always in the form
  - N⬜°E or N⬜°W
  - S⬜°E or S⬜°W

e.g.

The compass bearing of A from O is N72°E.

The compass bearing of B from O is S40°E.

⑰ Bird A and Bird B fly from the same nest in directions N56°E and N28°W respectively. Bird B is N75°W from Bird A. If the birds are 125 m apart, which bird is closer to the nest?

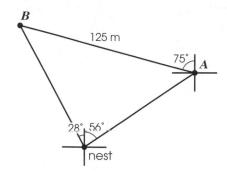

⑱ Ted uses a piece of rope to form a square with a side length of 23 cm. Then he uses the same rope to form a triangle with side lengths that are in the ratio of 6:8:9. The measure of the greatest angle in the triangle is 78.6°. Find the measures of the other two angles to one decimal place.

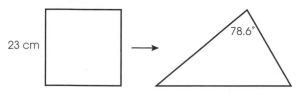

⑲ A piece of 40-cm-long wire is bent to form an isosceles triangle, of which one angle is 50°. What are the possible lengths of the sides of the triangle?

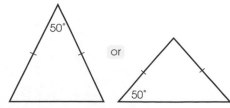

⑳ Mr. Duncan submitted a survey report on a piece of property to his supervisor. He was asked to redo the report after his supervisor checked his first drawing. Describe what is wrong with the drawing.

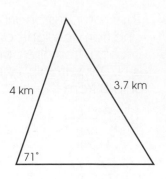

_____

㉑ Sam and Caleb both left a parking lot. They each drive in a straight line at an angle of 65° to each other. Sam is driving at a speed of 60 km/h. After 5 minutes, Caleb is N20°E from Sam. How far apart are they?

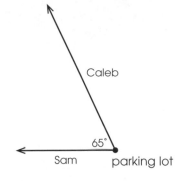

_____

㉒ Swing Sets A and B are on the opposite side of a slide. The slide is 200 m from Swing Set B. A triangular fence is to be built to enclose the swing sets and the slide. The angle formed by the fence at Swing Set B is 87° and the one at Swing Set A is 67°. What is the distance between the swing sets? How long is the fence?

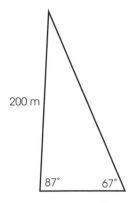

_____

㉓ A ceiling light is suspended from the ceiling by two wires. One wire is 125 cm long and forms an angle of 55° with the ceiling. The other wire is 45 cm longer. What is the angle formed by the longer wire with the ceiling?

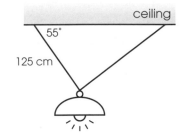

_____

㉔ On a ship sailing north at a speed of 15 km/h, Mr. Campbell noticed that a tower on a shore had a bearing of N24°E. After 15 minutes, Mr. Campbell observes that the bearing of the tower is now S80°E. How far is the ship from the tower?

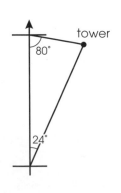

_____

   ISBN: 978-1-77149-221-8

Draw a labelled triangle using the information provided in each question. Then answer the question.

㉕ Mr. Scott measured a triangular playground which has sides of 200 m, 192 m, and 250 m and the smallest angle is 49°. What are the measures of the other two angles?

_____

㉖ In $\triangle ABC$, $\angle A = 58°$, $\angle C = 74°$, and $b = 4.8$ cm. What are the area and the perimeter of $\triangle ABC$?

_____

㉗ Two ships are sailing from Halifax. The Nina is sailing due east and the Pinta is sailing in the direction of S43°E. After an hour, the Nina has travelled 115 km and the distance between the two ships is 90 km. How far from Halifax is the Pinta?

_____

㉘ In $\triangle PQR$, $\angle Q$ is 72°, r is 7.8 cm, and q has a length between 9 cm and 10.2 cm. What is the greatest measure of $\angle R$?

_____

㉙ On a map, Kevin is on the east side of a 450-m-wide canyon and Wayne is on the west. There is a bird's nest at the angles of depression of 60° and 72° from Kevin and Wayne respectively. How far are they from the nest?

_____

8.3 The Cosine Law

Example

Find the length of c.

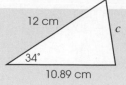
12 cm
c
34°
10.89 cm

Solution: Apply the cosine law.

$c^2 = a^2 + b^2 - 2ab \cos C$ ⟵ cosine law

$c^2 = 10.89^2 + 12^2 - 2(10.89)(12) \cos 34°$

$c^2 \doteq 45.91$ | $a = 10.89$ $b = 12$ $C = 34°$ |

$c \doteq 6.78$

The length of c is about 6.78 cm.

TRY THIS

Find the length of c.

5 cm
c
50°
5 cm

Check the correct equation for each triangle. Then solve for the unknown.

①
x
7.3 cm
85°
2.6 cm

(A) $2.6^2 = x^2 + 7.3^2 - 2(x)(7.3) \cos 85°$

(B) $x^2 = 2.6^2 + 7.3^2 - 2(2.6)(7.3) \cos 85°$

②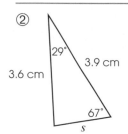
29°
3.6 cm
3.9 cm
67°
s

(A) $s^2 = 3.6^2 + 3.9^2 - 2(3.6)(3.9) \cos 29°$

(B) $s^2 = 3.6^2 + 3.9^2 - 2(3.6)(3.9) \cos 67°$

③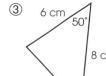
6 cm
50°
8 cm
m

(A) $8^2 = 6^2 + m^2 - 2(6)(m) \cos 50°$

(B) $m^2 = 6^2 + 8^2 - 2(6)(8) \cos 50°$

④
y
12 cm
80°
15.66 cm

(A) $y^2 = 12^2 + 15.66^2 - 2(12)(15.66) \cos 80°$

(B) $15.66^2 = y^2 + 12^2 - 2(y)(12) \cos 80°$

⑤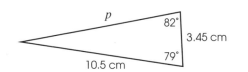
p
82°
3.45 cm
79°
10.5 cm

(A) $p^2 = 10.5^2 + 3.45^2 - 2(10.5)(3.45) \cos 82°$

(B) $p^2 = 10.5^2 + 3.45^2 - 2(10.5)(3.45) \cos 79°$

ISBN: 978-1-77149-221-8

Circle the triangles that have sufficient information for the cosine law to be applied. Then find the unknowns.

⑥

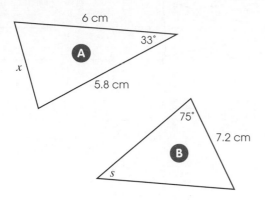

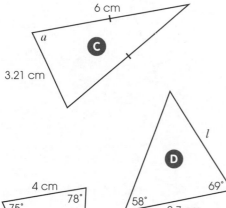

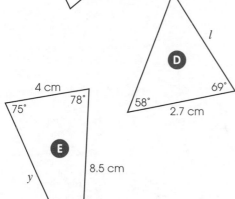

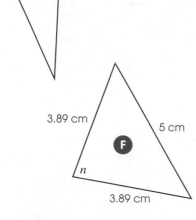

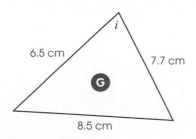

Triangle ◯

_____

Triangle ◯

_____

Triangle ◯

_____

Triangle ◯

_____

Triangle ◯

Find the missing lengths and angles.

⑦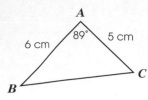

BC = _____
$\angle B$ = _____

⑧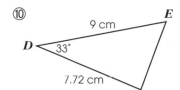

$\angle R$ = _____
$\angle Q$ = _____

⑨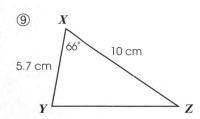

YZ = _____
$\angle Z$ = _____

⑩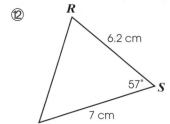

EF = _____
$\angle E$ = _____

⑪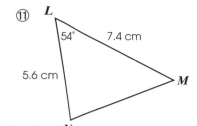

MN = _____
$\angle M$ = _____

⑫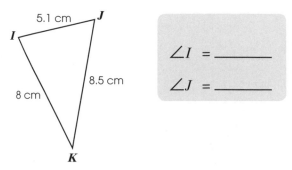

$\angle R$ = _____
RT = _____

⑬

$\angle I$ = _____
$\angle J$ = _____

⑭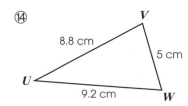

$\angle V$ = _____
$\angle W$ = _____

ISBN: 978-1-77149-221-8

**Check whether the cosine law can be applied to each triangle to solve for x. The markings,
• and ▲, indicate the lengths and angles that are given. Then answer the questions.**

⑮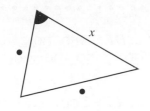

Yes / No

⑯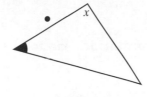

Yes / No

⑰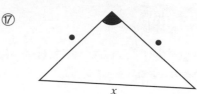

Yes / No

⑱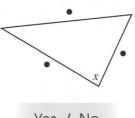

Yes / No

⑲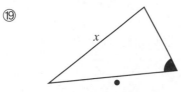

Yes / No

⑳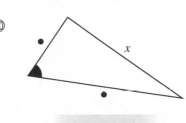

Yes / No

㉑ Consider the acute triangle shown. List the least additional information necessary for the cosine law to be applicable to solve for each unknown.

a. solving for a when

 • b and c are given

 _____

 • b and $\angle A$ are given

 _____

b. solving for $\angle A$ when

 • a and c are given

 _____

 • b and $\angle B$ are given

 _____

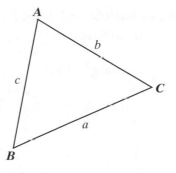

㉒ Consider the given right triangle.

a. Use the cosine law to find the value of b.

 _____

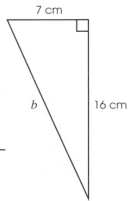

b. Describe the relationship between the Pythagorean theorem and the cosine law when there is a right angle in the triangle. Show your reasoning.

_____

ISBN: 978-1-77149-221-8

8.4 Solving Problems Using the Cosine Law

Example

Consider △ABC with the given information. Find the measure of ∠B.

$$AB = 4.6 \text{ cm} \quad AC = 6.2 \text{ cm} \quad BC = 5.6 \text{ cm}$$

Solution: Make a sketch of the triangle and label it with the given information. Then solve for ∠B.

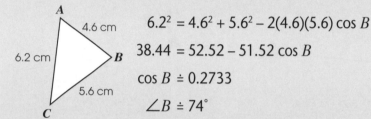

$$6.2^2 = 4.6^2 + 5.6^2 - 2(4.6)(5.6)\cos B$$

$$38.44 = 52.52 - 51.52 \cos B$$

$$\cos B \doteq 0.2733$$

$$\angle B \doteq 74°$$

The measure of ∠B is 74°.

> **Try This**
>
> Consider △DEF with the given information. Find the length of DE.
>
> $DF = 4.3 \text{ cm} \quad EF = 5 \text{ cm} \quad \angle F = 35°$

Make a sketch of each triangle as described. Then solve for the unknown.

① **Triangle XYZ**   Length of XZ:
- $XY = 3.16$ cm
- $YZ = 4$ cm
- $\angle Y = 40°$

② **Triangle LMN**   Length of LM:
- $LN = 15.66$ cm
- $MN = 12$ cm
- $\angle N = 65°$

③ **Triangle IJK**   Measure of ∠I:
- $IJ = 7$ cm
- $IK = 4.5$ cm
- $JK = 6$ cm

④ **Triangle PQR**   Measure of ∠P:
- $PQ = 12.5$ cm
- $PR = 12$ cm
- $QR = 5$ cm

ISBN: 978-1-77149-221-8

Solve for the unknowns.

⑤

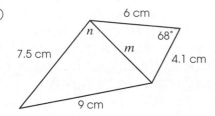

$x = $ _____ $y = $ _____

⑥

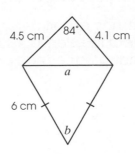

$a = $ _____ $b = $ _____

⑦

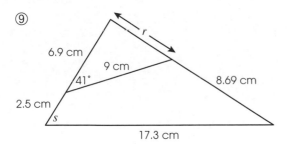

$m = $ _____ $n = $ _____

⑧

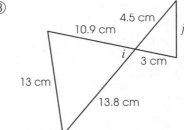

$i = $ _____ $j = $ _____

⑨

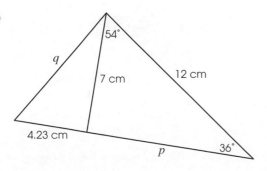

$r = $ _____ $s = $ _____

⑩

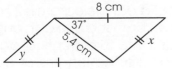

$p = $ _____ $q = $ _____

ISBN: 978-1-77149-221-8

Make a sketch of each shape. Answer the questions.

⑪ An isosceles triangle has a perimeter of 21 cm and the lengths of the identical sides are 8 cm each. What are the measures of its angles?

⑫ The perimeter of a parallelogram is 20 cm, one of its sides is 3 cm, and one of its angles is 68°. Joe folds it into two identical acute triangles. What are the lengths of each triangle?

⑬ Triangle ABC is inside a circle where AB is the diameter with a length of 10 cm. Vertex C is on the circle such that AC is 3 cm. What is the measure of $\angle A$?

⑭ Two isosceles triangles are attached to form a kite. The small triangle has identical sides of 4 cm and their contained angle is 30°. The identical sides of the big triangle are 6 cm each. What are the measures of the angles in the big triangle?

⑮ A polygon is cut into identical isosceles triangles. Each triangle has side lengths of 12 cm, 12 cm, and 9.18 cm.

   a. What are the measures of the angles in each triangle?

   b. How many sides does the polygon have?

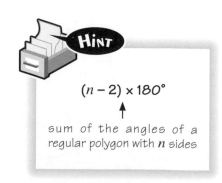

HINT

$(n - 2) \times 180°$

↑

sum of the angles of a regular polygon with n sides

ISBN: 978-1-77149-221-8

Solve the problems with the given diagrams.

⑯ Melissa wants to shoot a soccer ball into a net. What angle should she shoot within to score?

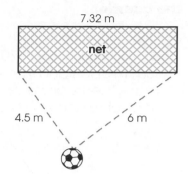

_____

⑰ What is the distance between the tips of the hour hand and the minute hand?

_____

⑱ Tarzan takes a 14-m-long vine and swings 62° to cross a ravine. What is the width of the ravine that he swung across?

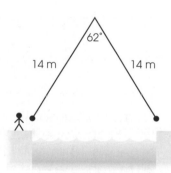

_____

⑲ Jason is in a hot-air balloon. From the sky, he sees Ada on one side and Ellen on the other side. How far apart are Ada and Ellen?

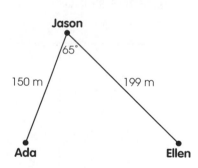

_____

⑳ A leaning tree is supported by a stick to keep it from falling. How long is the stick?

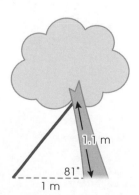

_____

ISBN: 978-1-77149-221-8   **COMPLETE MathSmart (Grade 10)**   **169**

Label each diagram with the correct measurements to illustrate each scenario. Then answer the question.

㉑ Two routes diverge at a treasure chest to two islands at 70°. The islands are 35 km apart and they are equal distances from the treasure chest. How far apart is each island from the treasure chest?

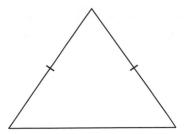

㉒ Tessa fences an area enclosed by three posts. The distances between the posts are 2 m, 3 m, and 2.5 m. What is the measure of the largest angle that the fencing makes?

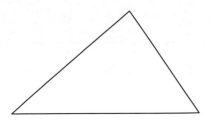

㉓ From Ivy's school, there is a hot dog stand N50°E and one N30°W. She knows the school is 18 m from the west stand and 30 m from the east stand. How far apart are the stands?

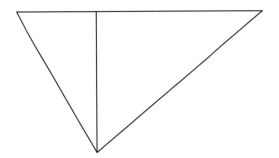

㉔ Amy and Juno left their home at the same time. Amy drove S70°E at 60 km/h and Juno drove N30°E at 70 km/h. How far apart will they be after 2 hours?

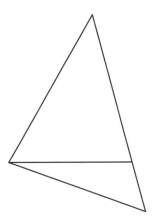

Sketch a diagram to illustrate each scenario. Solve the problem. Show your work.

㉕ Loretta's and Jane's kites are tangled in the air. The kites' strings are 12 m and 16 m long and the angle made between the strings is 36°. How far apart are the girls?

㉖ A scuba diver sees two dolphins above him. He sees one at an angle of elevation of 30° and the other one in the opposite direction at an angle of elevation of 40°. The diver is at an equal distance of 50 m from both dolphins. How far apart are the dolphins?

㉗ Andrei was practising for a triathlon. He swam 2 km N60°E, biked 10 km S24°W, and then ran back toward the starting point. How far did he run?

㉘ A triangular flag has side lengths of 1 m and 2.5 m and their contained angle is 67°. What is the perimeter of the flag?

㉙ A parallelogram has side lengths of 4 cm and 7 cm and an acute angle of 73.4°. Can you find the area of the parallelogram? If so, show your work.

8.5   Applying the Sine Law and the Cosine Law

Example

Find the measure of θ.

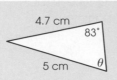

Solution:

The information given are the side lengths of two sides and the angle that is opposite to one of the sides. Use the sine law.

$$\frac{5}{\sin 83°} = \frac{4.7}{\sin \theta}$$

Applying the sine law

$a = 5 \qquad A = 83°$
$b = 4.7 \qquad B = \theta$

$$\frac{5}{0.99} \doteq \frac{4.7}{\sin \theta}$$

$$\sin \theta \doteq 0.9306$$

$$\theta \doteq 69°$$

The measure of θ is 69°.

Try This

Find the length of XY.

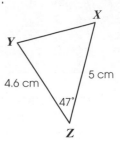

For each triangle, check to show whether each unknown can be solved using the sine law or the cosine law. Solve it and show your work.

① Find the size of $\angle C$.

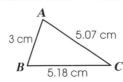

- (A) sine law
- (B) cosine law

② Find the length of DE.

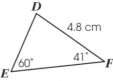

- (A) sine law
- (B) cosine law

③ Find the size of $\angle P$.

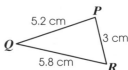

- (A) sine law
- (B) cosine law

④ Find the length of MN.

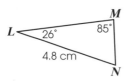

- (A) sine law
- (B) cosine law

⑤ Find the size of $\angle J$.

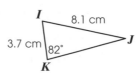

- (A) sine law
- (B) cosine law

⑥ Find the length of VW.

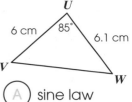

- (A) sine law
- (B) cosine law

ISBN: 978-1-77149-221-8

Apply both laws to find the unknowns.

⑦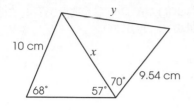

⑧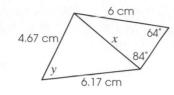

⑨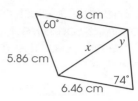

⑩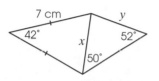

⑪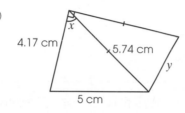

⑫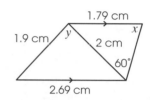

Make a sketch of each triangle. Then find the measures.

⑬ △*ABC*

- an acute triangle
- Point *D* lies on *AB*
- Point *E* lies on *AC*
- *DE* bisects *AB* and *AC*
- *AB* = 10 cm, *AC* = 12 cm,
  ∠*A* = 48°

a. Length of *DE*:

b. Size of ∠*C*:

⑭ △*XYZ*

- an isosceles triangle
- Point *M* lies on *YZ*
- *XM* bisects *YZ*
- ∠*X* = 40°, ∠*Z* = 70°,
  YZ = 10 cm

a. Length of *XY*:

b. Area of △*XYZ*:

ISBN: 978-1-77149-221-8

Solve the problems with the given diagrams.

⑮ A theatre is east of Jon's house and a library is southwest of the theatre. What is the angle of the routes diverged at the theatre?

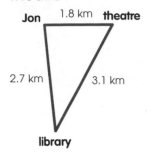

⑯ A picture is hung crooked on a wall. Find the length of the picture.

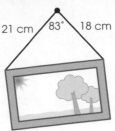

⑰ A playground slide is as shown. What is the length of the stairs?

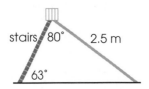

⑱ A swimmer panicked while swimming. Lifeguards A and B were on duty as shown. How much closer was Lifeguard B than Lifeguard A to the swimmer?

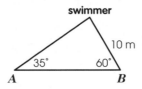

⑲ Four students are playing with a hacky sack. Their positions are as shown. How far apart are Students A and B?

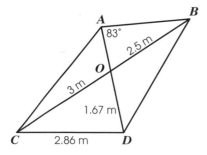

⑳ A wooden tower is as shown. What is its height?

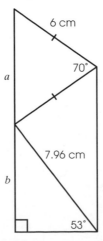

ISBN: 978-1-77149-221-8

Draw a diagram to illustrate each scenario. Solve the problem. Show your work.

㉑ A parallelogram has side lengths of 18 cm and 20 cm. Its shorter diagonal is 24 cm. What are the sizes of the angles of the parallelogram?

㉒ A chimney is on a roof. Katrina stands 10 m away from the base of the house and looks up at an angle of elevation of 27° and 29° respectively to the roof and the top of the chimney. How tall is the chimney?

㉓ Nora is on a swing. The angle that she is swinging at is 75° and the horizontal distances from one side to the other is 2.2 m. What is the length of the swing?

㉔ Ken has driven 10 km N20°E and then 5 km S15°E from home. How far away is he from home?

㉕ Stanley is on his balcony and is looking at the base of the building across the street at an angle of depression of 5° and its roof at an angle of elevation of 51°. The building is 53 m tall. How far apart are Stanley's house and the building?

ISBN: 978-1-77149-221-8

Complete MathSmart 10
Cumulative Review

In this review, the questions are classified into the four categories below.

- **K** Knowledge and Understanding
- **A** Application
- **C** Communication
- **T** Thinking

The icons beside the question numbers indicate in which categories the questions belong.

ISBN: 978-1-77149-221-8

Circle the correct answers.

①

K

Consider the given parabola.

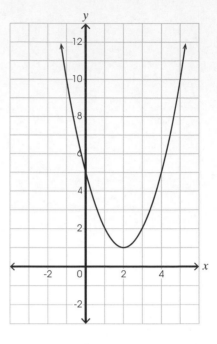

a. Which of the following statements are true?

A. The x-intercept is $(0,5)$.

B. $(2,1)$ is the vertex.

C. The minimum value is 1.

D. $(1,2)$ is the vertex.

b. What is the y-intercept of the graph?

A. $(5,0)$

B. $(0,5)$

C. $(4,5)$

D. $(5,4)$

c. What are the zeros of the graph?

A. $x = 0$

B. $y = 5$

C. $x = 2$

D. It has no zeros.

d. Which of the following is the equation of the graph?

A. $y = (x + 2)^2 + 1$

B. $y = (x - 2)^2 - 1$

C. $y = (x - 2)^2 + 1$

D. $y = (x + 2)^2 - 1$

e. If the parabola contains a reflection in the x-axis, which parameter of the original equation will be changed, given that $y = a(x - h)^2 + k$?

A. a

B. h

C. k

D. All parameters will be changed.

ISBN: 978-1-77149-221-8

② Consider △ABC.

K a. What is Point D?

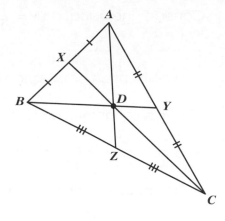

    A. a centroid

    B. a circumcentre

    C. an orthocentre

    D. a vertex

b. Which of the following statements are correct?

    A. AZ is a perpendicular bisector of BC.

    B. Y is the midpoint of AC.

    C. If $AC = BC$, then CX is a perpendicular bisector of AB.

    D. all of the above

c. How does AC relate to BY?

    A. BY is the altitude of AC.

    B. BY is the perpendicular bisector of AC.

    C. BY is the median of AC.

    D. none of the above

③ Consider the given circle. What is its equation?

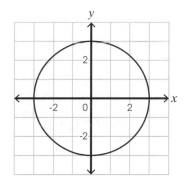

K

    A. $x^2 + y^2 = 3$

    B. $x + y = 9$

    C. $x^2 + y^2 = 9$

    D. insufficient information

④ Which of the following can be used to solve for x?

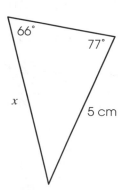

K

    A. sine law

    B. cosine law

    C. Pythagorean relationship

    D. midpoint formula

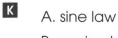 ISBN: 978-1-77149-221-8

⑤ K Consider the equation $y = \frac{1}{3}(x - 1)^2 + 2$. Which of the following transformations is applied to $y = x^2$?

A. a horizontal compression by a factor of $\frac{1}{3}$

B. a translation of 2 units to the left

C. a translation of 1 unit to the right

D. a vertical stretch by a factor of 3

⑥ K What can you conclude about $\triangle ABC$ and $\triangle XYZ$?

A. $\triangle ABC \cong \triangle XYZ$

B. $\triangle ABC \sim \triangle XYZ$

C. They are neither congruent nor similar.

D. insufficient information

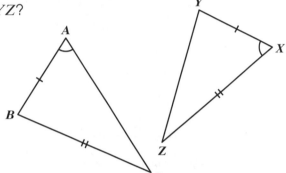

⑦ K Consider the given line segment.

a. Which of the following finds the midpoint?

A. $(x,y) = (\frac{-4 - 4}{2}, \frac{1 - (-1)}{2})$

B. $(x,y) = (\frac{-4 + 4}{2}, \frac{1 + (-1)}{2})$

C. $(x,y) = (\frac{1 + (-1)}{2}, \frac{-4 + 4}{2})$

D. $(x,y) = (\frac{1 - (-1)}{2}, \frac{-4 - 4}{2})$

b. Which of the following finds the distance, d, between the points?

A. $d = \sqrt{(4 - (-4))^2} + \sqrt{(-1 - 1)^2}$

B. $d = \sqrt{(4 + (-4))^2} + \sqrt{(-1 + 1)^2}$

C. $d = \sqrt{(4 - (-4))^2 + (-1 - 1)^2}$

D. $d = \sqrt{(4 + (-4))^2 + (-1 + 1)^2}$

ISBN: 978-1-77149-221-8

⑧ Which of the following is the fully factored form of $x^3 + x^2 - 6x$?

A. $x^2(x + 1) - 6x$

B. $x(x^2 + x - 6)$

C. $x(x - 2)(x + 3)$

D. $x^3 + x(x - 6)$

⑨ Which of the following describe the lines in a linear system that has no solutions?

A. They do not intersect.

B. They are parallel.

C. They coincide.

D. none of the above

⑩ Consider $\triangle ABC$.

a. Which angle is θ if $\sin \theta = \dfrac{8}{10}$?

    A. $\angle A$

    B. $\angle B$

    C. $\angle C$

    D. insufficient information

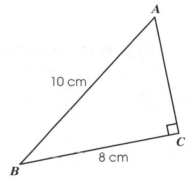

b. Which of the following finds the measure of $\angle B$?

    A. $\sin B = \dfrac{10}{8}$

    B. $\tan B = \dfrac{10}{8}$

    C. $\cos B = \dfrac{8}{10}$

    D. $\sin^{-1} B = \dfrac{8}{10}$

c. What is the measure of α if $\cos \alpha = \dfrac{8}{10}$?

    A. $45°$

    B. $30°$

    C. $90°$

    D. $37°$

ISBN: 978-1-77149-221-8

For each statement, circle T for true and F for false.

⑪ **K** The slopes of all 3 sides of a triangle must be different.　　　　**T / F**

⑫ **T** If a point is the centroid, the circumcentre, and also the orthocentre of a triangle, then it must be an equilateral triangle.　　　　**T / F**

⑬ **K** The equation of a circle is $x^2 + y^2 = \sqrt{4^2}$. Its area is $4^2\pi$ square units.　　　　**T / F**

⑭ **K** Two relations that have solutions must intersect at only one point.　　　　**T / F**

⑮ **T** A quadratic relation with $a < 0$ and $k < 0$ must have no solutions.　　　　**T / F**

⑯ **T** In an acute triangle, if the measures of two angles and two sides are given, then the sine law can be applied to find the remaining side.　　　　**T / F**

⑰ **K** All quadratic equations can be solved using the quadratic formula.　　　　**T / F**

Factor each polynomial fully.

⑱ **K** $2x^2 - 6x - 8$

⑲ **K** $-12x^2 - 24x - 12$

⑳ **K** $b^2 - 36$

㉑ **T** $a^4 - 16$

㉒ **T** $\dfrac{1}{6}x^2 - \dfrac{1}{2}x - 3$

㉓ **T** $3a^6 - 5a^3 - 2$

㉔ Write an equation for each line in slope y-intercept form and graph it.

K

a. slope = $\frac{1}{2}$
   y-intercept = 3

b. passes through
   (-2,3) and (1,-3)

c. x-intercept = 5
   y-intercept = -2

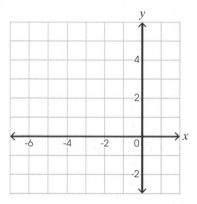

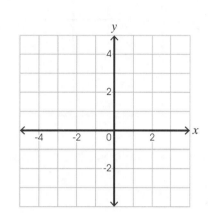

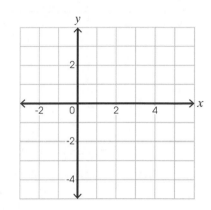

㉕ Find the centroid of $\triangle ABC$.

K

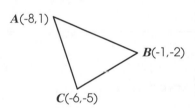

A(-8,1)

B(-1,-2)

C(-6,-5)

㉖ Find the orthocentre of $\triangle XYZ$.

K

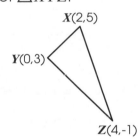

X(2,5)

Y(0,3)

Z(4,-1)

㉗ Find the area of $\triangle PQR$.

T

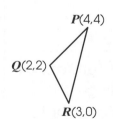

P(4,4)

Q(2,2)

R(3,0)

㉘ Prove that $\triangle IJK$ is a right scalene triangle.

T

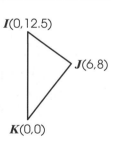

I(0,12.5)

J(6,8)

K(0,0)

 ISBN: 978-1-77149-221-8

Sketch the graph of each relation. Then answer the questions.

㉙ K

$y = 2(x - 1)^2$

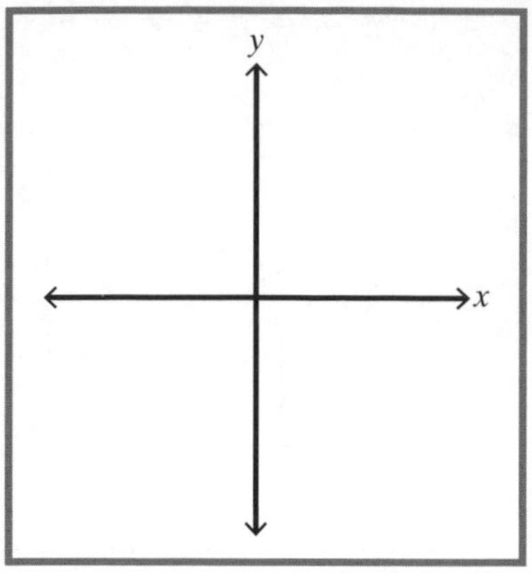

$y = -2x^2 - x + 1$

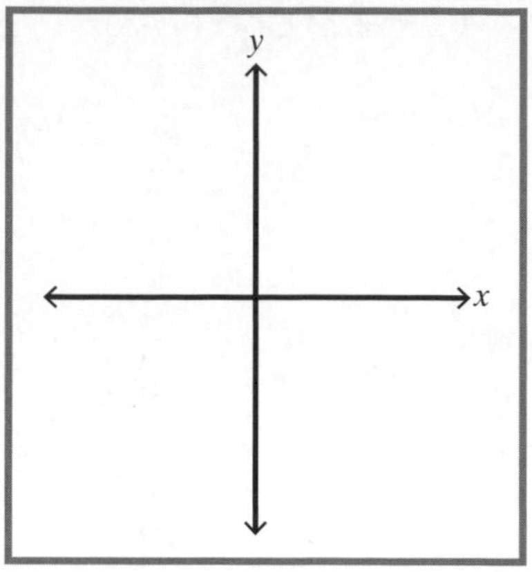

$y = -x^2 - 4$

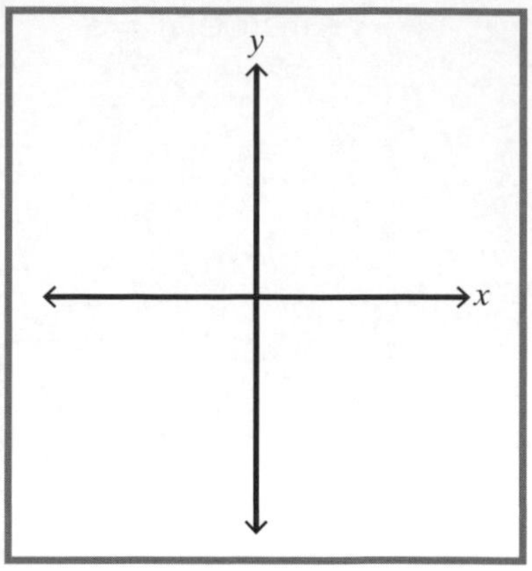

㉚ C Answer the questions about the relations above. Describe your reasoning.

a. Which relation has a minimum?

____

b. Which relation has no solutions?

____

Write a quadratic equation with the given descriptions.

㉛ K
- maximum at (0,4)
- (2,-4) lies on it

㉜ K
- x-intercepts at (-2,0) and (-8,0)
- minimum value of -4.5

㉝ K
- vertex at (3,5)
- zero at (8,0)

㉞ T
- y-intercept at (0,0)
- passes through (-4,0) and (-5,-5)

㉟ T
- axis of symmetry at $x = 4$
- passes through (0,0)
- maximum value of 7

㊱ T
- zeros at (2,0) and (3,0)
- minimum value of -5

ISBN: 978-1-77149-221-8

Find the unknowns. Then answer the questions.

㊲
K

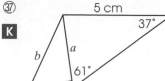

5 cm
37°
a
b
61°
2.15 cm

㊳
K

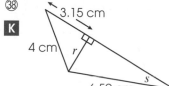

3.15 cm
4 cm   *r*
6.59 cm   *s*

㊴
K

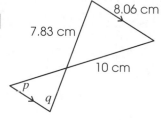

8.06 cm
7.83 cm
10 cm
p
q

㊵
T

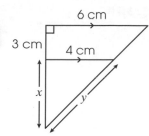

6 cm
3 cm   4 cm
x
y

㊶
T

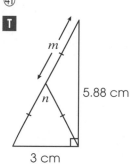

m
5.88 cm
n
3 cm

㊷
C
List the properties that similar triangles have. Out of the 5 pairs of triangles above, 2 of them are similar triangles. Circle them.

_____

_____

㊸
C
Two sides of an acute triangle are known. To find the length of the remaining side using the cosine law, which measure of the triangle is needed?

_____

_____

㊹
C
If two angles and one side of an acute triangle are known, is it guaranteed that the remaining sides of the triangle can be found using the sine law? Explain.

_____

_____

ISBN: 978-1-77149-221-8

Write each relation in vertex form. Then describe the transformations applied to $y = x^2$ and sketch its graph.

45 $y = -2x^2 + 16x - 27$

K
C

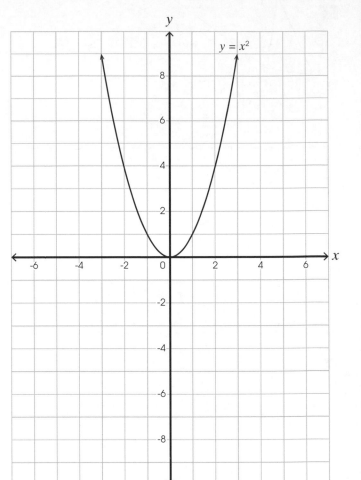

Transformation:

_____

_____

_____

46 $y = \frac{1}{2}(x - 2)(x + 2)$

K
C

Transformation:

_____

_____

_____

47 A transformation of 3 units to the left, 2 units down, and a vertical compression by a factor

C of $\frac{1}{2}$ is applied to $y = -2x^2 + 16x - 27$.

a. What is the new relation?

_____

_____

b. Describe the transformations applied to $y = x^2$ to create the graph of the new relation.

_____

_____

c. What transformations must be applied to the new relation if its graph is identical to $y = x^2$?

_____

_____

ISBN: 978-1-77149-221-8

Find the solutions for the systems of linear equations algebraically. Then identify the relationship of the lines for each system of equations.

㊽ $2x + y = 1$
K $4x - y = -7$

㊾ $3x + y - 8 = 0$
K $6x + 2y = -5$

㊿ $5x + 6y = 35$
K $x + 1.2y - 7 = 0$

The lines _____

_____ .

_____

_____

_____

_____

(51) 7 cookies and 6 doughnuts at a store cost $15. 6 cookies and 7 doughnuts cost $14.90.
A   How much do 12 cookies and 6 doughnuts cost?

_____

(52) Karen has two jars of juice with 10% and 20% sugar content. She wants to mix the juice
A   so that there is 18% sugar content. If she wants 8 L of juice in all, how much of each jar of
    juice does she need?

_____

(53) Elle jogged at 180 m/min and walked at half of that speed. If she travelled 4.95 km in half
A   an hour, how long did she jog and walk for in minutes?

_____

(54) The slope of Line A is the negative reciprocal of that of Line B. The slopes of Line B and
T   Line C are the same. Line C and Line D are perpendicular. Are there solutions to the
    equations of Lines A and D? If so, how many are there?

_____

_____

Answer the questions.

⑤⑤ T Consider $x^2 - kx + 144 = 0$. Find k such that the equation has

a. no real roots:

b. 2 real and distinct roots:

⑤⑥ T A graph has its zeros at $x = 2$ and $x = 6$ and its vertex at (3,2). Can the graph be a parabola? Explain.

Solve the problems. Show your work.

⑤⑦ A A farmer needs to wall off 3 pens as shown. With 180 m of fencing, what must the width of the pens be to maximize the area?

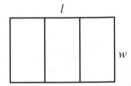

⑤⑧ A Cassi is 1.54 m tall and her shadow is 1.65 m long. How tall is her brother if his shadow is 1.7 m long?

⑤⑨ T Tickets to a school play are $2 each and the expected number of attendees is 150. For every 10¢ increase in price, 2 fewer people would attend. At what price will the revenue be maximized?

ISBN: 978-1-77149-221-8

60 At 12 m away from a building, the angle of elevation to the top of the building is 50°.

A a. How tall is the building?

_____

b. A 2.5-m flagpole stands at the top of the building. What is the difference between the angles of elevation to the top of the flagpole and to the top of the building?

_____

61 Billy, Chris, and Doug stand in a triangle. Billy stands 7.5 m away from Chris and Doug, who are 9 m apart. What are the angles of the triangle formed?

A

_____

62 Farmer Brown drives at 60 km/h from his farm at (12,14) to a horse show at (32,-2). If each unit on the grid represents 1 km, how long will the drive be?

A

_____

63 Hazel ran 5 km N70°E and then 3 km south. She then ran back to the starting point in a straight line. How far and in what direction and angle did she run?

T

_____

ISBN: 978-1-77149-221-8

ISBN: 978-1-77149-221-8

Handy Reference

Quadratic Relations

Polynomials

- **Simplifying Polynomials**

  1st Rearrange to group the like terms.

  2nd Simplify.

  e.g. $-x^2 + 3x + 5x^2 - 2 - 8x + 1$

  $= -x^2 + 5x^2 + 3x - 8x - 2 + 1$ ← group like terms

  $= 4x^2 - 5x - 1$ ← simplify

- **Expanding Polynomials**

  Applying the distributive property of multiplication to expand polynomials

  $a(x + y) = ax + ay$

  $(a + b)(x + y) = ax + ay + bx + by$

  e.g. $3(x + y)$

  $= 3x + 3y$

  e.g. $(x + 2)(x - 3)$

  $= x^2 - 3x + 2x - 6$

  $= x^2 - x - 6$

- **Factoring Polynomials**

  - distributive property

  $ax + ay = a(x + y)$

  e.g. $4x + 4y$ ← common factor: 4

  $= 4(x + y)$

  e.g. $xz + yz - 3x - 3y$

  $= z(x + y) - 3(x + y)$ ← common factors: z, -3

  $= (z - 3)(x + y)$

  - For quadratic relations, $ax^2 + bx + c$, find two integers such that they have a sum that equals b and a product that equals $a \times c$.

  e.g. $3x^2 + 7x + 2$

  $= 3x^2 + 6x + x + 2$ ← $\begin{array}{l} 6 + 1 = 7 \\ 6 \times 1 = 6 \end{array}$

  $= 3x(x + 2) + (x + 2)$

  $= (3x + 1)(x + 2)$

  - It may help you factor a polynomial if it is one of the three special cases below:

  $a^2 + 2ab + b^2 = (a + b)^2$ ⎤
  $a^2 - 2ab + b^2 = (a - b)^2$ ⎦ ← perfect-square trinomials

  $a^2 - b^2 = (a + b)(a - b)$ ← difference of squares

  e.g. $x^2 + 4xy + 4y^2$

  $= (x + 2y)^2$

  e.g. $x^2 - 4xy + 4y^2$

  $= (x - 2y)^2$

  e.g. $x^2 - 4y^2$

  $= (x + 2y)(x - 2y)$

Handy Reference

Properties of Quadratic Relations

x-intercept: the point at which the x-axis and a graph meet

y-intercept: the point at which the y-axis and a graph meet

direction of opening: a parabola opens either upward or downward

axis of symmetry: the line which divides a parabola into equal halves

vertex: the lowest or the highest point of a parabola

maximum/minimum value: the y-value of the vertex

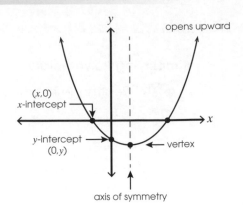

e.g.

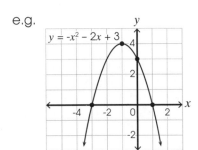

x-intercepts: (-3,0), (1,0)

y-intercept: (0,3)

direction of opening: downward

axis of symmetry: $x = -1$

vertex: (-1,4)

maximum value: $y = 4$

Forms of Quadratic Relations

Standard Form	**Factored Form**	**Vertex Form**
$y = ax^2 + bx + c$	$y = a(x - r)(x - s)$	$y = a(x - h)^2 + k$
y-intercept	zeros	vertex at (h,k)

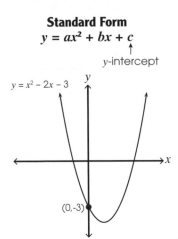

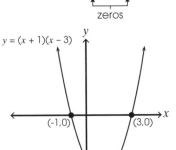

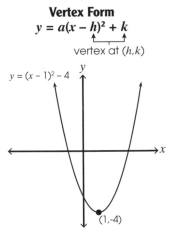

Some quadratic relations can be written in all three forms.

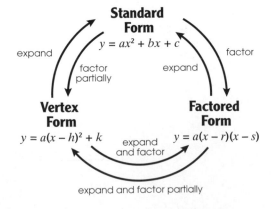

e.g. $x^2 - 2x - 3$ ⟵ standard form
$= (x + 1)(x - 3)$ ⟵ factored form

$x^2 - 2x - 3$ ⟵ standard form
$= (x^2 - 2x + 1) - 1 - 3$
$= (x - 1)^2 - 4$ ⟵ vertex form

$(x - 1)^2 - 4$ ⟵ vertex form
$= (x - 1)(x - 1) - 4$
$= x^2 - 2x - 3$ ⟵ standard form

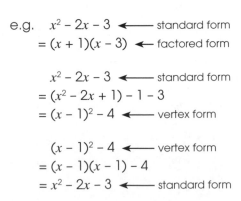

ISBN: 978-1-77149-221-8

Handy Reference

To change a quadratic relation in standard form to vertex form, two methods can be used:

Partial Factoring

1st Partially factor the relation.

2nd Find the axis of symmetry.

3rd Substitute the value of the axis of symmetry to find the vertex.

4th Write the relation in vertex form.

e.g. $y = x^2 + 6x + 4$ $0 = x(x + 6)$ axis of symmetry

$y = x(x + 6) + 4$ $x = 0$ or $x = -6$ $\dfrac{0 + (-6)}{2} = -3$

$y = (-3)^2 + 6(-3) + 4$ ➡ vertex: $(-3, -5)$
$y = -5$

So, $y = (x + 3)^2 - 5$

Completing the Square

$$x^2 + bx + c = x^2 + bx + (\tfrac{b}{2})^2 - (\tfrac{b}{2})^2 + c$$
$$= (x + \tfrac{b}{2})^2 + (-(\tfrac{b}{2})^2 + c)$$

e.g. $y = x^2 + 6x + 4$

$y = (x^2 + 6x + 9) - 9 + 4$

$y = (x + 3)^2 - 5$

Transformations of Quadratic Relations

Consider the parameters a, h, and k in the vertex form $y = a(x - h)^2 + k$ of a quadratic relation. The following transformations are applied to $y = x^2$ with the stated values of the parameters.

Parameter a

- $a > 0$:
  opens upward
- $a < 0$:
  opens downward
- $a > 1$ or $a < -1$:
  vertically stretched by a factor of a
- $0 < a < 1$ or $0 > a > -1$:
  vertically compressed by a factor of a

Parameter h

- $h > 0$:
  translated h units to the right
- $h < 0$:
  translated h units to the left

Parameter k

- $k > 0$:
  translated k units up
- $k < 0$:
  translated k units down

e.g.

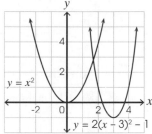

Transformations applied:

- vertically stretched by a factor of 2

- translated 3 units to the right and 1 unit down

Solving Quadratic Relations

To solve an equation, you may write the equation in factored form and find its roots, or you may use the quadratic formula if it is difficult or impossible to find the factored form of the equation.

Factoring

e.g. $2x^2 + 2x - 12 = 0$
      $2(x^2 + x - 6) = 0$
      $2(x - 2)(x + 3) = 0$

   $x - 2 = 0$ or $x + 3 = 0$
      $x = 2$ $x = -3$

So, x is 2 or -3.

Quadratic Formula

$$x = \dfrac{-b \pm \sqrt{b^2 - 4ac}}{2a}$$

Discriminant

$b^2 - 4ac > 0$: 2 real roots
$b^2 - 4ac = 0$: 1 real root
$b^2 - 4ac < 0$: no real roots

e.g. $x^2 + 6x + 4$ ← cannot be fully factored

   $a = 1$, $b = 6$, $c = 4$

$$x = \dfrac{-6 \pm \sqrt{6^2 - 4(1)(4)}}{2(1)}$$

$x \doteq -0.76$ or -5.24

ISBN: 978-1-77149-221-8

Handy Reference

Analytic Geometry

Linear Systems

You may solve for the variables in a system of linear equations in three ways:

↔ by graphing

1st Graph the lines.

2nd Their intersection, if any, is the solution.

e.g.

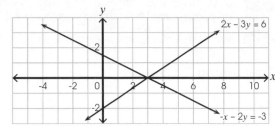

∴ Solution: $x = 3$, $y = 0$

↔ by substitution

1st Isolate one of the variables in one of the equations.

2nd Substitute the expression representing the isolated variable into another equation.

3rd Solve.

4th Substitute the known value to solve for the isolated variable.

e.g.
$$2x - 3y = 6$$
$$-x - 2y = -3 \leftarrow x = -2y + 3$$

$$2x - 3y = 6 \qquad -x - 2(0) = -3$$
$$2(-2y + 3) - 3y = 6 \qquad -x = -3$$
$$-7y + 6 = 6 \qquad x = 3$$
$$y = 0$$

∴ Solution: $x = 3$, $y = 0$

↔ by elimination

1st Multiply one of the equations or both of them so that they have one identical term.

2nd Add or subtract the equations to eliminate the identical term.

3rd Solve.

4th Substitute the known value to solve for the other variable.

e.g.
$$2x - 3y = 6 \ ①$$
$$-x - 2y = -3 \ ②$$

$$\begin{array}{r} 2x - 3y = 6 \ ① \\ +) \ -2x - 4y = -6 \ ② \times 2 \\ \hline -7y = 0 \\ y = 0 \end{array} \qquad \begin{array}{r} 2x - 3(0) = 6 \\ 2x = 6 \\ x = 3 \end{array}$$

∴ Solution: $x = 3$, $y = 0$

The three possible kinds of solutions of a linear system tell you the relationships of the lines in the system.

one solution	no solutions	infinite number of solutions
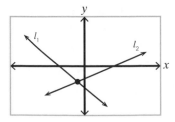	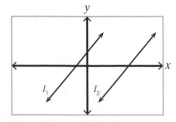	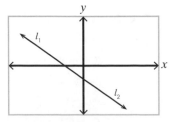
• lines intersect at one point • different slopes	• lines are parallel • same slope • different y-intercepts	• lines coincide • same slope • same y-intercept

ISBN: 978-1-77149-221-8

Handy Reference

Line Segments and Intersections

Distance Formula

$d = \sqrt{(x_2 - x_1)^2 + (y_2 - y_1)^2}$

e.g. $A(-4,2)$ $B(2,-5)$
Length of $AB = \sqrt{(2 - (-4))^2 + (-5 - 2)^2}$
$= \sqrt{85}$
$\doteq 9.22$

Midpoint Formula:

$(x,y) = (\dfrac{x_1 + x_2}{2}, \dfrac{y_1 + y_2}{2})$

Midpoint of $AB = (\dfrac{-4 + 2}{2}, \dfrac{2 + (-5)}{2})$
$= (-1,-1.5)$

Medians and Centroids

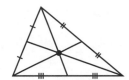

Finding the centroid of a triangle:

1st   Find the three equations of the medians. To do so, find the coordinates of each midpoint and the slope of each median.

2nd   Solve for x and y for the coordinates of the centroid.

Perpendicular Bisectors and Circumcentres

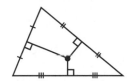

Finding the circumcentre of a triangle:

1st   Find the three equations of the perpendicular bisectors. To do so, find the coordinates of each midpoint and the slope of each perpendicular bisector.

2nd   Solve for x and y for the coordinates of the circumcentre.

Altitudes and Orthocentres

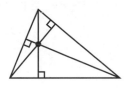

Finding the orthocentre of a triangle:

1st   Find the three equations of the altitudes. To do so, find the slopes of the perpendicular lines first.

2nd   Solve for x and y for the coordinates of the orthocentre.

Equation of a Circle

$x^2 + y^2 = r^2$
↑
radius

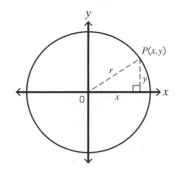

Consider a point at (x,y).

• It lies on the circle if $x^2 + y^2 = r^2$.
• It lies within the circle if $x^2 + y^2 < r^2$.
• It lies outside the circle if $x^2 + y^2 > r^2$.

e.g.

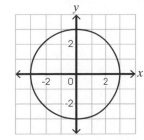

radius: 3 units
equation: $x^2 + y^2 = 3^2$
$x^2 + y^2 = 9$

ISBN: 978-1-77149-221-8

Handy Reference

Trigonometry

Congruent Triangles and Similar Triangles

Congruent Triangles

corresponding angles and corresponding sides with equal measures

Properties

- side-side-side (SSS)
- side-angle-side (SAS)
- angle-side-angle (ASA)
- angle-angle-side (AAS)
- right angle-hypotenuse-side (RHS)

Similar Triangles

corresponding angles with equal measures and corresponding sides in the same ratio

Properties

- all three corresponding angles are equal
- the corresponding sides are in the same ratio

Trigonometric Ratios

Consider any right triangle and one of its acute angles, θ.

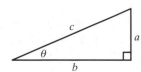

e.g.

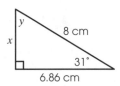

Primary Ratios

$$\sin \theta = \frac{\text{opposite}}{\text{hypotenuse}} = \frac{a}{c}$$

$$\cos \theta = \frac{\text{adjacent}}{\text{hypotenuse}} = \frac{b}{c}$$

$$\tan \theta = \frac{\text{opposite}}{\text{adjacent}} = \frac{a}{b}$$

Inverses

$\sin \theta = x$
  $\theta = \sin^{-1}x$
$\cos \theta = x$
  $\theta = \cos^{-1}x$
$\tan \theta = x$
  $\theta = \tan^{-1}x$

$\sin 31° = \dfrac{x}{8}$

$0.52 \doteq \dfrac{x}{8}$

$x \doteq 4.16$

$\cos y = \dfrac{4.16}{8}$

$\cos y = 0.52$

$y = \cos^{-1}(0.52)$

$y \doteq 59°$

Sine Law and Cosine Law

Consider any acute triangle.

e.g.

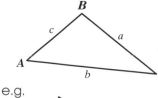

Sine Law

$$\frac{a}{\sin A} = \frac{b}{\sin B} = \frac{c}{\sin C}$$

$$\frac{5}{\sin 67°} = \frac{x}{\sin 70°}$$

$$x \doteq 5.1$$

Cosine Law

$$c^2 = a^2 + b^2 - 2ab \cos C$$

$y^2 = 5^2 + 5.1^2 - 2(5)(5.1) \cos 43°$

$y^2 \doteq 13.71$

$y \doteq 3.7$

ISBN: 978-1-77149-221-8

1   Basic Skills

1.1   Order of Operations

Try This (p. 6)

3 ; 3 ; 3 ; -4   4 ; -2 ; 4 ; 4 ; 8

1. $= 16 \div 16 - 1$
   $= 0$

2. $= 17 - 18 \div 9 + 4$
   $= 19$

3. $= -3 + (5 + 6) + 34$
   $= 42$

4. $= 16 - (81 - 25)$
   $= -40$

5. $= -3 \times 36 \div 4$
   $= -27$

6. $= -10 \div (4 + 1)$
   $= -2$

7. $= (5 - 2) \times \frac{4}{9}$
   $= \frac{4}{3}$

8. $= 36 - 16 \times \frac{1}{8}$
   $= 34$

9. $= \left(\frac{(2 - 6 + 8)^2}{-2 + 9 \times 2}\right)^{-1}$
   $= \left(\frac{4^2}{16}\right)^{-1}$
   $= 1$

10. $= \left(\frac{(-5)\frac{1}{5}}{(3^2)\frac{1}{9}}\right)^3$
    $= \left(\frac{-1}{1}\right)^3$
    $= -1$

11. $= (\frac{1}{6} - \frac{1}{3} + 3 \times \frac{1}{6}) + \frac{1}{4}$
    $= (\frac{1}{6} - \frac{1}{3} + \frac{1}{2}) + \frac{1}{4}$
    $= \frac{7}{12}$

12. $= \frac{\sqrt{3(3)}}{27 \times \frac{1}{3}}$
    $= \frac{\sqrt{9}}{9}$
    $= \frac{1}{3}$

13. $= 2(-\sqrt{9^2} \times \sqrt{5^2}) - \frac{1}{(\sqrt{\frac{1}{9}})^2}$
    $= 2(-9 \times 5) - \frac{1}{\frac{1}{9}}$
    $= -90 - 9$
    $= -99$

14. $= (\frac{3 + 2}{\sqrt{13}})^2$
    $= \frac{25}{13}$

15. $= \sqrt{\frac{4 - 3}{(3^{-1})^{-2} - 5}}$
    $= \sqrt{\frac{1}{3^2 - 5}}$
    $= \frac{1}{2}$

16. $= (1 - 12 \times \frac{1}{12})(1319^{9-8})$
    $= (1 - 1)(1319^1)$
    $= 0$

17. $(8 - 4)^2 = 4^2 = 16$
    $8^2 - 4^2 = 64 - 16 = 48$
    No, it is not true.

18. $(\sqrt{2})^3 = \sqrt{2} \times \sqrt{2} \times \sqrt{2} = 2\sqrt{2}$
    Yes, it is true.

19. $\sqrt{\frac{(-2 + 9)^2}{(9 - 2)^2}}$
    $= \sqrt{\frac{7^2}{7^2}}$
    $= \sqrt{1}$
    $= 1$
    Yes, it is true.

20. $\sqrt{(-2 - 6)^2} = \sqrt{(-8)^2} = \sqrt{64} = 8$
    $\sqrt{(-2)^2} - \sqrt{6^2}$
    $= \sqrt{4} - \sqrt{36}$
    $= 2 - 6$
    $= -4$
    No, it is not true.

21. $(78 + 2) \times (1 - 10\%) = 72$
    Adam's final score is 72.

22. Before: $\$168 \times (1 - 20\%) - \$20 = \$114.40$
    After: $(\$168 - \$20) \times (1 - 20\%) = \$118.40$
    It will be cheaper if the employee discount is applied before using the voucher.

23. $(\sqrt{\frac{12}{3}})^6 - 2 = 2^6 - 2 = 62$
    Adam's grandfather is 62 years old.

1.2   Algebraic Expressions

1. $3(4 - 2) - 8$
   $= 3(2) - 8$
   $= -2$

2. $\frac{3^3 - 3^2}{6}$
   $= \frac{27 - 9}{6}$
   $= 3$

3. $(10 - 1\frac{1}{2} \times 6)^{-2}$
   $= (10 - 9)^{-2}$
   $= 1$

4. $2(0.5) + 6(-1)$
   $= 1 - 6$
   $= -5$

5. $2(-1) - (-\frac{2}{1})^2$
   $= -2 - 4$
   $= -6$

6. $\frac{(-5)^2}{10} \times (-5 - 10)$
   $= \frac{25}{10} \times (-15)$
   $= -\frac{75}{2}$

7. $8\sqrt{9} + 9 \times \frac{5}{6}$
   $= 8 \times 3 + \frac{15}{2}$
   $= 31\frac{1}{2}$

8. $((-2)^3(\sqrt{25}))^{-2}$
   $= ((-8)5)^{-2}$
   $= \frac{1}{(-40)^2}$
   $= \frac{1}{1600}$

9. $\sqrt{-(-2)(8)} - (-2)^{-2} \times 8$
   $= \sqrt{16} - \frac{1}{4} \times 8$
   $= 2$

10. $= 10k^2 - 6k - 5$

11. $= 6a^2 + 2 - 7a + 28$
    $= 6a^2 - 7a + 30$

12. $= 2d^2 + 4d + 5d - 10$
    $= 2d^2 + 9d - 10$

13. $= -x + 3y + 3z$

14. $= 4x^2 + 7xy - 3y^2$

15. $= j^3 + 3j^2k + 3jk^2 + k^3$

16. $= a^3 + a^2b^2 - a^2b^2 + bc$
    $= a^3 + bc$

17. $= -de^2 - d + 4de^2 + 4e^2$
    $= 3de^2 + 4e^2 - d$

18.

$= 12p^2 + 18pq - 7pq$	$= \frac{6}{8}l - \frac{1}{8}l + 5\frac{2}{6}w - \frac{1}{6}w$	$= a^4 - ab - a^4 + 6b$
$= 12p^2 + 11pq$	$= \frac{5}{8}l + 5\frac{1}{6}w$	$= -ab + 6b$
$p = -3 \quad q = 2$	$l = 8 \quad w = \sqrt{36}$	$a = -9 \quad b = 3^{-1}$
$12(-3)^2 + 11(-3)(2)$	$\frac{5}{8}(-8) + 5\frac{1}{6}(\sqrt{36})$	$-(-9)(3^{-1}) + 6(3^{-1})$
$= 12(9) + 11(-6)$	$= -5 + \frac{31}{6}(6)$	$= 3 + 2$
$= 42$	$= 26$	$= 5$

19. P: $(x + 1) + 3 + x = 2x + 4$; $2(1.5) + 4 = 7$
    A: $(x)(3) \div 2 = 1.5x$; $1.5(1.5) = 2.25$

20. P: $2x + 1 + 2x + 2x + 1 + 2 + 7 = 6x + 11$; $6(1.5) + 11 = 20$
    A: $(2x + 1)(2x) + (2x)(2) \div 2 = 4x^2 + 2x + 2x = 4x^2 + 4x$;
    $4(1.5)^2 + 4(1.5) = 15$

21. P: $2\pi x \div 2 + x + 2x + x \doteq 3.14x + 4x = 7.14x$; $7.14(1.5) = 10.71$
    A: $2x(x) - \pi x^2 \div 2 \doteq 2x^2 - 1.57x^2 = 0.43x^2$; $0.43(1.5)^2 \doteq 0.97$

22. B ; 64
    $(2 \times 7 - 6)^2$
    $= (14 - 6)^2$
    $= 64$

23. B ; 61
    $x + 1.25x + 1.5625x$
    $= 3.8125x$
    $= 3.8125(16)$
    $= 61$

24. $(n + n)^2 - (2n - 1) = (2n)^2 - 2n + 1 = 4n^2 - 2n + 1$
    $4(-9)^2 - 2(-9) + 1 = 324 + 18 + 1 = 343$
    The difference is 343.

25. $b + \frac{1}{4}b + 100 = 1\frac{1}{4}b + 100$
    $1\frac{1}{4} \times 32 + 100 = 40 + 100 = 140$
    They have $140 in all.

26. $(n + 1) \times n \div 2$
    $(99 + 1) \times 99 \div 2 = 4950$
    The sum is 4950.

ISBN: 978-1-77149-221-8

ANSWERS

1.3 Equations

1. $3x = 15$
   $x = 5$

2. $-x = 29$
   $x = -29$

3. $6a - 3a = 12 - 6$
   $3a = 6$
   $a = 2$

4. $8p = 4$
   $p = \dfrac{1}{2}$

5. $2p + 6 = 3p + 3$
   $p = 3$

6. $a + 6 = \dfrac{9}{10}a + 27$
   $\dfrac{1}{10}a = 21$
   $a = 210$

7. $3n + 8 = 6n - 46$
   $3n = 54$
   $n = 18$

8. $8x - 4 = 2x + 2$
   $6x = 6$
   $x = 1$

9. $6x + 12 = 3x - 9$
   $3x = -21$
   $x = -7$

10. $x = \dfrac{-x - 3}{2}$
    $2x = -x - 3$
    $3x = -3$
    $x = -1$

11. $\dfrac{3 + 4}{12} = \dfrac{7}{12}x$
    $x = 1$

12. $x + 2 = 3x + 12$
    $2x = -10$
    $x = -5$

13. $12x - 11x = 4$ Check: LS: 4 ; 44
    $x = 4$ RS: 4 ; 44

14. $7a - 14 = 5a + 20$ Check: LS: 7(17 – 2) = 105
    $2a = 34$ RS: 5(17 + 4) = 105
    $a = 17$

15. $3a - 1 = 5a - 5$ Check: LS: $\dfrac{2}{5} - \dfrac{1}{15} = \dfrac{1}{3}$
    $2a = 4$ RS: $\dfrac{2}{3} - \dfrac{1}{3} = \dfrac{1}{3}$
    $a = 2$

16. $(2w + 3 + w) \times 2 = 27$
    $(3w + 3) \times 2 = 27$
    $6w + 6 = 27$
    $6w = 21$
    $w = 3.5$

17. $\pi(3w - 5) = 49\pi$
    $3w - 5 = 49$
    $3w = 54$
    $w = 18$

18. $2(l + 1) = 16(l - 13)$
    $2l + 2 = 16l - 208$
    $14l = 210$
    $l = 15$

19. $x + 8 = 7x - 4$
    $6x = 12$
    $x = 2$

20. $\dfrac{6(x - 1\frac{1}{2})}{2} = 4\dfrac{1}{2}$
    $3x - 4\dfrac{1}{2} = 4\dfrac{1}{2}$
    $3x = 9$
    $x = 3$

21. $\dfrac{2(b - 3 + 2b)}{2} = 24$
    $3b - 3 = 24$
    $3b = 27$
    $b = 9$

22. $x + 2x - 2 = 3x - \dfrac{1}{2} - \dfrac{3}{2}$
    $3x - 2 = 3x - 2$
    $x = x$
    They are both correct because there is an infinite number of solutions.

23. $7x - 18x + 12 = 14 - 10x - x$
    $-11x + 12 = 14 - 11x$
    $0x = 2$
    There is no solution. Daniel is correct.

24. Let n be one of the numbers.
    $n + \dfrac{3n - 2}{2} = -21$
    $2n + 3n - 2 = -42$
    $5n = -40$
    $n = -8$
    $\dfrac{3(-8) - 2}{2} = \dfrac{-24 - 2}{2} = -13$
    The numbers are -8 and -13.

25. $3x + 6 = 159$
    $x = 51$ The number was 51. He
    $51 \times 3 - 6 = 147$ was supposed to get 147.

26. Let j be the amount of money Jason has.
    $j + \dfrac{7}{9}j + (\dfrac{3}{4})(\dfrac{7}{9})j = 680$
    $\dfrac{85}{36}j = 680$ Derek: $288 \times \dfrac{7}{9} = 224$
    $j = 288$ Billy: $224 \times \dfrac{3}{4} = 168$
    Billy has $168, Derek has $224, and Jason has $288.

27. Let s be the amount of time Sophie took.
    $\dfrac{s + (s + 0.1) + (s + 0.1 + 0.04)}{3} = 9.88$
    $s = 9.8$
    It took Sophie 9.8 s.

28. Let m be the length of the medium string.
    $m + (m - 2) + (2m - 1) = 21$
    $m = 6$
    Short: $6 - 2 = 4$
    Long: $2(6) - 1 = 11$
    The side lengths are 4 cm, 6 cm, and 11 cm.

1.4 Simple Linear Equations

1. $y = 3x - 2$
   $y - 2 = -\dfrac{1}{4}(x - 4)$
   $3x - y - 2 = 0$
   $y - 4 = 3(x - 2)$
   $4x + y - 3 = 0$
   $y = -\dfrac{1}{2}x$

   Slope y-intercept Form
   Standard Form
   Point-slope Form

2. A: $y = 2x + 3$ B: $4y = -3x + 8$
                                    $y = -\dfrac{3}{4}x + 2$
   C: $y = -3x - 6 + 5$ D: $2y = 4x + 3$
      $y = -3x - 1$ $y = 2x + \dfrac{3}{2}$
   E: $y = \dfrac{1}{4}x + 1\dfrac{1}{4}$ F: $y = 1.5x - 6 + 1.5$
                                    $y = 1.5x - 4.5$

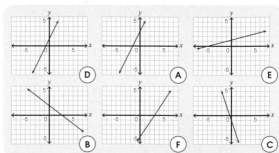

3. $y = 4x + 3$
   4 ; 3

4. $y = 3x + 1$
   3 ; 1

5. $4y = -x + 4$
   $y = -\dfrac{1}{4}x + 1$
   $-\dfrac{1}{4}$; 1

6. $y = 3x - 2$
   3 ; -2

7a. Their slopes are the same.
  b. Their slopes are negative reciprocals.

ISBN: 978-1-77149-221-8

8a. • Line A:

$(y - (-1)) = 3(x - (-1))$

$y + 1 = 3(x + 1)$

$y = 3x + 2$

$3x - y + 2 = 0$

• Line B:

$x - 1 = 0$

• Line C:

$y - 0 = -\frac{1}{3}(x - (-6))$

$3y = -x - 6$

$x + 3y + 6 = 0$

b. Yes, Line A and Line C are perpendicular because their slopes are the negative reciprocals of each other.

9. T　　　　10. T　　　　11. F

12. T　　　　13. F

14. $y = 60 - 80x$
$y = -80x + 60$

15. $x + y = 1$
$y = -x + 1$

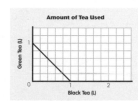

16. $3x + 2y = 18$
$y = -\frac{3}{2}x + 9$

2　Systems of Linear Equations

2.1　Graphing Systems of Linear Equations

Try This (p. 18)

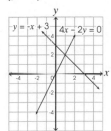

(1,2)

1.

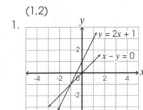

(-1,-1)

2.

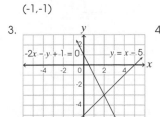

$(\frac{3}{2},-3)$

3.

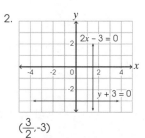

(2,-3)

4.

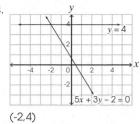

(-2,4)

5.

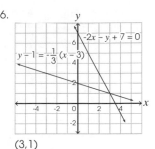

(-3,-1)

6.

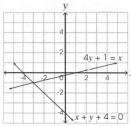

(3,1)

7. $y = -2x$

LS	RS
2	-2(-1) = 2 ✔

It is a solution.

$y = x + 3$

LS	RS
2	-1 + 3 = 2 ✔

8. $x + y - 8 = 0$

LS	RS
3 + 5 - 8 = 0	0 ✔

It is not a solution.

$2x - y = -1$

LS	RS
2(3) - 5 = 1	-1 ✗

9. $y = -\frac{1}{2}x - 6$

LS	RS
-8	$-\frac{1}{2}(4) - 6 = -8$ ✔

It is not a solution.

$y = -\frac{1}{2}x$

LS	RS
-8	$-\frac{1}{2}(4) = -2$ ✗

10. $y = -x$

LS	RS
$\frac{3}{2}$	$-(-\frac{3}{2}) = \frac{3}{2}$ ✔

It is a solution.

$2x + 4y - 3 = 0$

LS	RS
$2(-\frac{3}{2}) + 4(\frac{3}{2}) - 3$ $= -3 + 6 - 3 = 0$	0 ✔

11.

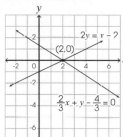

$2y = x - 2$

LS	RS
2(0) = 0	2 - 2 = 0 ✔

$\frac{2}{3}x + y - \frac{4}{3} = 0$

LS	RS
$\frac{2}{3}(2) + 0 - \frac{4}{3} = 0$	0 ✔

12.

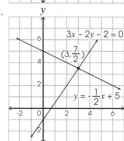

$3x - 2y - 2 = 0$

LS	RS
$3(3) - 2(\frac{7}{2}) - 2$ $= 9 - 7 - 2 = 0$	0 ✔

$y = -\frac{1}{2}x + 5$

LS	RS
$\frac{7}{2}$	$-\frac{1}{2}(3) + 5$ $= -\frac{3}{2} + \frac{10}{2} = \frac{7}{2}$ ✔

13a. $y - 2 = -\frac{1}{2}(x - 1)$

$2y - 4 = -x + 1$

$x + 2y - 5 = 0$

b.

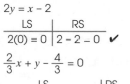

14a. (Suggested answer)
$l_2: y = 1$
$l_3: x - y + 1 = 0$

b.

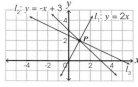

15. $y = 50x$

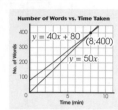

$y = 40(x + 2)$
$y = 40x + 80$

They will type the same number of words after 8 min.

16. $3x + 3y = 54$
$x + y = 18$

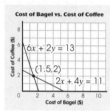

$7x + 10y = 150$
$y = -\frac{7}{10}x + 15$

Each DVD costs $10 and each book costs $8.

17. $6x + 2y = 13$
$y = -3x + 6.5$

$2x + 4y = 11$
$y = -\frac{1}{2}x + 2.75$

Each bagel costs $1.50 and each cup of coffee costs $2.

2.2 Solving by Substitution

Try This (p. 22)

$3x + y = 16$ ①
$2x + 3y = 20$ ②

1st: Isolate y in equation ①.
$y = -3x + 16$

2nd: Substitute y into equation ②.
$2x + 3(-3x + 16) = 20$
$2x - 9x + 48 = 20$
$-7x = 20 - 48$
$-7x = -28$
$x = 4$

3rd: Substitute 4 for x into equation ①.
$3(4) + y = 16$
$y = 4$

The solution is $x = 4$ and $y = 4$.

1. $m = 4 - 3n$
$(4 - 3n) - 2n = -1$
$4 - 5n = -1$
$n = 1$
$m = 4 - 3(1) = 1$
$\therefore m = 1, n = 1$

2. $4x - (2x + 3) = 1$
$2x - 3 = 1$
$x = 2$
$y = 2(2) + 3 = 7$
$\therefore x = 2, y = 7$

3. $b = \frac{24 - 3a}{2}$
$3a - 2(\frac{24 - 3a}{2}) = -12$
$3a - 24 + 3a = -12$
$6a = 12$
$a = 2$
$b = \frac{24 - 3(2)}{2} = 9$
$\therefore a = 2, b = 9$

4. $x = 19 - 3y$
$5(19 - 3y) + 3y = 35$
$95 - 15y + 3y = 35$
$y = 5$
$x = 19 - 3(5) = 4$
$\therefore x = 4, y = 5$

5. $p = \frac{5 - 3q}{2}$
$8(\frac{5 - 3q}{2}) + 6q = 0$
$20 - 12q + 6q = 0$
$6q = 20$
$q = \frac{10}{3}$
$p = \frac{5 - 3(\frac{10}{3})}{2} = -\frac{5}{2}$
$\therefore p = -\frac{5}{2}, q = \frac{10}{3}$

6. $s = 2s - 3 - 1$
$s = 4$
$t = 2(4) - 3 = 5$
$\therefore s = 4, t = 5$

7. $x = 1 - 2y$
$3(1 - 2y) - 2y = 0$
$3 - 6y - 2y = 0$
$y = \frac{3}{8}$
$x = 1 - 2(\frac{3}{8}) = \frac{1}{4}$
$\therefore x = \frac{1}{4}, y = \frac{3}{8}$

8. $x = \frac{7 - 9y}{6}$
$7(\frac{7 - 9y}{6}) - 5y = 3$
$49 - 63y - 30y = 18$
$-93y = -31$
$y = \frac{1}{3}$
$x = \frac{7 - 9(\frac{1}{3})}{6} = \frac{2}{3}$
$\therefore x = \frac{2}{3}, y = \frac{1}{3}$

9. $w + l = 21$
$\frac{1}{2}l - 3 + l = 21$
$\frac{3}{2}l = 24$
$l = 16$
$w + 16 = 21$
$w = 5$
$\therefore w = 5, l = 16$

10. $x = 5 - 3y$
$-7(5 - 3y) + 21y = 28$
$-35 + 21y + 21y = 28$
$y = \frac{3}{2}$
$x = 5 - 3(\frac{3}{2}) = \frac{1}{2}$
$\therefore x = \frac{1}{2}, y = \frac{3}{2}$

11. $a = \frac{8 - 3b}{5}$
$4(\frac{8 - 3b}{5}) + 2b = -2$
$32 - 12b + 10b = -10$
$b = 21$
$a = \frac{8 - 3(21)}{5} = -11$
$\therefore a = -11, b = 21$

12. $x = \frac{26 + 5y}{7}$
$-6(\frac{26 + 5y}{7}) + 7y = -6$
$-156 - 30y + 49y = -42$
$y = 6$
$x = \frac{26 + 5(6)}{7} = 8$
$\therefore x = 8, y = 6$

13. $x = \frac{3 - 3y}{2}$
$4(\frac{3 - 3y}{2}) - 6y + 2 = 0$
$6 - 6y - 6y + 2 = 0$
$y = \frac{2}{3}$
$x = \frac{3 - 3(\frac{2}{3})}{2} = \frac{1}{2}$
$(\frac{1}{2}, \frac{2}{3})$

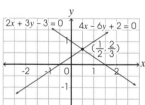

14. $\frac{1}{2}x + 4 = -x + 1$
$\frac{3}{2}x = -3$
$x = -2$
$y = -(-2) + 1 = 3$
$(-2, 3)$

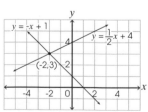

15. $x + 3(-\frac{1}{3}x - 1) - 6 = 0$
$x - x - 3 - 6 = 0$
$0x = 9$
No solutions

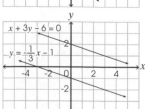

ISBN: 978-1-77149-221-8

16. $2n - 7 = \frac{1}{2}(3n + 3)$

$2n - 7 = \frac{3}{2}n + \frac{3}{2}$

$\frac{1}{2}n = \frac{17}{2}$

$n = 17$

$m = 3(17) + 3 = 54$

$\therefore m = 54, n = 17$

Check:
$54 = 3(17) + 3$
$2(17) - 7 = \frac{1}{2}(54)$

17. $0.03(10\,000 - y) + 0.012y = 282$
$-0.018y = -18$
$y = 1000$
$x = 10\,000 - 1000 = 9000$
$\therefore x = 9000, y = 1000$
Check: $9000 + 1000 = 10\,000$
$0.03(9000) + 0.012(1000) = 282$

18. $0.4(240 - y) + 0.15y = 72$
$-0.25y = -24$
$y = 96$
$x = 240 - 96 - 144$
$\therefore x = 144, y = 96$

Check:
$0.4(144) + 0.15(96) = 72$
$144 + 96 = 240$

19. $0.1h + 0.2(25 - 2h) = 1.01$
$-0.3h = -3.99$
$h = 13.3$
$m = 25 - 2(13.3) = -1.6$
$\therefore m = -1.6, h = 13.3$

Check:
$2(13.3) + (-1.6) = 25$
$0.1(13.3) + 0.2(-1.6) = 1.01$

20. $2.5(10 - j) + 0.5j = 17$
$-2j = -8$
$j = 4$
$i = 10 - 4 = 6$
$\therefore i = 6, j = 4$

Check:
$2.5(6) + 0.5(4) = 17$
$10 - 6 - 4 = 0$

21a. No, it does not matter because the order of which variable is solved first does not change the values of the variables.

b. (Suggested answer)
Yes. If the equations are solved by substitution, we should isolate y in equation ② and then solve for x first.

c. No. He should substitute the value of y into equation ① to solve for x.

22. $11x + y = 144$
$12.5x + 1.25y = 165$

$12.5x + 1.25(144 - 11x) = 165$
$1.25x = 15$
$x = 12$
$y = 144 - 11 \times 12 = 12$
The club bought 12 T-shirts and 12 badges.

23. $x + 2y = 17$
$x - y = 5$

$y + 5 + 2y = 17$
$3y = 12$
$y = 4$
$x = 5 + 4 = 9$

The integers are 4 and 9.

24. $x + y = \frac{3}{4}$

$2x + 6y = 3$

$2(\frac{3}{4} - y) + 6y = 3$
$\frac{3}{2} - 2y + 6y = 3$
$4y = \frac{3}{2}$
$y = \frac{3}{8}$
$x = \frac{3}{4} - \frac{3}{8} = \frac{3}{8}$

Walk: $2 \times \frac{3}{8} = \frac{3}{4}$ Run: $6 \times \frac{3}{8} = 2\frac{1}{4}$

She walked $\frac{3}{4}$ km and ran $2\frac{1}{4}$ km.

25. Way 1:
$x + 2y = 21$
$x - y = 3$
$3 + y + 2y = 21$
$3y = 18$
$y = 6$
$x = 3 + 6 = 9$

Way 2:
$x + 2y = 21$
$y - x = 3$
$y - 3 + 2y = 21$
$3y = 24$
$y = 8$
$x = 8 - 3 = 5$

The side lengths are either 9 cm, 6 cm, and 6 cm, or 8 cm, 8 cm, and 5 cm.

2.3 Solving by Elimination

Try This (p. 26)

$m + 3n = 16$ ①
$2m + 5n = 24$ ②

1st: Multiply ① by 2.
$2m + 6n = 32$

2nd: Subtract.
$\quad 2m + 6n = 32$
$-)\ 2m + 5n = 24$
$\quad\quad\quad\quad n = 8$

3rd: Substitute $n = 8$ into ①.
$m + 3(8) = 16$
$m = -8$
The solution is $m = -8$ and $n = 8$.

1. $\quad a + 3b = 4$ ①
$-)\ a - 4b = -3$ ②
$\quad\quad 7b = 7$
$\quad\quad\ b = 1$
$a + 3(1) = 4$
$a = 1$
$\therefore a = 1, b = 1$

2. $\quad 3x - y = 2$ ①
$+)\ -3x - 3y = 18$ ② × 3
$\quad\quad -4y = 20$
$\quad\quad\quad y = -5$
$-x - (-5) = 6$
$x = -1$
$\therefore x = -1, y = -5$

3. $\quad 3p + 12q = 6$ ① × 3
$-)\ 3p + 5q = -1$ ②
$\quad\quad 7q = 7$
$\quad\quad\ q = 1$
$p + 4(1) = 2$
$p = -2$
$\therefore p = -2, q = 1$

4. $\quad 2g + 7h = -46$ ①
$+)\ 35g - 7h = 231$ ② × 7
$\quad\quad 37g = 185$
$\quad\quad\ g = 5$
$5(5) - h = 33$
$h = -8$
$\therefore g = 5, h = -8$

5. $\quad 14x + 2y = 66$ ① × 2
$+)\ 9x - 2y = -20$ ②
$\quad\quad 23x = 46$
$\quad\quad\ x = 2$
$7(2) + y = 33$
$y = 19$
$\therefore x = 2, y = 19$

6. $\quad 12i + 3j = 243$ ① × 3
$-)\ 3i + 3j = 81$ ②
$\quad\quad 9i = 162$
$\quad\quad\ i = 18$
$4(18) + j = 81$
$j = 9$
$\therefore i = 18, j = 9$

7. $\quad 6d - 8e = 10$ ① × 2
$-)\ 2d - 8e = -34$ ②
$\quad\quad 4d = 44$
$\quad\quad\ d = 11$
$3(11) - 4e = 5$
$e = 7$
$\therefore d = 11, e = 7$

8. $\quad 14r - 4s = -2$ ① × 2
$+)\ 3r + 4s = 53$ ②
$\quad\quad 17r = 51$
$\quad\quad\ r = 3$
$7(3) - 2s = -1$
$s = 11$
$\therefore r = 3, s = 11$

9. $\quad 4v + 6w = 10$ ① × 2
$+)\ 9v - 6w = 42$ ② × 3
$\quad\quad 13v = 52$
$\quad\quad\ v = 4$
$2(4) + 3w = 5$
$w = -1$
$\therefore v = 4, w = -1$

10. $\quad 20x + 15y = -5$ ① × 5
$+)\ 18x - 15y = -261$ ② × 3
$\quad\quad 38x = -266$
$\quad\quad\ x = -7$
$4(-7) + 3y = -1$
$y = 9$
$\therefore x = -7, y = 9$

11.
$$16e + 18f = 14 \quad ① \times 2$$
$$+) \ 30e - 18f = 9 \quad ② \times 3$$
$$46e = 23$$
$$e = \frac{1}{2}$$
$$8(\tfrac{1}{2}) + 9f = 7$$
$$f = \frac{1}{3}$$
$$\therefore e = \frac{1}{2}, f = \frac{1}{3}$$

12.
$$-12a + 10b = -4 \quad ① \times 2$$
$$+) \ 12a + 4b = 11 \quad ②$$
$$14b = 7$$
$$b = \frac{1}{2}$$
$$-6a + 5(\tfrac{1}{2}) = -2$$
$$a = \frac{3}{4}$$
$$\therefore a = \frac{3}{4}, b = \frac{1}{2}$$

13.
$$3x + 6y + 3 = 0 \quad ①$$
$$-)12x + 6y - 42 = 0 \quad ② \times 6$$
$$-9x + 45 = 0$$
$$x = 5$$
$$y = -2(5) + 7$$
$$y = -3$$
$$(5, -3)$$

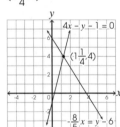

14.
$$10x - 4y - 20 = 0 \quad ① \times 2$$
$$+) \ 7x + 4y - 14 = 0 \quad ②$$
$$17x - 34 = 0$$
$$x = 2$$
$$5(2) - 2y - 10 = 0$$
$$y = 0$$
$$(2, 0)$$

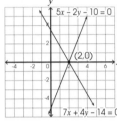

15.
$$\frac{8}{5}x + y - 6 = 0 \quad ①$$
$$+) \ \ 4x - y - 1 = 0 \quad ②$$
$$\frac{28}{5}x - 7 = 0$$
$$x = 1\frac{1}{4}$$
$$-\frac{8}{5}(1\tfrac{1}{4}) = y - 6$$
$$y = 4$$
$$(1\tfrac{1}{4}, 4)$$

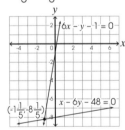

16.
$$36x - 6y - 6 = 0 \quad ① \times 6$$
$$-) \ \ x - 6y - 48 = 0 \quad ②$$
$$35x + 42 = 0$$
$$x = -1\frac{1}{5}$$
$$6(-1\tfrac{1}{5}) - y - 1 = 0$$
$$y = -8\frac{1}{5}$$
$$(-1\tfrac{1}{5}, \ -8\tfrac{1}{5})$$

17.
$$x + 3(y - 1) = 27 \quad \rightarrow \quad x + 3y - 30 = 0 \quad ①$$
$$y = 2x + 3 \quad \rightarrow \quad 2x - y + 3 = 0 \quad ②$$
$$x + 3y - 30 = 0 \quad ①$$
$$+) \ 6x - 3y + 9 = 0 \quad ② \times 3$$
$$7x - 21 = 0$$
$$x = 3$$
$$y = 2(3) + 3 = 9$$
The integers are 3 and 9.

18.
$$x + 6 = 2(y + 6) \quad \rightarrow \quad x = 2y + 6 \quad ①$$
$$x - 2 = 3(y - 2) + 1 \quad \rightarrow \quad x = 3y - 3 \quad ②$$
$$x = 2y + 6 \quad ①$$
$$-) \ x = 3y - 3 \quad ②$$
$$0 = -y + 9$$
$$y = 9$$
$$x = 2(9) + 6 = 24$$
Brandon is 24 years old and Debbie is 9 years old.

19.
$$4x + 3y = 45 \quad ①$$
$$4x - 3y = 3 \quad ②$$

$$4x + 3y = 45 \quad ①$$
$$+) \ 4x - 3y = 3 \quad ②$$
$$8x = 48$$
$$x = 6$$
$$4(6) + 3y = 45$$
$$y = 7$$
The side length of the square is 6 cm and the side length of the triangle is 7 cm.

20.
$$4x + 2y = 5 \quad ①$$
$$x + y = 1.5 \quad ②$$

$$4x + 2y = 5 \quad ①$$
$$-) \ 2x + 2y = 3 \quad ② \times 2$$
$$2x = 2$$
$$x = 1$$
$$y = 1.5 - 1 = 0.5$$
Jackson ran for 1 h and walked for 0.5 h.

21.
$$x + y = 38 \quad ①$$
$$2x + 4y = 118 \quad ②$$

$$2x + 4y = 118 \quad ②$$
$$-) \ 2x + 2y = 76 \quad ① \times 2$$
$$2y = 42$$
$$y = 21$$
$$x = 38 - 21 = 17$$
There are 17 chickens and 21 rabbits.

22.
$$\frac{x}{8} + \frac{y}{6} = \frac{13}{24} \quad \rightarrow \quad 3x + 4y = 13 \quad ①$$
$$\frac{y}{8} + \frac{x}{6} = \frac{5}{8} \quad \rightarrow \quad 3y + 4x = 15 \quad ②$$
$$12x + 16y = 52 \quad ① \times 4$$
$$-) \ 12x + 9y = 45 \quad ② \times 3$$
$$7y = 7$$
$$y = 1$$
$$3x + 4(1) = 13$$
$$x = 3$$
The two fractions are $\frac{3}{8}$ and $\frac{1}{6}$.

23.
$$x + y + 20 = 236 \quad \rightarrow \quad x + y = 216$$
$$0.1x + 0.25y + 20 \times 0.05 = 30.7 \quad \rightarrow \quad 0.1x + 0.25y = 29.7$$
$$0.1(216 - y) + 0.25y = 29.7$$
$$21.6 - 0.1y + 0.25y = 29.7$$
$$0.15y = 8.1$$
$$y = 54$$
$$x = 216 - 54 = 162$$
54 of his coins are quarters.

24.
$$120x + 130y = 3.7 \rightarrow x = \frac{3.7 - 130y}{120}$$
$$90x + 160y = 3.4$$
$$90(\frac{3.7 - 130y}{120}) + 160y = 3.4$$
$$333 - 11\,700y + 19\,200y = 408$$
$$y = 0.01$$
$$x = \frac{3.7 - 130(0.01)}{120} = 0.02$$
The costs of dark and white chocolate are \$0.02/g and \$0.01/g respectively.

25.
$$60x + 120y = 240$$
$$x + y = 2\frac{1}{3}$$

$$60(2\tfrac{1}{3} - y) + 120y = 240$$
$$140 - 60y + 120y = 240$$
$$60y = 100$$
$$y = 1\frac{2}{3}$$
$$x = 2\tfrac{1}{3} - 1\tfrac{2}{3} = \frac{2}{3}$$
Distance: $60 \times \frac{2}{3} = 40$
The distance is 40 km.

26.
$$x + y = 6$$
$$0.6x + 0.1y = 0.25 \times 6$$

$$0.6x + 0.1(6 - x) = 1.5$$
$$0.6x + 0.6 - 0.1x = 1.5$$
$$x = 1.8$$
$$y = 6 - 1.8 = 4.2$$
She needs 1.8 L of 60% alcohol solution and 4.2 L of 10% solution.

2.4 Possible Solutions

1.
System A	System B	System C
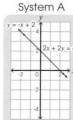		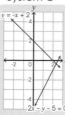

2. System A has an infinite number of solutions. The two equations represent the same line. They have the same slope of -1.

3. System B has no solutions. The two lines are parallel and they both have a slope of -1.

4. System C has exactly one solution. The two lines intersect at one point and their slopes are different.

5. It is System B.

6. $x = \dfrac{12 - 5y}{2}$

$\dfrac{1}{5}(\dfrac{12 - 5y}{2}) + \dfrac{1}{2}y = -1$

$12 - 5y + 5y = -10$

$0y = -22$

They have no solutions.
∴ These two lines are parallel.

7. $y = -\dfrac{1}{2}x + \dfrac{3}{2}$

$0.7x + 1.4(-\dfrac{1}{2}x + \dfrac{3}{2}) = 2.1$

$0.7x - 0.7x + 2.1 = 2.1$

$0x = 0$

They have an infinite number of solutions.
∴ These two lines coincide.

8. $y = \dfrac{11 + 7x}{12}$

$13x + 18(\dfrac{11 + 7x}{12}) = 16\dfrac{1}{2}$

$26x + 33 + 21x = 33$

$x = 0$

$y = \dfrac{11 + 7(0)}{12} = \dfrac{11}{12}$

They have one solution.
∴ These two lines intersect at one point.

9. $y = \dfrac{-5x + 2}{6}$

$\dfrac{1}{3}x + \dfrac{2}{5}(\dfrac{-5x + 2}{6}) = \dfrac{2}{15}$

$10x - 10x + 4 = 4$

$0x = 0$

They have an infinite number of solutions.
∴ These two lines coincide.

10. $4x - (4x + 98) + 3\dfrac{1}{9} = 0$

$4x - 4x - 98 + 3\dfrac{1}{9} = 0$

$0x = 94\dfrac{8}{9}$

They have no solutions.
∴ These two lines are parallel.

11. $3x + 4y = 2 \rightarrow y = -\dfrac{3}{4}x + \dfrac{1}{2}$

$3x - 4y = 7 \rightarrow y = \dfrac{3}{4}x - \dfrac{7}{4}$

1 ; They have different slopes, so they must intersect at one point.

12. $x + 3y - 2 = 0 \rightarrow y = -\dfrac{1}{3}x + \dfrac{2}{3}$

$18x + 54y = 36 \rightarrow y = -\dfrac{1}{3}x + \dfrac{2}{3}$

infinitely many ; They have the same slope and y-intercept. Therefore, they must coincide and have infinitely many solutions.

13. $2x - y - 7 = 0 \qquad \rightarrow y = 2x - 7$
$0.5x - 0.25y - 0.3 = 0 \rightarrow y = 2x - 1.2$
no solutions ; They have the same slope but different y-intercepts. Therefore, they are parallel lines which have no intersections.

14-15. (Suggested answers)

14a. $x + y = 5$ b. $3x - 2y + 1 = 0$ c. $6x - 4y + 14 = 0$

15a. $6x - 7y + 4 = 0$ b. $7x + 6y = 0$

16. $l_1: y = -\dfrac{1}{2}x + \dfrac{6}{7}$ $l_2: y = \dfrac{k}{5}x + \dfrac{3}{5}$

Having "no solutions" implies that they have the same slope.

$-\dfrac{1}{2} = \dfrac{k}{5}$

$k = -\dfrac{5}{2}$

k is $-\dfrac{5}{2}$.

17. (Suggested answers)

a. $l_1: y = 3x + 2$ $l_2: y = -\dfrac{A}{B}x - \dfrac{C}{B}$

$-\dfrac{A}{B} = 3$ and $-\dfrac{C}{B} = 2$

$A = -6, B = 2, C = -4$

b. $-\dfrac{A}{B} = 3$ and $-\dfrac{C}{B} \neq 2$

$A = -6, B = 2, C = 4$

18a. $2x + 5y - 8 = 0 \rightarrow y = -\dfrac{2}{5}x + \dfrac{8}{5}$

$2x + 5y + 4 = 0 \rightarrow y = -\dfrac{2}{5}x - \dfrac{4}{5}$

They are parallel lines. This system of equations has no solutions.

b. (Suggested answer) $y = -\dfrac{2}{5}x + 5$

19. (Suggested answer)
Find a line that is parallel to l_2.
$l_2: y = 3x + 2$
New line: $y = 3x + 4$

20. $2(x - 3) = y - 3 \qquad \rightarrow 2x - y - 3 = 0$
$2(x + 2) - 5 = y + 2 \rightarrow 2x - y - 3 = 0$
No, Jane cannot find their ages because neither x nor y can be isolated without isolating the other one as well.

21. $3x + 2y = 0.3 \times 5 \qquad \rightarrow 3x + 2y = 1.5$
$6x + 4y = 0.3 \times 10 \qquad \rightarrow 3x + 2y = 1.5$
The salt concentrations cannot be found.

22. Maxine: $10 + 5x$ $10 + 5x = 6 + 5.5x$
    Natalie: $6 + 5.5x$ $0.5x = 4$
                       $x = 8$
They would have run the same total distance after 8 days.

23. $3x + 3y = 12.15 \rightarrow 6x + 6y = 24.3$
$2x + 2y = 8.1 \qquad \rightarrow 6x + 6y = 24.3$
The cost of 1 bag of chips cannot be found.

24. $0.5x + 0.8y = 46$ ①
$0.25x + 0.6y = 27$ ②
    $0.5x + 0.8y = 46$ ①
-) $\underline{0.5x + 1.2y = 54}$ ② × 2
           $-0.4y = -8$
               $y = 20$
$0.5x + 0.8(20) = 46$
            $x = 60$
Dice: $x + x = 60 + 60 = 120$
He bought 120 dice in all.

ANSWERS

3 Analytic Geometry

3.1 Length of a Line Segment

Try This (p. 36)

$GH^2 = 2^2 + 7^2$

$GH \doteq 7.28$

The length is about 7.28 units.

1. $MN^2 = 2^2 + 5^2$

   $MN \doteq 5.39$

   MN is about 5.39 units.

2. $OP^2 = 4^2 + 7^2$

   $OP \doteq 8.06$

   OP is about 8.06 units.

3. $QR^2 = 3^2 + 8^2$

   $QR \doteq 8.54$

   QR is about 8.54 units.

4. $ST^2 = 6^2 + 4^2$

   $ST \doteq 7.21$

   ST is about 7.21 units.

5. $d = \sqrt{(9-4)^2 + (7-5)^2}$

   $= \sqrt{29}$

6. $d = \sqrt{(4-2)^2 + (3-(-4))^2}$

   $= \sqrt{53}$

7. $d = \sqrt{(2-(-1))^2 + (18-5)^2}$

   $= \sqrt{178}$

8. $d = \sqrt{(4-2.5)^2 + (9-7)^2}$

   $= \sqrt{6.25}$

   $= 2.5$

9. $d = \sqrt{(9-0)^2 + (\frac{1}{2}-(-5))^2}$

   $= \sqrt{111.25}$

10. $d = \sqrt{(-\frac{1}{2}-(-3))^2 + (0-(-1))^2}$

    $= \sqrt{7.25}$

11. **1st:** slope = 1

    $y - 0 = 1(x - 0)$

    $y = x$

    2nd: $y = -x + 3$ $y = x$

    $x = -x + 3$

    $x = \frac{3}{2}$ and $y = \frac{3}{2}$

    Point of intersection: $(\frac{3}{2}, \frac{3}{2})$

    3rd: $d = \sqrt{(\frac{3}{2}-0)^2 + (\frac{3}{2}-0)^2}$

    $= \sqrt{4.5}$

    $\doteq 2.12$

12. **1st:** Find the equation of the perpendicular line, l.

    $4x + y - 4 = 0$ $y - (-5) = \frac{1}{4}(x - (-2))$

    $y = -4x + 4$ $4y + 20 = x + 2$

    slope of $l = \frac{1}{4}$ $4y - x + 18 = 0$

    2nd: Find the point of intersection.

    $4x + y - 4 = 0$ $4(4y + 18) + y - 4 = 0$

    $4y - x + 18 = 0$ $16y + 72 + y - 4 = 0$

    $y = -4$

    $4(-4) - x + 18 = 0$

    $x = 2$

    Point of intersection: $(2, -4)$

    3rd: Distance between $(2, -4)$ and $(-2, -5)$:

    $d = \sqrt{(-2-2)^2 + (-5-(-4))^2}$

    $= \sqrt{17}$

    $\doteq 4.12$

13. Team A: $\sqrt{(1-(-4))^2 + (-2-17)^2} = \sqrt{386}$

    Team B: $\sqrt{(1-6)^2 + (-2-13)^2} = \sqrt{250}$

    No, Team B is closer to the prize.

14. $AB = \sqrt{(-1-(-10))^2 + (9-7)^2} \doteq 9.22$

    $BC = \sqrt{(8-(-1))^2 + (-1-9)^2} \doteq 13.45$

    $CD = \sqrt{(11-8)^2 + (-4-(-1))^2} \doteq 4.24$

    Total length: $AB + BC + CD = 26.91$

    The cable is about 26.91 units long.

15a. Distance between Wilson's home and the coffee shop:

    $\sqrt{(3-2)^2 + (15-18)^2} \doteq 3.16$

    Tea store: $(2, 18 + 3.16) = (2, 21.16)$

    The tea store will be at $(2, 21.16)$.

   b. $\sqrt{(2-3)^2 + (21.16-15)^2} \doteq 6.24$

    The tea store will be about 6.24 km from the coffee shop.

16. l is perpendicular to $y = 2x - 6$ and passes through $(1, 2.5)$.

    slope of l: $-\frac{1}{2}$ $y = 2x - 6$ ①

    $y - 2.5 = -\frac{1}{2}(x - 1)$ $x + 2y = 6$ ②

    $2y - 5 = -x + 1$ $x + 2(2x - 6) = 6$

    $x + 2y = 6$ $5x = 18$

    $x = 3.6$

    $y = 2(3.6) - 6$

    $y = 1.2$

    Point of intersection: $(3.6, 1.2)$

    $d = \sqrt{(3.6-1)^2 + (1.2-2.5)^2}$

    $\doteq 2.91$

    Distance in m: 10 m × 2.91 = 29.1 m

    He travels about 29.1 m.

3.2 Midpoint of a Line Segment

Try This (p. 39)

$(x, y) = (\frac{4 + (-1)}{2}, \frac{5 + (-3)}{2}) = (\frac{3}{2}, 1)$

The midpoint is $(\frac{3}{2}, 1)$.

1. Line MN: $(x, y) = (\frac{2+4}{2}, \frac{1+7}{2}) = (3, 4)$

   Line OP: $(x, y) = (\frac{2+(-3)}{2}, \frac{5+7}{2}) = (-\frac{1}{2}, 6)$

   Line QR: $(x, y) = (\frac{-1+(-2)}{2}, \frac{4+(-5)}{2}) = (-\frac{3}{2}, -\frac{1}{2})$

   Line ST: $(x, y) = (\frac{3+(-3)}{2}, \frac{-4+2}{2}) = (0, -1)$

2. $(x, y) = (\frac{-3+4}{2}, \frac{1+(-1)}{2})$

   $= (\frac{1}{2}, 0)$

3. $(x, y) = (\frac{-2+5}{2}, \frac{-4+0}{2})$

   $= (\frac{3}{2}, -2)$

4. $(x, y) = (\frac{0+5}{2}, \frac{\frac{1}{2}+3}{2})$

   $= (\frac{5}{2}, \frac{7}{4})$

5. $(x, y) = (\frac{a+1}{2}, \frac{a-1}{2})$

6. $(x, y) = (\frac{\frac{a}{2}+(-2)}{2}, \frac{-1+a}{2})$

   $= (\frac{a-4}{4}, \frac{-1+a}{2})$

7. $(x, y) = (\frac{2a-1+a}{2}, \frac{1+2a}{2})$

   $= (\frac{3a-1}{2}, \frac{1+2a}{2})$

8. -4 ; -3 ; -4 ; -3

9. $3 = \frac{x+6}{2}$ $7 = \frac{y+(-1)}{2}$

   $x = 0$ $y = 15$

   $(0, 15)$

10. $6\frac{1}{2} = \frac{x+4}{2}$ $15 = \frac{y+12}{2}$

    $x = 9$ $y = 18$

    $(9, 18)$

11. $0 = \frac{x+(-\frac{3}{2})}{2}$ $-5\frac{1}{2} = \frac{y+0}{2}$

    $x = \frac{3}{2}$ $y = -11$

    $(\frac{3}{2}, -11)$

12. $0 = \frac{x+(-4)}{2}$ $0 = \frac{y+5}{2}$

    $x = 4$ $y = -5$

    $(4, -5)$

13. $-2.5 = \frac{x+1.5}{2}$ $0 = \frac{y+4}{2}$

    $x = -6.5$ $y = -4$

    $(-6.5, -4)$

14. $a = \frac{x+a-1}{2}$ $-1 = \frac{y+a}{2}$

    $x = a + 1$ $y = -a - 2$

    $(a + 1, -a - 2)$

15. $-1 = \frac{x+0}{2}$ $a = \frac{y+a+1}{2}$

    $x = -2$ $y = a - 1$

    $(-2, a - 1)$

16. $a = \frac{x+a+1}{2}$ $a = \frac{y+2a}{2}$

    $x = a - 1$ $y = 0$

    $(a - 1, 0)$

17a. $(x, y) = (\frac{0+4}{2}, \frac{6+0}{2})$

    $= (2, 3)$

    Point M is at $(2, 3)$.

   b. $4 = \frac{x+0}{2}$ $0 = \frac{y+6}{2}$

    $x = 8$ $y = -6$

    Point C is at $(8, -6)$.

   c. $AC = \sqrt{(8-0)^2 + (-6-6)^2}$

    $= \sqrt{208}$

    The length is $\sqrt{208}$ units.

   d. $\frac{y-6}{x-0} = \frac{-6-6}{8-0}$

    $2(y - 6) = -3x$

    $3x + 2y - 12 = 0$

18. **1st:** $(x,y) = (\frac{6+8}{2}, \frac{2+(-4)}{2}) = (7,-1)$

　　2nd: slope $= \frac{-1-0}{7-(-4)} = -\frac{1}{11}$　**3rd:**　$y - (-1) = -\frac{1}{11}(x-7)$

　　　　　　　　　　　　　　　　　$11y + 11 = -x + 7$
　　　　　　　　　　　　　　　　　$x + 11y + 4 = 0$

19. **1st:** $M(x,y) = (\frac{-3+5}{2}, \frac{-3+(-2)}{2}) = (1, -\frac{5}{2})$

　　2nd: slope $= \dfrac{-\frac{5}{2} - 1}{1 - (-1)} = -\frac{7}{4}$

　　3rd:　$y - 1 = -\frac{7}{4}(x - (-1))$

　　　　　　$4y - 4 = -7x - 7$
　　　　$7x + 4y + 3 = 0$

$D(-1,1)$　$E(-3,-3)$　M　$F(5,-2)$

20. Median from Vertex K:

　　1st: $M_1(x,y) = (\frac{4+1}{2}, \frac{-3+1}{2}) = (\frac{5}{2}, -1)$

　　2nd: slope $= \dfrac{-7-(-1)}{-2 - \frac{5}{2}} = \frac{4}{3}$

　　3rd:　$y - (-7) = \frac{4}{3}(x - (-2))$
　　　　　　$3y + 21 = 4x + 8$
　　　　　$4x - 3y - 13 = 0$

　　Median from Vertex J:

　　1st: $M_2(x,y) = (\frac{1+(-2)}{2}, \frac{1+(-7)}{2}) = (-\frac{1}{2}, -3)$

　　2nd: slope $= \dfrac{-3-(-3)}{-\frac{1}{2} - 4} = 0$

　　3rd: $y - (-3) = 0(x - (-\frac{1}{2}))$
　　　　　　　　$y = -3$

$I(1,1)$　M_1　M_2　$J(4,-3)$　$K(-2,-7)$

21. $-1 = \dfrac{k+3+3}{2}$　　$-4 = \dfrac{2+l+2}{2}$
　　$k - -8$　　　　　　　$l = -12$

　　The values of k and l are -8 and -12 respectively.

22. Midpoint of AD: $(\frac{-7+(-1)}{2}, \frac{2+7}{2}) = (-4, \frac{9}{2})$

　　Midpoint of BC: $(\frac{-2+(-6)}{2}, \frac{3+6}{2}) = (-4, \frac{9}{2})$

　　Yes, the diagonals have the same midpoint at $(-4, \frac{9}{2})$.

23. $(x,y) = (\frac{5+(-1)}{2}, \frac{3+(-5)}{2}) = (2,-1)$

　　Diameter: $\sqrt{(5-(-1))^2 + (3-(-5))^2} = 10$

　　The coordinates are $(2,-1)$. The diameter is 10 units.

24a. $(0,0)$ is the midpoint of RQ.

　　$0 = \dfrac{x+6}{2}$　　$0 = \dfrac{y+1}{2}$
　　$x = -6$　　　　$y = -1$

　　The coordinates of R are $(-6,-1)$.

 b. $PQ = \sqrt{(6-(-2))^2 + (1-5)^2} = \sqrt{80} \doteq 8.94$
　　$QR = \sqrt{(6-(-6))^2 + (1-(-1))^2} = \sqrt{148} \doteq 12.17$
　　$RP = \sqrt{(-2-(-6))^2 + (5-(-1))^2} = \sqrt{52} \doteq 7.21$
　　Perimeter: $8.94 + 12.17 + 7.21 = 28.32$
　　The perimeter of $\triangle PQR$ is about 28.32 units.

3.3 Equation of a Circle

Try This (p. 43)

　　$x^2 + y^2 = r^2$
　　$2^2 + 4^2 = r^2$
　　　　$r^2 = 20$

　　The equation is $x^2 + y^2 = 20$.

1a. $x^2 + y^2 = 2.25$; B　　b. $x^2 + y^2 = 4$; C
 c. $x^2 + y^2 = 36$; F　　d. $x^2 + y^2 = 16$; A
 e. $x^2 + y^2 = 1$; E　　f. $x^2 + y^2 = 6.25$; D
2. $2^2 + 3^2 = 13 > 10$　　3. $(-7)^2 + 2^2 = 53 > 50$
　　outside the circle　　　　outside the circle

4. $2^2 + (-5)^2 = 29$
　　on the circle

5. $(-4)^2 + (-6)^2 = 52 < 81$
　　within the circle

6. $\frac{2}{12}\pi r^2 = 37.5\pi$
　　　$r^2 = 225$
　　　$r = 15$

　　The coordinates would be $(15,0)$.

7. 　$x^2 + y^2 = r^2$　　　Total distance:
　　$20^2 + 21^2 = r^2$　　$3\pi d = 3 \times 3.14 \times 2 \times 29$
　　　　　$r = 29$　　　　　　　$= 546.36$

　　The sailboat will travel 546.36 units.

8. $x^2 + y^2 = 12.65^2$
　　$x^2 + y^2 \doteq 160.02$
　　Ruffland: $(-4)^2 + 11^2 = 137 < 160.02$
　　Kinfield: $12^2 + 5^2 = 169 > 160.02$
　　No, Kinfield is not within the range.

3.4 Medians and Centroids

Try This (p. 45)

　　Midpoint of AC: $(x,y) = (\frac{0+(-4)}{2}, \frac{7+1}{2}) = (-2,4)$

　　slope of median $= \dfrac{-5-4}{6-(-2)} = -\frac{9}{8}$

　　　　　　　　$y - 4 = -\frac{9}{8}(x - (-2))$
　　　　　　$8(y - 4) = -9(x + 2)$
　　　　　$9x + 8y - 14 = 0$

　　The equation is $9x + 8y - 14 = 0$.

1. • Median XM:

　　$(x,y) = (6,2)$

　　slope $= \dfrac{2-2}{6-(-8)} = 0$

　　$y = 2$

　• Median YM:

　　$(x,y) = (0,0)$

　　slope $= \dfrac{6-0}{4-0} = \frac{3}{2}$

　　$y = \frac{3}{2}x$

　　$3x - 2y = 0$

　• Median ZM:

　　$(x,y) = (-2,4)$

　　slope $= \dfrac{-2-4}{8-(-2)} = -\frac{3}{5}$

　　$y - 4 = -\frac{3}{5}(x - (-2))$

　　$5y - 20 - -3x$　　6

　　$3x + 5y - 14 = 0$

2. • Median PM:

　　$(x,y) = (\frac{2+5}{2}, \frac{4+3}{2})$

　　　　$= (3.5, 3.5)$

　　slope $= \dfrac{3.5-1}{3.5-1} = 1$

　　$y - 1 = x - 1$

　　$x - y = 0$

　• Median QM:

　　$(x,y) = (3,2)$

　　slope $= \dfrac{4-2}{2-3} = -2$

　　$y - 2 = -2(x - 3)$

　　$y - 2 = -2x + 6$

　　$2x + y - 8 = 0$

　• Median RM:

　　$(x,y) = (\frac{1+2}{2}, \frac{1+4}{2})$

　　　　$= (\frac{3}{2}, \frac{5}{2})$

　　slope $= \dfrac{3 - \frac{5}{2}}{5 - \frac{3}{2}} = \frac{1}{7}$

　　$y - 3 = \frac{1}{7}(x - 5)$

　　$7y - 21 = x - 5$

　　$x - 7y + 16 = 0$

3. **1st:** *IM:* $(x,y) = (\frac{5+6}{2}, \frac{10+3}{2}) = (\frac{11}{2}, \frac{13}{2})$

   slope $= \frac{\frac{13}{2} - 2}{\frac{11}{2} - 1} = 1$ $\qquad$ $y - 2 = x - 1$
   $\qquad\qquad\qquad\qquad\qquad$ $x - y + 1 = 0$

   JM: $(x,y) = (\frac{1+6}{2}, \frac{2+3}{2}) = (\frac{7}{2}, \frac{5}{2})$

   slope $= \frac{10 - \frac{5}{2}}{5 - \frac{7}{2}} = 5$ $\qquad$ $y - 10 = 5(x - 5)$
   $\qquad\qquad\qquad\qquad\qquad$ $5x - y - 15 = 0$

   KM: $(x,y) = (\frac{1+5}{2}, \frac{2+10}{2}) = (3,6)$

   slope $= \frac{3-6}{6-3} = -1$ $\qquad$ $y - 3 = -(x - 6)$
   $\qquad\qquad\qquad\qquad\qquad$ $x + y - 9 = 0$

   2nd:
   $x - y + 1 = 0$
   $\underline{+)\ x + y - 9 = 0}$
   $\quad 2x - 8 = 0$
   $\qquad\quad x = 4$
   $4 - y + 1 = 0$
   $\qquad\quad y = 5$
   Centroid: (4,5)

   3rd:
   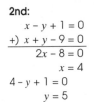

4. **1st:** *DM:* $(x,y) = (\frac{2+4}{2}, \frac{7+0}{2}) = (3, \frac{7}{2})$

   slope $= \frac{-1 - \frac{7}{2}}{-3 - 3} = \frac{3}{4}$ $\qquad$ $y - (-1) = \frac{3}{4}(x - (-3))$
   $\qquad\qquad\qquad\qquad\qquad$ $3x - 4y + 5 = 0$

   EM: $(x,y) = (\frac{-3+4}{2}, \frac{-1+0}{2}) = (\frac{1}{2}, -\frac{1}{2})$

   slope $= \frac{7 - (-\frac{1}{2})}{2 - \frac{1}{2}} = 5$ $\qquad$ $y - 7 = 5(x - 2)$
   $\qquad\qquad\qquad\qquad\qquad$ $5x - y - 3 = 0$

   FM: $(x,y) = (\frac{-3+2}{2}, \frac{-1+7}{2}) = (-\frac{1}{2}, 3)$

   slope $= \frac{0-3}{4-(-\frac{1}{2})} = -\frac{2}{3}$ $\qquad$ $y - 0 = -\frac{2}{3}(x - 4)$
   $\qquad\qquad\qquad\qquad\qquad$ $2x + 3y - 8 = 0$

   2nd:
   $3x - 4y - 5 = 0$
   $5x - y - 3 = 0$
   $3x - 4(5x - 3) + 5 = 0$
   $\qquad\qquad\qquad x = 1$
   $5(1) - y - 3 = 0$
   $\qquad\qquad y = 2$
   Centroid: (1,2)

   3rd:
   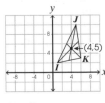

5. **1st:** *XM:* $(x,y) = (\frac{1+2}{2}, \frac{2+(-1)}{2}) = (\frac{3}{2}, \frac{1}{2})$

   slope $= \frac{1 - \frac{1}{2}}{-2 - \frac{3}{2}} = -\frac{1}{7}$ $\qquad$ $y - 1 = -\frac{1}{7}(x - (-2))$
   $\qquad\qquad\qquad\qquad\qquad$ $x + 7y - 5 = 0$

   YM: $(x,y) = (\frac{-2+2}{2}, \frac{1+(-1)}{2}) = (0,0)$

   slope $= \frac{2-0}{1-0} = 2$ $\qquad$ $y - 2 = 2(x - 1)$
   $\qquad\qquad\qquad\qquad\qquad$ $-2x + y = 0$

   ZM: $(x,y) = (\frac{-2+1}{2}, \frac{1+2}{2}) = (-\frac{1}{2}, \frac{3}{2})$

   slope $= \frac{-1 - \frac{3}{2}}{2 - (-\frac{1}{2})} = -1$ $\qquad$ $y - (-1) = -(x - 2)$
   $\qquad\qquad\qquad\qquad\qquad$ $x + y - 1 = 0$

   2nd:
   $-2x + y = 0$
   $\underline{-)\ x + y - 1 = 0}$
   $\quad -3x + 1 = 0$
   $\qquad\quad x = \frac{1}{3}$
   $\frac{1}{3} + y - 1 = 0$
   $\qquad\quad y = \frac{2}{3}$
   Centroid: $(\frac{1}{3}, \frac{2}{3})$

   3rd:
   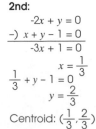

6. Location of treasure: $(\frac{12+(-1)}{2}, \frac{-2+(-4)}{2}) = (\frac{11}{2}, -3)$

   slope $= \frac{4-(-3)}{6 - \frac{11}{2}} = 14$ $\qquad$ $y - 4 = 14(x - 6)$
   $\qquad\qquad\qquad\qquad\qquad\qquad$ $y = 14x - 80$
   $\therefore y = 14x - 80$
   The equation of his route is $y = 14x - 80$.

7. Midpoint of *AB*: $(\frac{-1+5}{2}, \frac{-4+4}{2}) = (2,0)$

   $\frac{y-0}{x-2} = \frac{-3-0}{6-2}$
   $\qquad y = -\frac{3}{4}(x - 2)$
   $3x + 4y - 6 = 0$
   The equation of Emma's route is $3x + 4y - 6 = 0$.

8. The line from *P* to the midpoint of *QR*:

   $(x,y) = (\frac{7+13}{2}, \frac{16+8}{2}) = (10,12)$
   slope $= \frac{0-12}{0-10} = \frac{6}{5}$ $\qquad\qquad\quad$ $y = \frac{6}{5}x$
   $\qquad\qquad\qquad\qquad\qquad\qquad$ $6x - 5y = 0$ ①

   The line from *Q* to the midpoint of *PR*:

   $(x,y) = (\frac{13+0}{2}, \frac{8+0}{2}) = (\frac{13}{2}, 4)$
   slope $= \frac{16-4}{7 - \frac{13}{2}} = 24$ $\qquad$ $y - 16 = 24(x - 7)$
   $\qquad\qquad\qquad\qquad\qquad$ $24x - y - 152 = 0$ ②
   $24x - (\frac{6}{5}x) - 152 = 0$
   $\qquad\qquad\qquad x = \frac{20}{3}$
   $y = \frac{6}{5}(\frac{20}{3}) = 8$
   The coordinates are $(\frac{20}{3}, 8)$.

9. The line from *A* to the midpoint of *BC*:

   $(x,y) = (\frac{-1+7}{2}, \frac{3+1}{2}) = (3,2)$
   slope $= \frac{-4-2}{-6-3} = \frac{2}{3}$ $\qquad$ $y - (-4) = \frac{2}{3}(x - (-6))$
   $\qquad\qquad\qquad\qquad\qquad$ $2x - 3y = 0$ ①

   The line from *B* to the midpoint of *AC*:

   $(x,y) = (\frac{-6+7}{2}, \frac{-4+1}{2}) = (\frac{1}{2}, -\frac{3}{2})$
   slope $= \frac{3 - (-\frac{3}{2})}{-1 - \frac{1}{2}} = -3$ $\qquad$ $y - 3 = -3(x - (-1))$
   $\qquad\qquad\qquad\qquad\qquad$ $3x + y = 0$ ②
   $2x - 3(-3x) = 0$
   $\qquad\quad x = 0$
   $y = -3(0) = 0$
   Centroid: (0,0)
   The coordinates are (0,0).

3.5 Perpendicular Bisectors and Circumcentres

Try This (p. 48)

Midpoint of *XY*: $(\frac{-6+4}{2}, \frac{2+6}{2}) = (-1,4)$

$m_{XY} = \frac{2-6}{-6-4} = \frac{2}{5}$ $\qquad$ $m_\perp = -\frac{5}{2}$

$y - 4 = -\frac{5}{2}(x - (-1))$
$\qquad y = -\frac{5}{2}x + \frac{3}{2}$
The equation is $y = -\frac{5}{2}x + \frac{3}{2}$.

1. $P(1,1)$, $Q(2,4)$, $R(5,3)$

   PQ: Midpoint of *PQ*: $(\frac{1+2}{2}, \frac{1+4}{2}) = (\frac{3}{2}, \frac{5}{2})$

   $m_{PQ} = \frac{4-1}{2-1} = 3$ $\qquad$ $m_\perp = -\frac{1}{3}$

   $y - \frac{5}{2} = -\frac{1}{3}(x - \frac{3}{2})$
   $\qquad\quad y = -\frac{1}{3}x + 3$

 ISBN: 978-1-77149-221-8

PR: Midpoint of PR: $(\frac{1+5}{2}, \frac{1+3}{2}) = (3,2)$

$m_{PR} = \frac{3-1}{5-1} = \frac{1}{2}$ $\quad m_\perp = -2$

$y - 2 = -2(x - 3)$
$\quad y = -2x + 8$

QR: Midpoint of QR: $(\frac{2+5}{2}, \frac{4+3}{2}) = (\frac{7}{2}, \frac{7}{2})$

$m_{QR} = \frac{4-3}{2-5} = -\frac{1}{3}$ $\quad m_\perp = 3$

$y - \frac{7}{2} = 3(x - \frac{7}{2})$

$\quad y = 3x - 7$

2.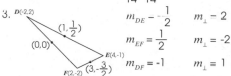

$m_{GH} = \frac{5}{2}$ $\quad m_\perp = -\frac{2}{5}$

$m_{GI} = -1$ $\quad m_\perp = 1$

$m_{HI} = \frac{1}{6}$ $\quad m_\perp = -6$

Perpendicular bisector of GH: $y - \frac{3}{2} = -\frac{2}{5}(x - 0)$

$\quad y = -\frac{2}{5}x + \frac{3}{2}$

Perpendicular bisector of GI: $y - 2 = 1(x - 3)$

$\quad y = x - 1$

Perpendicular bisector of HI: $y - (-\frac{1}{2}) = -6(x - 2)$

$\quad y = -6x + 11\frac{1}{2}$

Circumcentre of $\triangle GHI$:

$y = -\frac{2}{5}x + \frac{3}{2}$ ① $\qquad x - 1 = -\frac{2}{5}x + \frac{3}{2}$

$y = x - 1$ ② $\qquad\qquad x = \frac{25}{14}$

$\qquad\qquad\qquad y = \frac{25}{14} - 1 = \frac{11}{14}$

The circumcentre is $(\frac{25}{14}, \frac{11}{14})$.

3.

$m_{DE} = -\frac{1}{2}$ $\quad m_\perp = 2$

$m_{EF} = \frac{1}{2}$ $\quad m_\perp = -2$

$m_{DF} = -1$ $\quad m_\perp = 1$

Perpendicular bisector of DE: $y - \frac{1}{2} = 2(x - 1)$

$\quad y = 2x - \frac{3}{2}$

Perpendicular bisector of EF: $y - (-\frac{3}{2}) = -2(x - 3)$

$\quad y = -2x + \frac{9}{2}$

Perpendicular bisector of DF: $y - 0 = 1(x - 0)$

$\quad y = x$

Circumcentre of $\triangle DEF$:

$y = 2x - \frac{3}{2}$ ① $\qquad x = 2x - \frac{3}{2}$

$y = x$ ② $\qquad\qquad x = \frac{3}{2}$

$\qquad\qquad\qquad y = \frac{3}{2}$

The circumcentre is $(\frac{3}{2}, \frac{3}{2})$.

4.

$m_{AB} = -\frac{7}{6}$ $\quad m_\perp = \frac{6}{7}$

$m_{BC} = \frac{5}{2}$ $\quad m_\perp = -\frac{2}{5}$

$m_{AC} = -\frac{1}{4}$ $\quad m_\perp = 4$

Perpendicular bisector of AB: $y - \frac{1}{2} = \frac{6}{7}x$

$\quad y = \frac{6}{7}x + \frac{1}{2}$

Perpendicular bisector of BC: $y - (-\frac{1}{2}) = -\frac{2}{5}(x - 4)$

$\quad y = -\frac{2}{5}x + \frac{11}{10}$

Perpendicular bisector of AC: $y - 3 = 4(x - 1)$

$\quad y = 4x - 1$

Circumcentre of $\triangle ABC$:

$y = \frac{6}{7}x + \frac{1}{2}$ ① $\qquad \frac{6}{7}x + \frac{1}{2} = 4x - 1$

$y = 4x - 1$ ② $\qquad\qquad x = \frac{21}{44}$

$\qquad\qquad y = 4(\frac{21}{44}) - 1 = \frac{10}{11}$

The circumcentre is $(\frac{21}{44}, \frac{10}{11})$.

5. $\triangle ABC$: Midpoint of AB: $(-\frac{5}{2}, -\frac{3}{2})$ $\quad m_{AB} = 3$
Perpendicular bisector of AB: $y = -\frac{1}{3}x - \frac{7}{3}$
Midpoint of AC: $(1, -1)$ $\quad m_{AC} = -2$
Perpendicular bisector of AC: $y = \frac{1}{2}x - \frac{3}{2}$
Midpoint of BC: $(-\frac{1}{2}, -\frac{11}{2})$ $\quad m_{BC} = \frac{1}{7}$
Perpendicular bisector of BC: $y = -7x - 9$
Circumcentre: $(-1, -2)$

$\triangle PQR$: Midpoint of PQ: $(-9, 3)$ $\quad m_{PQ} = -3$
Perpendicular bisector of PQ: $y = \frac{1}{3}x + 6$
Midpoint of PR: $(-6, 4)$ $\quad m_{PR} = -\frac{1}{2}$
Perpendicular bisector of PR: $y = 2x + 16$
Midpoint of QR: $(-5, 1)$ $\quad m_{QR} = \frac{1}{3}$
Perpendicular bisector of QR: $y = -3x - 14$
Circumcentre: $(-6, 4)$

$\triangle HIJ$: Midpoint of HI: $(11, 3)$ $\quad m_{HI} = -1$
Perpendicular bisector of HI: $y = x - 8$
Midpoint of HJ: $(8, 2)$ $\quad m_{HJ} = 3$
Perpendicular bisector of HJ: $y = -\frac{1}{3}x + \frac{14}{3}$
Midpoint of IJ: $(10, 0)$ $\quad m_{IJ} = \frac{1}{3}$
Perpendicular bisector of IJ: $y = -3x + 30$
Circumcentre: $(9\frac{1}{2}, 1\frac{1}{2})$

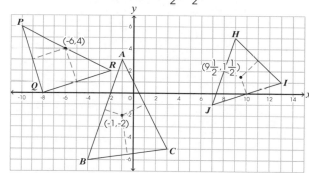

6a. • Midpoint of AB:

$(x, y) = (\frac{3}{2}, 6)$ $\qquad y - 6 = -\frac{1}{4}(x - \frac{3}{2})$

$m_{AB} = 4$ $\quad m_\perp = -\frac{1}{4}$ $\qquad y = -\frac{1}{4}x + \frac{51}{8}$

• Midpoint of BC:

$(x, y) = (6, \frac{15}{2})$ $\qquad y - \frac{15}{2} = \frac{2}{3}(x - 6)$

$m_{BC} = -\frac{3}{2}$ $\quad m_\perp = \frac{2}{3}$ $\qquad y = \frac{2}{3}x + \frac{7}{2}$

• Midpoint of AC:

$(x, y) = (\frac{9}{2}, \frac{3}{2})$ $\qquad y - \frac{3}{2} = -3(x - \frac{9}{2})$

$m_{AC} = \frac{1}{3}$ $\quad m_\perp = -3$ $\qquad y = -3x + 15$

b. $y = \frac{2}{3}x + \frac{7}{2}$ ① $\qquad \frac{2}{3}x + \frac{7}{2} = -3x + 15$

$y = -3x + 15$ ② $\qquad\qquad x = \frac{69}{22}$

$\qquad\qquad y = -3(\frac{69}{22}) + 15 = \frac{123}{22}$

Circumcentre: $(\frac{69}{22}, \frac{123}{22})$

The coordinates are $(\frac{69}{22}, \frac{123}{22})$.

ISBN: 978-1-77149-221-8

7a. $A(5,5)$, $B(-5,-5)$, $C(5,-5)$

• Midpoint of AB:
$(x,y) = (0,0)$
$m_{AB} = 1 \qquad m_\perp = -1$
$y = -x$

• Midpoint of AC:
$(x,y) = (5,0)$
$m_{AC} = $ undefined $\qquad m_\perp = 0$
$y = 0$

The circumcentre is $(0,0)$.

• Midpoint of BC:
$(x,y) = (0,-5)$
$m_{BC} = 0 \quad m_\perp = $ undefined
$x = 0$

b. (Suggested answer)
$P(1,7)$, $Q(1,-7)$, $R(7,1)$

• Midpoint of PQ:
$(x,y) = (1,0)$
$m_{PQ} = $ undefined $\quad m_\perp = 0$
$y = 0$

• Midpoint of QR:
$(x,y) = (4,-3)$
$m_{QR} = \dfrac{4}{3} \qquad m_\perp = -\dfrac{3}{4}$
$y - (-3) = -\dfrac{3}{4}(x - 4)$
$y = -\dfrac{3}{4}x$

• Midpoint of PR:
$(x,y) = (4,4)$
$m_{PR} = -1 \qquad m_\perp = 1$
$y - 4 = x - 4$
$y = x$

The circumcentre is $(0,0)$.
Yes, it has the same circumcentre as Tori's.

3.6 Altitudes and Orthocentres

Try This (p. 52)

slope of $BC = m_{BC} = \dfrac{2 - (-4)}{4 - (-5)} = \dfrac{2}{3} \qquad m_\perp = -\dfrac{3}{2}$

$y - 4 = -\dfrac{3}{2}(x - (-6))$
$y - 4 = -\dfrac{3}{2}x - 9$
$y = -\dfrac{3}{2}x - 5$

1.

$m_{ZX} = \dfrac{6 - 2}{2 - (-6)} = \dfrac{1}{2}$
$m_{YQ} = -2$
Equation of YQ:
$y - 0 = -2(x - 2)$
$y = -2x + 4$

$m_{XY} = \dfrac{6 - 0}{2 - 2} = $ undefined
$m_{ZP} = 0$
Equation of ZP:
$y - 2 = 0(x - (-6))$
$y = 2$
$m_{ZY} = \dfrac{2 - 0}{-6 - 2} = -\dfrac{1}{4}$
$m_{XR} = 4$
Equation of XR:
$y - 6 = 4(x - 2)$
$y = 4x - 2$

2.

$P(1,5)$, $Q(-3,1)$, $R(2,-2)$

$m_{QR} = \dfrac{-2 - 1}{2 - (-3)} = -\dfrac{3}{5}$
$m_{PB} = \dfrac{5}{3}$
Equation of PB:
$y - 5 = \dfrac{5}{3}(x - 1)$
$y = \dfrac{5}{3}x + \dfrac{10}{3}$

$m_{PQ} = \dfrac{5 - 1}{1 - (-3)} = 1$
$m_{RC} = -1$
Equation of RC:
$y - (-2) = -(x - 2)$
$y = -x$
$m_{PR} = \dfrac{5 - (-2)}{1 - 2} = -7$
$m_{QA} = \dfrac{1}{7}$
Equation of QA:
$y - 1 = \dfrac{1}{7}(x - (-3))$
$y = \dfrac{1}{7}x + \dfrac{10}{7}$

3. $m_1 = \dfrac{1 - (-7)}{2 - (-6)} = 1$
$m_\perp = -1$
$y - (-5) = -1(x - (-10))$
$y = -x - 15$

$m_2 = \dfrac{-5 - (-7)}{-10 - (-6)} = -\dfrac{1}{2}$
$m_\perp = 2$
$y - 1 = 2(x - 2)$
$y = 2x - 3$

$m_3 = \dfrac{1 - (-5)}{2 - (-10)} = \dfrac{1}{2}$
$m_\perp = -2$
$y - (-7) = -2(x - (-6))$
$y = -2x - 19$
$y = -x - 15$; $y = 2x - 3$; $y = -2x - 19$; $(-4,-11)$

$-x - 15 = 2x - 3$
$x = -4$
$y = -(-4) - 15 = -11$

4. $m_1 = \dfrac{5 - (-3)}{4 - 0} = 2$
$m_\perp = -\dfrac{1}{2}$
$y - 3 = -\dfrac{1}{2}(x - 8)$
$y = -\dfrac{1}{2}x + 7$
$m_3 = \dfrac{5 - 3}{4 - 8} = -\dfrac{1}{2}$
$m_\perp = 2$
$y - (-3) = 2(x - 0)$
$y = 2x - 3$

$m_2 = \dfrac{-3 - 3}{0 - 8} = \dfrac{3}{4}$
$m_\perp = -\dfrac{4}{3}$
$y - 5 = -\dfrac{4}{3}(x - 4)$
$y = -\dfrac{4}{3}x + \dfrac{31}{3}$
$-\dfrac{1}{2}x + 7 = 2x - 3$
$x = 4$
$y = 2(4) - 3 = 5$

$y = -\dfrac{1}{2}x + 7$; $y = -\dfrac{4}{3}x + \dfrac{31}{3}$; $y = 2x - 3$; $(4,5)$

5. $m_1 = \dfrac{2 - (-6)}{1 - (-3)} = 2$
$m_\perp = -\dfrac{1}{2}$
$y - 0 = -\dfrac{1}{2}(x - 5)$
$y = -\dfrac{1}{2}x + \dfrac{5}{2}$
$m_3 = \dfrac{2 - 0}{1 - 5} = -\dfrac{1}{2}$
$m_\perp = 2$
$y - (-6) = 2(x - (-3))$
$y = 2x$

$m_2 = \dfrac{0 - (-6)}{5 - (-3)} = \dfrac{3}{4}$
$m_\perp = -\dfrac{4}{3}$
$y - 2 = -\dfrac{4}{3}(x - 1)$
$y = -\dfrac{4}{3}x + \dfrac{10}{3}$
$-\dfrac{1}{2}x + \dfrac{5}{2} = 2x$
$x = 1$
$y = 2(1) = 2$

$y = -\dfrac{1}{2}x + \dfrac{5}{2}$; $y = -\dfrac{4}{3}x + \dfrac{10}{3}$; $y = 2x$; $(1,2)$

6a.

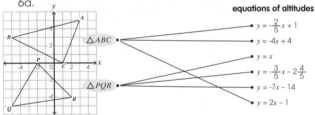

equations of altitudes

$y = -\dfrac{2}{5}x + 1$

$y = -4x + 4$

$y = x$

$y = -\dfrac{3}{5}x - 2\dfrac{4}{5}$

$y = -7x - 14$

$y = 2x - 1$

b. $\triangle ABC$:
$y = -4x + 4$ ①
$y = 2x - 1$ ②
$2x - 1 = -4x + 4$
$6x = 5$
$x = \dfrac{5}{6}$
$y = 2\left(\dfrac{5}{6}\right) - 1 = \dfrac{2}{3}$
Orthocentre: $\left(\dfrac{5}{6}, \dfrac{2}{3}\right)$

$\triangle PQR$:
$y = x$ ①
$y = -7x - 14$ ②
$x = -7x - 14$
$8x = -14$
$x = -\dfrac{7}{4}$
$y = -\dfrac{7}{4}$
Orthocentre: $\left(-\dfrac{7}{4}, -\dfrac{7}{4}\right)$

7. $m_{BC} = \dfrac{-4 - (-3)}{-1 - 6} = \dfrac{1}{7}$
$m_\perp = -7$
Equation of altitude from A:
$y - 4 = -7(x - 5)$
$y = -7x + 39$
Equation of AC:
$\dfrac{y - 4}{x - 5} = \dfrac{-3 - 4}{6 - 5}$
$y - 4 = -7(x - 5)$
$y = -7x + 39$
∴ AC is an altitude of the triangle.

$A(5,4)$, $B(-1,-4)$, $C(6,-3)$

8. The orthocentre of a right triangle is the vertex at its right angle.

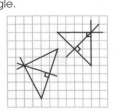

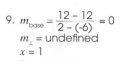

9. $m_{base} = \dfrac{12-12}{2-(-6)} = 0$
$m_\perp =$ undefined
$x = 1$
The equation is $x = 1$.

10. Length of altitude: 8
Base of triangle: $20 \times 2 \div 8 = 5$
Coordinates of Q: $(0,-5)$

$m_{base} = \dfrac{-5-0}{0-0} =$ undefined
$y = -3$
The coordinates of Q are $(0,-5)$. The equation is $y = -3$.

11. Solve for C.
$$\begin{array}{r} 4x + 3y + 12 = 0 \\ -)\ 4x + 5y + 20 = 0 \\ \hline -2y - 8 = 0 \\ y = -4 \end{array}$$
$4x + 3(-4) + 12 = 0$
$x = 0$
Coordinates of C: $(0,-4)$

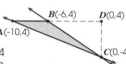

$m_{AC} = \dfrac{-4-4}{0-(-10)} = -\dfrac{4}{5}$ $m_\perp = \dfrac{5}{4}$
$y - 4 = \dfrac{5}{4}(x - (-6))$
$y = \dfrac{5}{4}x + \dfrac{23}{2}$
Coordinates of D: $(0,4)$
Base of triangle: $-6 - (-10) = 4$
Height of triangle: $4 - (-4) = 8$
Area: $4 \times 8 \div 2 = 16$
The equation is $y = \dfrac{5}{4}x + \dfrac{23}{2}$. The area is 16 square units.

12. $m_{BC} = \dfrac{-4-(-2)}{1-(-5)} = -\dfrac{1}{3}$

$m_\perp = 3$
Altitude of BC:
$y - 2 = 3(x - a)$
$y = 3x - 3a + 2$
Substitute $(-2,-1)$ into altitude of BC.
$-1 = 3(-2) - 3a + 2$
$a = -1$

3.7 Classifying Shapes

Try This (p. 56)

l_{PQ}: $\sqrt{(-6-(-3))^2 + (2-(-4))^2} = \sqrt{45}$
l_{QR}: $\sqrt{(-3-7)^2 + (-4-1)^2} = \sqrt{125}$
l_{PR}: $\sqrt{(-6-7)^2 + (2-1)^2} = \sqrt{170}$
All three sides have different lengths. It is a scalene triangle.

1. l_{XY}: $\sqrt{(0-(-6))^2 + (7-(-11))^2} = \sqrt{360}$
l_{YZ}: $\sqrt{(-6-6)^2 + (-11-(-5))^2} = \sqrt{180}$
l_{XZ}: $\sqrt{(0-6)^2 + (7-(-5))^2} = \sqrt{180}$
It is an isosceles triangle.
$m_{XY} = \dfrac{7-(-11)}{0-(-6)} = 3$ $m_{YZ} = \dfrac{-11-(-5)}{-6-6} = \dfrac{1}{2}$
$m_{XZ} = \dfrac{7-(-5)}{0-6} = -2$
$YZ \perp XZ$; It is a right triangle.

2. l_{DE}: $\sqrt{(-1-(-4))^2 + (3-(-6))^2} = \sqrt{90}$
l_{EF}: $\sqrt{(-4-5)^2 + (-6-1)^2} = \sqrt{130}$
l_{DF}: $\sqrt{(-1-5)^2 + (3-1)^2} = \sqrt{40}$
It is a scalene triangle.
$m_{DE} = \dfrac{3-(-6)}{-1-(-4)} = 3$ $m_{EF} = \dfrac{-6-1}{-4-5} = \dfrac{7}{9}$
$m_{DF} = \dfrac{3-1}{-1-5} = -\dfrac{1}{3}$
$DE \perp DF$; It is a right triangle.

3. l_{AB}: $\sqrt{(2-4)^2 + (1-4)^2} = \sqrt{13}$
l_{BC}: $\sqrt{(4-4)^2 + (4-(-2))^2} = \sqrt{36} = 6$
l_{AC}: $\sqrt{(2-4)^2 + (1-(-2))^2} = \sqrt{13}$
It is an isosceles triangle.
$m_{AB} = \dfrac{4-1}{4-2} = \dfrac{3}{2}$ $m_{BC} = \dfrac{-2-4}{4-4} =$ undefined
$m_{AC} = \dfrac{-2-1}{4-2} = -\dfrac{3}{2}$
It is not a right triangle.

4. l_{PQ}: $\sqrt{(-8-0)^2 + (3-7)^2} = \sqrt{80}$
l_{QR}: $\sqrt{(0-2)^2 + (7-3)^2} = \sqrt{20}$
l_{PR}: $\sqrt{(-8-2)^2 + (3-3)^2} = \sqrt{100} = 10$
It is a scalene triangle.
$m_{PQ} = \dfrac{3-7}{-8-0} = \dfrac{1}{2}$ $m_{QR} = \dfrac{7-3}{0-2} = -2$
$m_{PR} = \dfrac{3-3}{-8-2} = 0$
$PQ \perp QR$; It is a right triangle.

5. $d_{WX} = \sqrt{(5-1)^2 + (8-4)^2} = \sqrt{32}$
$d_{YZ} = \sqrt{(14-10)^2 + (5-1)^2} = \sqrt{32}$
$d_{XY} = \sqrt{(14-5)^2 + (5-8)^2} = \sqrt{90}$
$d_{WZ} = \sqrt{(10-1)^2 + (1-4)^2} = \sqrt{90}$
Opposite sides have the same length.

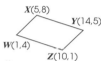

$m_{WX} = \dfrac{8-4}{5-1} = 1$ $m_{YZ} = \dfrac{5-1}{14-10} = 1$
$m_{XY} = \dfrac{8-5}{5-14} = -\dfrac{1}{3}$ $m_{WZ} = \dfrac{4-1}{1-10} = -\dfrac{1}{3}$
$WX // YZ$ and $XY // WZ$
Quadrilateral $WXYZ$ is a parallelogram.

6. $d_{AB} = \sqrt{(2-1)^2 + (1-3)^2} = \sqrt{5}$
$d_{CD} = \sqrt{(5-6)^2 + (5-3)^2} = \sqrt{5}$
$d_{BC} = \sqrt{(5-1)^2 + (5-3)^2} = \sqrt{20}$
$d_{AD} = \sqrt{(6-2)^2 + (3-1)^2} = \sqrt{20}$
Opposite sides have the same length.

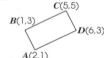

$m_{AB} = \dfrac{3-1}{1-2} = -2$ $m_{CD} = \dfrac{5-3}{6-6} = -2$
$m_{BC} = \dfrac{5-3}{5-1} = \dfrac{1}{2}$ $m_{AD} = \dfrac{3-1}{6-2} = \dfrac{1}{2}$
$AB // CD$, $BC // AD$, $AB \perp BC$, $CD \perp AD$
Quadrilateral $ABCD$ is a rectangle.

7. $d_{IL} = \sqrt{(-1-(-4))^2 + (4-(-3))^2} = \sqrt{58}$
$d_{JK} = \sqrt{(6-3)^2 + (1-(-6))^2} = \sqrt{58}$
$d_{IJ} = \sqrt{(-1-6)^2 + (4-1)^2} = \sqrt{58}$
$d_{KL} = \sqrt{(-4-3)^2 + (-3-(-6))^2} = \sqrt{58}$
Four sides have the same length.

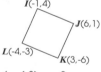

$m_{IJ} = \dfrac{1-4}{6-(-1)} = -\dfrac{3}{7}$ $m_{KL} = \dfrac{-6-(-3)}{3-(-4)} = -\dfrac{3}{7}$
$m_{IL} = \dfrac{4-(-3)}{-1-(-4)} = \dfrac{7}{3}$ $m_{JK} = \dfrac{1-(-6)}{6-3} = \dfrac{7}{3}$
$IJ // KL$, $IL // JK$, $IJ \perp IL$, $KL \perp JK$
Quadrilateral $IJKL$ is a square.

8. $d_{PQ} = \sqrt{(-1-1)^2 + (6-1)^2} = \sqrt{29}$
$d_{QR} = \sqrt{(1-(-1))^2 + (1-(-4))^2} = \sqrt{29}$
$d_{RS} = \sqrt{(-1-(-3))^2 + (-4-1)^2} = \sqrt{29}$
$d_{PS} = \sqrt{(-3-(-1))^2 + (1-6)^2} = \sqrt{29}$
Four sides have the same length.

$m_{PQ} = \dfrac{6-1}{-1-1} = -\dfrac{5}{2}$ $m_{QR} = \dfrac{1-(-4)}{1-(-1)} = \dfrac{5}{2}$
$m_{RS} = \dfrac{-4-1}{-1-(-3)} = -\dfrac{5}{2}$ $m_{PS} = \dfrac{1-6}{-3-(-1)} = \dfrac{5}{2}$
$PQ // RS$, $QR // PS$
Quadrilateral $PQRS$ is a rhombus.

9a. Midpoint of AB: $\left(\dfrac{-4+5}{2}, \dfrac{3+0}{2}\right) = \left(\dfrac{1}{2}, \dfrac{3}{2}\right)$

$m_{AB} = \dfrac{0-3}{5-(-4)} = -\dfrac{1}{3}$
$m_\perp = 3$
$y - \dfrac{3}{2} = 3\left(x - \dfrac{1}{2}\right)$
$y = 3x$
The equation is $y = 3x$.

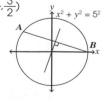

ISBN: 978-1-77149-221-8

b. Centre of circle = (0,0)
Substitute (0,0) into the equation $y = 3x$.
LS = 0   RS = 3(0) = 0
Yes, it passes through the centre of the circle.

10. $m_{ST} = \dfrac{-23 - 25}{-5 - 9} = \dfrac{24}{7}$ Equation of ST:

$$y - 25 = \frac{24}{7}(x - 9)$$
$$y = \frac{24}{7}x - \frac{41}{7}$$

Substitute (2,1) into the equation.
LS = 1   RS = $\dfrac{24}{7}(2) - \dfrac{41}{7} = 1$
∴ (2,1) lies on the equation.
ST is the diameter of the circle.

11. Milo should find the equation of the perpendicular bisector of XY. First, find the midpoint of XY and the slope of XY. The slope of the perpendicular bisector is the negative reciprocal of the slope of XY. Then use the point-slope form to find the equation of the perpendicular bisector which is the equation of the line that cuts the circle in half.

Midpoint of XY: $(\dfrac{10 + (-8)}{2}, \dfrac{0 + (-6)}{2}) = (1,-3)$

$m_{XY} = \dfrac{0 - (-6)}{10 - (-8)} = \dfrac{1}{3}$ $m_\perp = -3$
$y - (-3) = -3(x - 1)$
$y = -3x$
The equation of the line is $y = -3x$.

12a. Midpoint A: $(\dfrac{-6 + 4}{2}, \dfrac{2 + 6}{2}) = (-1,4)$

Midpoint B: $(\dfrac{4 + 8}{2}, \dfrac{6 + (-4)}{2}) = (6,1)$

Midpoint C: $(\dfrac{8 + (-2)}{2}, \dfrac{-4 + (-8)}{2}) = (3,-6)$

Midpoint D: $(\dfrac{-2 + (-6)}{2}, \dfrac{-8 + 2}{2}) = (-4,-3)$

$d_{AB} = \sqrt{(-1 - 6)^2 + (4 - 1)^2} = \sqrt{58}$
$d_{BC} = \sqrt{(6 - 3)^2 + (1 - (-6))^2} = \sqrt{58}$
$d_{CD} = \sqrt{(3 - (-4))^2 + (-6 - (-3))^2} = \sqrt{58}$
$d_{AD} = \sqrt{(-1 - (-4))^2 + (4 - (-3))^2} = \sqrt{58}$
Four sides have the same length.

$m_{AB} = \dfrac{1 - 4}{6 - (-1)} = -\dfrac{3}{7}$ $m_{BC} = \dfrac{-6 - 1}{3 - 6} = \dfrac{7}{3}$
$m_{CD} = \dfrac{-3 - (-6)}{-4 - 3} = -\dfrac{3}{7}$ $m_{AD} = \dfrac{4 - (-3)}{-1 - (-4)} = \dfrac{7}{3}$
$AB // CD$, $BC // AD$, $AB \perp BC$, $CD \perp AD$
The new shape is a square.

b. $\sqrt{58} \times \sqrt{58} = 58$
The area is 58 square units.

13a. $d_{PQ} = \sqrt{(-1 - 4)^2 + (6 - 4)^2} = \sqrt{29}$
$d_{QR} = \sqrt{(4 - 2)^2 + (4 - (-1))^2} = \sqrt{29}$
$d_{PQ} = d_{QR}$
$m_{PQ} = \dfrac{4 - 6}{4 - (-1)} = -\dfrac{2}{5}$ $m_{QR} = \dfrac{-1 - 4}{2 - 4} = \dfrac{5}{2}$
$PQ \perp QR$; $\triangle PQR$ is a right isosceles triangle.

b. $\triangle AQB = AQ \times QB \div 2$ $(AQ = \dfrac{1}{2}PQ$ and $QB = \dfrac{1}{2}QR)$
$= \dfrac{1}{2}PQ \times \dfrac{1}{2}QR \div 2$
$= \dfrac{1}{4}(PQ \times QR \div 2)$ $(\triangle PQR = PQ \times QR \div 2)$
$= \dfrac{1}{4}\triangle PQR$

14. $m_{BC} = $ undefined $m_{AB} = 0$
$AB \perp BC$; $\triangle ABC$ is a right triangle.
$d_{AB} = 10$
Area: $120 = 10 \times d_{BC} \div 2$ $\sqrt{(5 - 5)^2 + (b - (-12))^2} = 24$
$d_{BC} = 24$ $b + 12 = 24$
                                    $b = 12$

Midpoint of AC: $(\dfrac{-5 + 5}{2}, \dfrac{-12 + 12}{2}) = (0,0)$
The centre is at (0,0).

15. • Statement 1:
Diagonal JL (l_1):   Diagonal KM (l_2):
$m_{JL} = \dfrac{0 - 4}{3 - 1} = -2$ $m_{KM} = \dfrac{4 - 0}{6 - (-2)} = \dfrac{1}{2}$
They are perpendicular.

Midpoint of JL: $(\dfrac{1 + 3}{2}, \dfrac{4 + 0}{2}) = (2,2)$

Midpoint of KM: $(\dfrac{-2 + 6}{2}, \dfrac{0 + 4}{2}) = (2,2)$ $J(1,4)$ $K(6,4)$ $M(-2,0)$ $L(3,0)$

The diagonals intersect at their midpoints and the diagonals are perpendicular to each other. So the diagonals are right bisectors of each other.

• Statement 2:
Midpoint M: $(\dfrac{-2 + 6}{2}, \dfrac{3 + (-1)}{2}) = (2,1)$ $C(4,5)$ $A(-2,3)$ N M $B(6,-1)$
Midpoint N: $(\dfrac{4 + 6}{2}, \dfrac{5 + (-1)}{2}) = (5,2)$
$m_{MN} = \dfrac{2 - 1}{5 - 2} = \dfrac{1}{3}$ $m_{AC} = \dfrac{5 - 3}{4 - (-2)} = \dfrac{1}{3}$
∴ $MN // AC$
$d_{MN} = \sqrt{(5 - 2)^2 + (2 - 1)^2} = \sqrt{10}$
$d_{AC} = \sqrt{(4 - (-2))^2 + (5 - 3)^2} = \sqrt{40} = 2\sqrt{10} = 2d_{MN}$
∴ The length of MN is half of AC.

• Statement 3:
Midpoint of AB: $(\dfrac{-3 + 1}{2}, \dfrac{1 + 5}{2}) = (-1,3)$

$m_{AB} = \dfrac{5 - 1}{1 - (-3)} = 1$ $m_\perp = -1$
Perpendicular bisector of AB: $y - 3 = -1(x - (-1))$
$y = -x + 2$
Midpoint of BC: $(\dfrac{2 + 1}{2}, \dfrac{4 + 5}{2}) = (\dfrac{3}{2}, \dfrac{9}{2})$

$m_{BC} = \dfrac{5 - 4}{1 - 2} = -1$ $m_\perp = 1$
Perpendicular bisector of BC: $y - \dfrac{9}{2} = 1(x - \dfrac{3}{2})$
$y = x + 3$

Point of intersection: $-x + 2 = x + 3$
$x = -\dfrac{1}{2}$
$y = -\dfrac{1}{2} + 3 = \dfrac{5}{2}$

Circumcentre: $D(-\dfrac{1}{2}, \dfrac{5}{2})$ $B(1,5)$ $C(2,4)$ $A(-3,1)$
$d_{AD} = \sqrt{(-3 - (-\dfrac{1}{2}))^2 + (1 - \dfrac{5}{2})^2} = \sqrt{\dfrac{17}{2}}$
$d_{BD} = \sqrt{(1 - (-\dfrac{1}{2}))^2 + (5 - \dfrac{5}{2})^2} = \sqrt{\dfrac{17}{2}}$
$d_{CD} = \sqrt{(2 - (-\dfrac{1}{2}))^2 + (4 - \dfrac{5}{2})^2} = \sqrt{\dfrac{17}{2}}$
∴ The distances from the vertices to the circumcentre are the same.

16. $m_{AC} = \dfrac{5 - (-1)}{3 - 1} = 3$ $m_{BD} = \dfrac{3 - 1}{7 - (-3)} = \dfrac{1}{5}$
$y - (-1) = 3(x - 1)$ $y - 1 = \dfrac{1}{5}(x - (-3))$
$y = 3x - 4$ $y = \dfrac{1}{5}x + \dfrac{8}{5}$
$3x - 4 = \dfrac{1}{5}x + \dfrac{8}{5}$ $A(3,5)$ $D(-3,1)$ $B(7,3)$ $C(1,-1)$
$x = 2$
$y = 3(2) - 4 = 2$
They should set it up at (2,2).

17a. $m_1 = \dfrac{3 - 1}{5 - (-1)} = \dfrac{1}{3}$ $m_2 = \dfrac{-4 - 5}{4 - 1} = -3$
m_1 and m_2 are negative reciprocals.
Yes, the rods bisect each other perpendicularly.

b. To have a proper "kite" shape, it must have two pairs of sides with equal lengths.

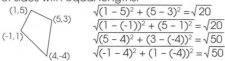

$\sqrt{(1-5)^2 + (5-3)^2} = \sqrt{20}$
$\sqrt{(1-(-1))^2 + (5-1)^2} = \sqrt{20}$
$\sqrt{(5-4)^2 + (3-(-4))^2} = \sqrt{50}$
$\sqrt{(-1-4)^2 + (1-(-4))^2} = \sqrt{50}$

Yes, it has a proper "kite" shape.

18.

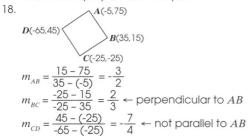

$m_{AB} = \dfrac{15-75}{35-(-5)} = -\dfrac{3}{2}$

$m_{BC} = \dfrac{-25-15}{-25-35} = \dfrac{2}{3}$ ← perpendicular to AB

$m_{CD} = \dfrac{45-(-25)}{-65-(-25)} = -\dfrac{7}{4}$ ← not parallel to AB

No, it is not in the shape of a square.

19. Let (a,b) be the coordinates of the forest.

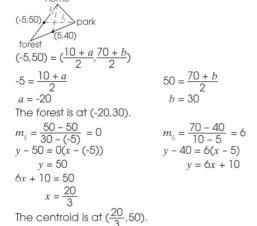

$(-5,50) = (\dfrac{10+a}{2}, \dfrac{70+b}{2})$

$-5 = \dfrac{10+a}{2}$ $50 = \dfrac{70+b}{2}$
$a = -20$ $b = 30$

The forest is at $(-20,30)$.

$m_{l_1} = \dfrac{50-50}{30-(-5)} = 0$ $m_{l_2} = \dfrac{70-40}{10-5} = 6$
$y - 50 = 0(x-(-5))$ $y - 40 = 6(x-5)$
$y = 50$ $y = 6x + 10$
$6x + 10 = 50$
$x = \dfrac{20}{3}$

The centroid is at $(\dfrac{20}{3}, 50)$.

4 Polynomials

4.1 Expanding and Factoring

Try This (p. 62)

$x^2 - 5x$; $x - 5$; $x^2 - 4x - 5$ $x^2 + 2x$; $-4x - 8$; $x^2 - 2x - 8$

1. $= x^2 + 4x + 3$
2. $= n^2 - 3n + 2$
3. $= k^2 + k - 6$
4. $= b^2 - 36$
5. $= a^2 - 5a - 14$
6. $= d^2 - 2d - 8$
7. $= 3x^2 + 2x - 1$
8. $= 2y^2 - 8$
9. $= 2t^2 + t - 3$
10. $= 3s^2 + 10s + 3$
11. $= 6h^2 - 11h - 2$
12. $= 4k^2 - 9k + 2$
13. $= x^2 + 2xy + y^2$
14. $= a^2 - 2ab + b^2$
15. $= 6y^2 - 4y - 2$
16. $= 10k^2 + 13k - 3$
17. $= 12j^2 + 5j - 2$
18. $= 3c^2 - 2cd - d^2$
19. $= 2x^2 - xy - 3y^2$
20. $= 6m^2 - 3mn - 3n^2$
21. $= 20x^2 + 20xy + 5y^2$

Try This (p. 63)

$= 2(x^2 - 3x + 4)$ $= 2x(4x^2 + x - 2)$

22. m ; $3n$
23. x^2y ; $= x^2y(2x + 1)$
24. xy ; $= xy(2x^2 + x + 3y)$
25. $3ab$; $= 3ab(a + 5 - 4b)$
26. $6x^2yz^2$; $= 6x^2yz^2(1 - 3xyz)$
27. $6c$; $= 6c(3ab - 2ac + 9b)$
28. 2 ; $= 2(2xy + 3yz + 4xz)$
29. $13mn$; $= 13mn(m^2n - 3mn + 7)$
30. x ; 3
31. $a(b-6) + 2(b-6)$
    $= (b-6)(a+2)$
32. $-2a(a-1) + (a-1)$
    $= (a-1)(-2a+1)$
33. $3m(n+1) - (n+1)$
    $= (n+1)(3m-1)$

34. $(x-1)^2 + 4(x-1)$
    $= (x-1)((x-1)+4)$
    $= (x-1)(x+3)$

35. $6p^2q + (5-x)p^2q$
    $= p^2q(6+(5-x))$
    $= p^2q(11-x)$

36. $x^2(x+y) - 2(x+y)^2$
    $= (x+y)(x^2 - 2(x+y))$
    $= (x+y)(x^2 - 2x - 2y)$

37. $mn(m-n)^2 - 2(m-n)$
    $= (m-n)(mn(m-n) - 2)$
    $= (m-n)(m^2n - mn^2 - 2)$

38. x ; y ; x ; y ; x ; y

39. $y(3-x) + z(3-x)$
    $= (y+z)(3-x)$

40. $= a(y+z) + b(y+z)$
    $= (a+b)(y+z)$

41. $= 6(x-2y) + x(x-2y)$
    $= (6+x)(x-2y)$

42. $= -2a(a+b) - 4(a+b)$
    $= (-2a-4)(a+b)$
    $= -2(a+2)(a+b)$

43. $= x^2y^2(x-y) + x(x-y)$
    $= (x^2y^2 + x)(x-y)$
    $= x(xy^2 + 1)(x-y)$

44. $= -3mn(n-2m) + (n-2m)$
    $= (-3mn+1)(n-2m)$

45. $= -2(2p-1) - pq^2(2p-1)$
    $= (-2 - pq^2)(2p-1)$
    $= -(2 + pq^2)(2p-1)$

46. $= i^2(i+j) - j^2(j+i)$
    $= (i^2 - j^2)(i+j)$

47. $(a+b)^3$
    $= (a+b)(a+b)(a+b)$
    $= (a^2 + 2ab + b^2)(a+b)$
    $= a^3 + 3a^2b + 3ab^2 + b^3$
    $\neq a^3 + b^3$
    They are not the same.

48. $(x+y)^2$
    $= x^2 + 2xy + y^2$
    They are the same.

49. $\dfrac{4x^3y^2 + xy^2}{xy^2}$
    $= \dfrac{xy^2(4x^2 + 1)}{xy^2}$
    $= 4x^2 + 1$
    $\neq 4x + 1$
    They are not the same.

50. $\dfrac{c^2d^2 + cd^3 + cd^2}{c+d+1}$
    $= \dfrac{cd^2(c+d+1)}{c+d+1}$
    $= cd^2$
    They are the same.

51a. $\dfrac{x^3 + x^2y + xy + y^2}{x^2 + y} = \dfrac{x^2(x+y) + y(x+y)}{x^2+y} = \dfrac{(x^2+y)(x+y)}{x^2+y}$
    $= x + y$
    The width is $(x+y)$.

  b. $x^3 + x^2y + xy + y^2 - x^3 = x^2y + xy + y^2 = y(x^2 + x + y)$
    The area will be $y(x^2 + x + y)$.

52. $a^3 - a^2b + ab - b^2 = a^2(a-b) + b(a-b) = (a^2 + b)(a-b)$

Area $= \dfrac{b \times h}{2}$

$(a^2 + b)(a-b) = \dfrac{b \times h}{2}$

$bh = 2(a^2 + b)(a-b)$

The possible base and height are $2(a^2 + b)$ and $a - b$.

4.2 Factorization of Trinomials (1)

Try This (p. 66)

$= (x+1)(x+3)$ $= (x-5)(x+1)$

1. -3 ; -2 ; -3 ; -2
   $= (x-3)(x-2)$
2. 2 ; 4 ; 2 ; 4
   $= (x+2)(x+4)$
3. 2 ; 3 ; 2 ; 3
   $= (x+2)(x+3)$
4. 1 ; 4 ; 1 ; 4
   $= (x+1)(x+4)$
5. 1 ; -2 ; 1 ; -2
   $= (x+1)(x-2)$
6. -1 ; 2 ; -1 ; 2
   $= (x-1)(x+2)$
7. -3 ; 5 ; -3 ; 5
   $= (x-3)(x+5)$
8. 1 ; 2 ; 1 ; 2
   $= (x+1)(x+2)$
9. -4 ; 3 ; -4 ; 3
   $= (x-4)(x+3)$
10. -4 ; 2 ; -4 ; 2
    $= (x-4)(x+2)$
11. $= (x-1)(x+4)$
12. $= (x+3)(x+4)$
13. $= (x-1)(x-8)$
14. $= (x+5)(x-2)$
15. $= (x+4)(x-5)$
16. $= (x+3)(x+6)$
17. $= (x+1)^2$
18. $= (x+2)^2$
19. $= (x+8)(x+1)$
20. $= (x-4)(x-5)$
21. $= (x+4)(x+6)$
22. $= (x+5)^2$
23. $= (x+7)^2$
24. $= (x+10)^2$

25. $= (x - 4)(x + 8)$

26. $= (x - 9)(x + 4)$

27. $2 ; 1$

28. $= (x + 2y)(x - y)$

29. $= (x - 2y)(x + y)$

30. $= (x - 2y)(x - y)$

31. $= (x - 3y)(x + y)$

32. $= (x + 3y)(x + y)$

33. $= (x - 3y)(x + 2y)$

34. $= (x - 3y)^2$

35. $= \dfrac{(x - 12)(x - 2)}{x - 2}$
    $= x - 12$

36. $= \dfrac{(x - 8)(x - 3)}{x - 8}$
    $= x - 3$

37. $= \dfrac{(x + 5)(x - 4)}{(x + 5)(x + 1)}$
    $= \dfrac{x - 4}{x + 1}$

38. $= \dfrac{(x - 12)(x + 4)}{2(x + 4)}$
    $= \dfrac{x - 12}{2}$

39. $= \dfrac{(x + 25)(x - 4)}{(x + 25)^2}$
    $= \dfrac{x - 4}{x + 25}$

40. $= \dfrac{(x - 6)(x - 1)}{(x - 1)^3}$
    $= \dfrac{x - 6}{(x - 1)^2}$

41. Think: two integers a and b
    $a + b = -2$
    $a \times b = 13 \leftarrow 1 \times 13$ or -1×-13
    If $a = 1$ and $b = 13$, $1 + 13 = 14 \neq -2$
    If $a = -1$ and $b = -13$, $-1 + (-13) = -14 \neq -2$
    $\therefore$ Anna is correct.

42. It was not done correctly.
    $-x^2 - 2x - 24 = -(x^2 + 2x + 24)$
    It cannot be factored further.

43. Linda's solution is correct.
    $x^2 + 6 + 5x$ Think: two integers a and b
    $= x^2 + 5x + 6$ $a + b = 5 \leftarrow 2 + 3 = 5$
    $= (x + 2)(x + 3)$ $a \times b = 6 \leftarrow 2 \times 3 = 6$
    The integers are 2 and 3.

44. $l \times w = x^2 + 4x - 21 = (x + 7)(x - 3)$
    Its possible dimensions are $(x + 7)$ and $(x - 3)$.

45. $(a + b) \times h \div 2 = x^2 + 2xy + y^2$
    $\quad (a + b) \times h = 2(x + y)(x + y)$
    Its possible height is $2(x + y)$.

46a. $x^2 + xy - 2y^2 = (x - y)(x + 2y)$
    If the number of eggs in the cartons is $x + 2y$, the number of cartons is $x - y$, or vice versa.

  b. No, it is because $x - y$ must be a number that is greater than 0. If x is less than y, then $x - y$ yields a negative number.

  c. If $y = 0$, the number of eggs in each carton is x and the number of cartons is x.

4.3 Factorization of Trinomials (2)

Try This (p. 70)

$2 ; 1$
$= 2x(x + 1) + (x + 1)$
$= (x + 1)(2x + 1)$

$-2 ; 3$
$= 2x(x - 1) + 3(x - 1)$
$= (x - 1)(2x + 3)$

1. $= 3x^2 + 3x + 2x + 2$
    $= 3x(x + 1) + 2(x + 1)$
    $= (x + 1)(3x + 2)$

2. $= 2x^2 - 6x - 3x + 9$
    $= 2x(x - 3) - 3(x - 3)$
    $= (x - 3)(2x - 3)$

3. $= 5x^2 + 10x + x + 2$
    $= 5x(x + 2) + (x + 2)$
    $= (x + 2)(5x + 1)$

4. $= 4x^2 - 2x - 2x + 1$
    $= 2x(2x - 1) - (2x - 1)$
    $= (2x - 1)^2$

5. $= 7x^2 - 28x + 2x - 8$
    $= 7x(x - 4) + 2(x - 4)$
    $= (x - 4)(7x + 2)$

6. $= 2x^2 - 12x + 19x - 114$
    $= 2x(x - 6) + 19(x - 6)$
    $= (x - 6)(2x + 19)$

7. $= 3x^2 + 6x - 2x - 4$
    $= 3x(x + 2) - 2(x + 2)$
    $= (x + 2)(3x - 2)$

8. $= 2x^2 - 4x + 5x - 10$
    $= 2x(x - 2) + 5(x - 2)$
    $= (x - 2)(2x + 5)$

9. $= 4x^2 + 8x - x - 2$
    $= 4x(x + 2) - (x + 2)$
    $= (x + 2)(4x - 1)$

10. $= 4x^2 - 6x + 2x - 3$
    $= 2x(2x - 3) + (2x - 3)$
    $= (2x - 3)(2x + 1)$

11. $= 6x^2 - 2x - 3x + 1$
    $= 2x(3x - 1) - (3x - 1)$
    $= (3x - 1)(2x - 1)$

12. $= 8x^2 + 12x - 2x - 3$
    $= 4x(2x + 3) - (2x + 3)$
    $= (2x + 3)(4x - 1)$

13. $= 9x^2 - 15x + 12x - 20$
    $= 3x(3x - 5) + 4(3x - 5)$
    $= (3x - 5)(3x + 4)$

14. $= 4x^2 + 10x - 6x - 15$
    $= 2x(2x + 5) - 3(2x + 5)$
    $= (2x + 5)(2x - 3)$

15. $= 8x^2 + 6x + 4x + 3$
    $= 2x(4x + 3) + (4x + 3)$
    $= (4x + 3)(2x + 1)$

16. $= 6x^2 - 9x + 4x - 6$
    $= 3x(2x - 3) + 2(2x - 3)$
    $= (2x - 3)(3x + 2)$

17. $= 2x^2 + 38x - x - 19$
    $= 2x(x + 19) - (x + 19)$
    $= (x + 19)(2x - 1)$

18. $= 6x^2 - 9x - 8x + 12$
    $= 3x(2x - 3) - 4(2x - 3)$
    $= (2x - 3)(3x - 4)$

19. The second step should be $6x^2 - 10x + 3x - 5$.
    $\quad 6x^2 - 7x - 5$
    $= 6x^2 - 10x + 3x - 5$
    $= 2x(3x - 5) + (3x - 5)$
    $= (3x - 5)(2x + 1)$

20. 1st way: 2nd way:
    $(4x^2 - 6x) + (2x - 3)$ $(4x^2 + 2x) - (6x + 3)$
    $= 2x(2x - 3) + (2x - 3)$ $= 2x(2x + 1) - 3(2x + 1)$
    $= (2x - 3)(2x + 1)$ $= (2x + 1)(2x - 3)$
    Both ways are correct.

21. $\quad 12x^2 - x - 1$
    $= 12x^2 - 4x + 3x - 1$
    $= 4x(3x - 1) + (3x - 1)$
    $= (3x - 1)(4x + 1)$
    The integers are $3x - 1$ and $4x + 1$.

22. $\quad 10x^2 - 27x + 5$
    $= 10x^2 - 2x - 25x + 5$
    $= 2x(5x - 1) - 5(5x - 1)$
    $= (5x - 1)(2x - 5)$
    Its possible base and height are $5x - 1$ and $2x - 5$.

23. $\quad 9x^2 - 9x + 2$
    $= 9x^2 - 3x - 6x + 2$
    $= 3x(3x - 1) - 2(3x - 1)$
    $= (3x - 1)(3x - 2)$
    The possible side lengths are $3x - 1$ and $3x - 2$.
    No, they cannot be the side lengths of a square because the side lengths of a square must be equal.

24. $\quad 6x^2 - 13x + 6$
    $= 6x^2 - 9x - 4x + 6$
    $= 3x(2x - 3) - 2(2x - 3)$
    $= (2x - 3)(3x - 2)$
    Joseph did not fully factor the polynomial. The polynomial can be fully factored as $(x + 1)(2x - 3)(3x - 2)$.

25. $\quad (2x - 1)(2x + 1)$
    $= 4x^2 - 2x + 2x - 1$
    $= 4x^2 - 1$
    So, $2x - 1$ and $2x + 1$ are the factors of $4x^2 - 1$. Katy is correct.

4.4 Perfect-square Trinomials and Differences of Squares

Try This (p. 73)

$x^2 ; 4 ; x ; 2 ; = (x + 2)^2$

1. $x ; -1$
    $= (x - 1)^2$

2. $x ; -4$
    $= (x - 4)^2$

3. $x ; -3$
    $= (x - 3)^2$

4. $x ; 5$
    $= (x + 5)^2$

5. $x ; 7$
    $= (x + 7)^2$

6. $x ; -6$
    $= (x - 6)^2$

7. $x ; -8$
    $= (x - 8)^2$

8. $x ; 6$
    $= (x + 6)^2$

9. $x ; 9$
    $= (x + 9)^2$

10. $x ; -12$
    $= (x - 12)^2$

11. $x ; y$
    $= (x + y)^2$

12. $x ; -2y$
    $= (x - 2y)^2$

13. $4x$; 3
    $= (4x + 3)^2$

14. $3x$; -1
    $= (3x - 1)^2$

15. $2x$; -5
    $= (2x - 5)^2$

16. $3x$; 2
    $= (3x + 2)^2$

17. $2x$; -3
    $= (2x - 3)^2$

18. $4x$; -y
    $= (4x - y)^2$

19-30. Perfect-square trinomials: 20, 22, 23, 24, 26, 27, 28, 30

20. $= (x - 7)^2$

22. $= (x + 1)^2$

23. $= (x + 8)^2$

24. $= (4x + 1)^2$

26. $= (5x - 1)^2$

27. $= (x - 1)^2$

28. $= (3x - 5)^2$

30. $= (4x + 3)^2$

31. A ; The signs of the perfect squares, a^2 and b^2, are both positive.

e.g. $(2x - 3)^2 = 4x^2 - 12x + 9$

    positive   positive

32. A

e.g. $(a + b)^2 = a^2 + 2ab + b^2$

Let $a = b = 2x$.

LS: $(2x + 2x)^2 = (4x)^2 = 16x^2$

RS: $(2x)^2 + 2(2x)(2x) + (2x)^2 = 4x^2 + 8x^2 + 4x^2 = 16x^2$

33. x ; 2 ; $= (x + 2)(x - 2)$ 34. x ; 6 ; $= (x + 6)(x - 6)$

35. x ; 1 ; $= (x + 1)(x - 1)$ 36. $2x$; 1 ; $= (2x + 1)(2x - 1)$

37. $3x$; 2 ; $= (3x + 2)(3x - 2)$ 38. $5x$; 1 ; $= (5x + 1)(5x - 1)$

39. $4x$; 3 ; $= (4x + 3)(4x - 3)$ 40. x^2 ; y ; $= (x^2 + y)(x^2 - y)$

41. $2x^2$; $3y$; $= (2x^2 + 3y)(2x^2 - 3y)$

42-53. Differences of squares: 43, 44, 46, 47, 50, 51, 53

43. $= (x + 4)(x - 4)$ 44. $= (2x + 4y)(2x - 4y)$

46. $= (4x + 1)(4x - 1)$ 47. $= (3x + y^2)(3x - y^2)$

50. $= (xy + 1)(xy - 1)$ 51. $= (5x^2 + 3y)(5x^2 - 3y)$

53. $= (x + 2y^2)(x - 2y^2)$

54. No, the difference can be negative.

e.g. $4^2 - 9^2 = (4 + 9)(4 - 9) = 13(-5) = -65$

$4^2 - 9^2$ gives a negative number.

55. $x^2 + kx + 6$

$a^2 = x^2$ $b^2 = 6$

$a = \pm x$ $b = \pm \sqrt{6}$

$2x(\sqrt{6}) = kx$ or $2x(-\sqrt{6}) = kx$

$k = 2\sqrt{6}$ $k = -2\sqrt{6}$

k will be $2\sqrt{6}$ or $-2\sqrt{6}$.

56. $152^2 - 148^2 = (152 + 148)(152 - 148) = 300(4) = 1200$

57. The two consecutive odd numbers are y and $y + 2$.

∴ $y(y + 2) + 1 = y^2 + 2y + 1 = (y + 1)^2$

$(y + 1)^2$ is a perfect square. Sally is correct.

58. $x^2 - 5^2 = (x + 5)(x - 5)$

Its area is $(x + 5)(x - 5)$.

59. $a^2 - b^2 = (a + b)(a - b)$

Its area is $(a + b)(a - b)$.

4.5 Factorization Strategy

Try This (p. 77)

x ; x ; $x + 3$; $x - 2$

1. $= y(y - 6)$

2. $= 2x(x^2 - 9)$
   $= 2x(x + 3)(x - 3)$

3. $= 3c(4ac - 25)$

4. $= (4a^2 + 9)(4a^2 - 9)$
   $= (4a^2 + 9)(2a + 3)(2a - 3)$

5. $= 4x(x - 3)$

6. $= (x^2 + y^2)(x^2 - y^2)$
   $= (x^2 + y^2)(x + y)(x - y)$

7. $= 3(2z^2 + z - 10)$
   $= 3(z - 2)(2z + 5)$

8. $= 2(b^2 - 6b + 9)$
   $= 2(b - 3)^2$

9. $= 3x(2x^2 - 3x - 2)$
   $= 3x(2x + 1)(x - 2)$

10. $= d(3d^2 - 5d - 2)$
    $= d(3d + 1)(d - 2)$

11. $= 2x(x^2 + 2x - 3)$
    $= 2x(x + 3)(x - 1)$

12. $= q(q^2 - 12q + 36)$
    $= q(q - 6)^2$

13. $= a^2(a - 4) + 2(a - 4)$
    $= (a^2 + 2)(a - 4)$

14. $= (x + y)(x - y) + 7(x + y)$
    $= (x - y + 7)(x + y)$

15. $= 2p(p + q) - 2(p + q)$
    $= (2p - 2)(p + q)$
    $= 2(p - 1)(p + q)$

16. $= i^2(i - 3) + 9(i - 3)$
    $= (i^2 + 9)(i - 3)$

17. $= x(x^2 - 7) + 2(x^2 - 7)$
    $= (x + 2)(x^2 - 7)$

18. $= y(x - 7) + 3(x - 7)$
    $= (y + 3)(x - 7)$

19. $= c^2 - d^2 + 2c - 2d$
    $= (c + d)(c - d) + 2(c - d)$
    $= (c + d + 2)(c - d)$

20. $= 2q + 6pq + 5 + 15p$
    $= 2q(1 + 3p) + 5(1 + 3p)$
    $= (2q + 5)(1 + 3p)$

21. $= 6xy + 4y - 15x - 10$
    $= 2y(3x + 2) - 5(3x + 2)$
    $= (2y - 5)(3x + 2)$

22. $= (x - y)^2 - (x - y)$
    $= (x - y - 1)(x - y)$

23. $= (3a + 1)^2 - 6b(1 + 3a)$
    $= (3a - 6b + 1)(3a + 1)$

24. $= x^2 + 4x + 4 - 3xy - 6y$
    $= (x + 2)^2 - 3y(x + 2)$
    $= (x - 3y + 2)(x + 2)$

25. $= (x^2 + y^2)(x^2 - y^2)$
    $= (x^2 + y^2)(x + y)(x - y)$

26. $= (8a^2)^2 - 1^2$
    $= (8a^2 - 1)(8a^2 + 1)$

27. $= (\frac{x^2}{3^2})^2 - (\frac{2^2}{5^2})^2$
    $= (\frac{x^2}{3^2} + \frac{2^2}{5^2})(\frac{x^2}{3^2} - \frac{2^2}{5^2})$
    $= (\frac{x^2}{9} + \frac{4}{25})(\frac{x}{3} + \frac{2}{5})(\frac{x}{3} - \frac{2}{5})$

28. $= 2mn(m^2 + 2mn + n^2 - p^2)$
    $= 2mn((m + n)^2 - p^2)$
    $= 2mn(m + n + p)(m + n - p)$

29. $(a^2 + b^2)$ does not equal $(a + b)(a - b)$ and cannot be factored.

So, $(a^2 + b^2)(a - 2b)$ is the answer.

30. $(6x^2 + 5x + 6)$ does not equal $(2x + 3)(3x + 2)$ and cannot be factored.

So, $-2(6x^2 + 5x + 6)$ is the answer.

31. $x^2 + 4\frac{1}{2}x + 4\frac{1}{2} = (2x + 3) \times 1 + \frac{1}{2}(2x + 3)(h - 1)$

$2x^2 + 9x + 9 = 2(2x + 3) + (2x + 3)(h - 1)$

$(2x + 3)(x + 3) = (2 + h - 1)(2x + 3)$

$x + 3 = h + 1$

$h = x + 2$

The height is $x + 2$.

32a. Let y be the side length of the square.

$y^2 = 121a^2 + 44a + 4$

$y^2 = (11a + 2)^2$

$y = 11a + 2$

Perimeter: $4(11a + 2)$

Its perimeter is $4(11a + 2)$.

b. $11a + 2 > 0$

$a > -\frac{2}{11}$

The possible value of a is greater than $-\frac{2}{11}$.

5 Graphs of Quadratic Relations

5.1 Properties of Quadratic Relations

Try This (p. 80)

A ; C ; E

1.

x	y
-2	4
-1	1
0	0
1	1
2	4

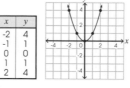

2.

x	y
-2	-4
-1	2
0	4
1	2
2	-4

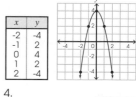

3.

x	y
-2	0
-1	-3
0	-4
1	-3
2	0

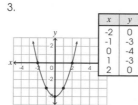

4.

x	y
-2	-4
-1	0
0	2
1	2
2	0

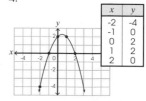

5.

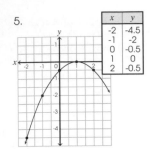

x	y
-2	-4.5
-1	-2
0	-0.5
1	0
2	-0.5

6.

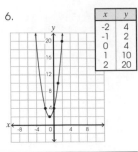

x	y
-2	4
-1	2
0	4
1	10
2	20

(-2, 0)(2, 0)	(-1,0) (2,0)	(1,0)	none
(0, -4)	(0,2)	(0,-0.5)	(0,4)
opens upward	opens downward	opens downward	opens upward
x = 0	x = 0.5	x = 1	x = -1
(0, -4)	(0.5,2.25)	(1,0)	(-1,2)
y = -4	y = 2.25	y = 0	y = 2

7. A:

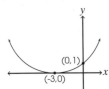

B: (Suggested answer)

(0,1)
(-3,0)
(1.5,0)
(0,-6)

C: (Suggested answer)

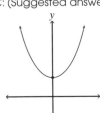

D:

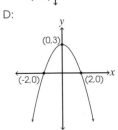

(0,3)
(-2,0) (2,0)

8a. opens upward
9a. opens upward
10a. opens downward
b. 7
b. a minimum value
b. (0,-2)
11. F   12. T   13. T   14. T
15a. T   b. T   c. T
16a. B
b. $y = 0.1x^2 - 2x$
$y = 0.1x(x - 20)$
x-intercepts: (0,0) and (20,0)
vertex: (10,-10)
The maximum water depth was -10 m.
17a. C
b. $y = -0.6x^2 + 2.7x + 1.5$
$y = -0.3(2x^2 - 9x - 5)$
$y = -0.3(2x + 1)(x - 5)$
x-intercepts: (-0.5,0) and (5,0)
Karen was 5 m away from the plants.

5.2 Finding Zeros

Try This (p. 84)

$y = (x + 2)(x - 1)$

$x + 2 = 0$ or $x - 1 = 0$
$x = -2$ $x = 1$
The zeros occur at (-2,0) and (1,0).

(-2,0) (1,0)

1. A: $(x - 1)(x + 3) = 0$
$x - 1 = 0$ or $x + 3 = 0$
$x = 1$ $x = -3$
(1,0)   (-3,0)

B: $(x + 4)(x - 4) = 0$
$x + 4 = 0$ or $x - 4 = 0$
$x = -4$ $x = 4$
(-4,0)   (4,0)

C: $(x + 2)(3 - x) = 0$
$x + 2 = 0$ or $3 - x = 0$
$x = -2$ $x = 3$
(-2,0)   (3,0)

D: $(4 - x)(x + 1) = 0$
$4 - x = 0$ or $x + 1 = 0$
$x = 4$ $x = -1$
(4,0)   (-1,0)

E: $(x - 2)^2 = 0$
$x - 2 = 0$
$x = 2$
(2,0)

F: $(x + 3)^2 = 0$
$x + 3 = 0$
$x = -3$
(-3,0)

B ; D
E ; A
F ; C

2. • y-intercept: -2 ; 2 ; -4 ; -4
• zeros: 2 ; 2 ; -2 ; -2
• axis of symmetry: 2 ; (-2) ; 0
• vertex: 0 ; 0 ; -2 ; 2 ; -4 ; (0,-4)

3. • y-intercept:
$y = (0 + 1)(2 - 0)$
$y = (1)(2)$
$y = 2$
(0,2)
• axis of symmetry:
$x = \dfrac{-1 + 2}{2}$
$x = \dfrac{1}{2}$

• zeros:
$x + 1 = 0$ or $2 - x = 0$
$x = -1$ $x = 2$
(-1,0)   (2,0)
• vertex:
$y = (\dfrac{1}{2} + 1)(2 - \dfrac{1}{2})$
$y = (\dfrac{3}{2})(\dfrac{3}{2})$
$y = \dfrac{9}{4}$
$(\dfrac{1}{2}, \dfrac{9}{4})$

4. • y-intercept:
$y = (0 - 1)^2$
$y = (-1)^2$
$y = 1$
(0,1)
• axis of symmetry:
$x = \dfrac{1 + 1}{2}$
$x = 1$

• zeros:
$x - 1 = 0$
$x = 1$
(1,0)
• vertex:
$y = (1 - 1)^2$
$y = 0$
(1,0)

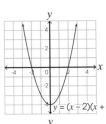
$y = (x - 2)(x + 2)$

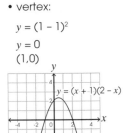
$y = (x + 1)(2 - x)$

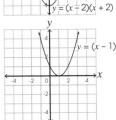
$y = (x - 1)^2$

5. • y-intercept:
$y = 2(0)^2 - 2(0) = 0$
(0,0)
• zeros:
$y = 2x(x - 1)$
$0 = 2x(x - 1)$
$x = 0$ or $x - 1 = 0$
(0,0) $x = 1$
                (1,0)
• axis of symmetry:
$x = \dfrac{0 + 1}{2} = \dfrac{1}{2}$
$x = \dfrac{1}{2}$

• vertex:
$y = 2(\dfrac{1}{2})^2 - 2(\dfrac{1}{2})$
$y = -\dfrac{1}{2}$
$(\dfrac{1}{2}, -\dfrac{1}{2})$

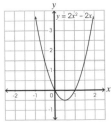
$y = 2x^2 - 2x$

ISBN: 978-1-77149-221-8

6. • y-intercept:
$y = -(0)^2 + 3(0) - 2 = -2$
(0,-2)
• zeros:
$y = -(x - 1)(x - 2)$
$0 = -(x - 1)(x - 2)$
$x - 1 = 0$ or $x - 2 = 0$
$x = 1$ $x = 2$
(1,0)   (2,0)
• axis of symmetry:
$x = \frac{1 + 2}{2} = \frac{3}{2}$
$x = \frac{3}{2}$

• vertex:
$y = -(\frac{3}{2})^2 + 3(\frac{3}{2}) - 2$
$y = \frac{1}{4}$
$(\frac{3}{2}, \frac{1}{4})$

7. • y-intercept:
$y = -3(0)^2 + 6(0) + 9 = 9$
(0,9)
• zeros:
$y = -3(x^2 - 2x - 3)$
$y = -3(x - 3)(x + 1)$
$0 = -3(x - 3)(x + 1)$
$x - 3 = 0$ or $x + 1 = 0$
$x = 3$ $x = -1$
(3,0)   (-1,0)
• axis of symmetry:
$x = \frac{3 + (-1)}{2} = 1$
$x = 1$

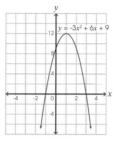

• vertex:
$y = -3(1)^2 + 6(1) + 9$
$y = 12$
(1,12)

Try This (p. 87)
$y = a(x - (-2))(x - 2)$
$y = a(x + 2)(x - 2)$
$8 = a(0 + 2)(0 - 2)$
$a = -2$
$y = -2(x + 2)(x - 2)$

8. $y = a(x - (-1))(x - 1)$
$y = a(x + 1)(x - 1)$
$-3 = a(0 + 1)(0 - 1)$
$a = 3$
$y = 3(x + 1)(x - 1)$

9. $y = a(x - (-4))(x - 2)$
$y = a(x + 4)(x - 2)$
$8 = a(0 + 4)(0 - 2)$
$a = -1$
$y = -(x + 4)(x - 2)$

10. $y = a(x - 2)(x - (-2))$
$y = a(x - 2)(x + 2)$
$-8 = a(0 - 2)(0 + 2)$
$a = 2$
$y = 2(x - 2)(x + 2)$

11. $y = a(x - 3)^2$
$-9 = a(0 - 3)^2$
$a = -1$
$y = -(x - 3)^2$

12-13. (Suggested answers)

12.

x	y
0	-2
0.5	-1
-3	4
2	4
-1	-2
1.5	1.5
-2	0

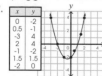

zeros: (-2,0) and (1,0)
y-intercept: (0,-2)
$y = (x + 2)(x - 1)$

13.

x	y
2	0
6	3.5
-1	-0.5
4	1
0	-0.5
-6	2.5
-4	1

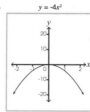

zeros: (2,0) and (-2.5,0)
y-intercept: (0,-0.5)
$y = 0.1(x - 2)(x + 2.5)$

14. $0 = -\frac{3}{4}(t - 2)(t + 1)$
$t - 2 = 0$ or $t + 1 = 0$
$t = 2$ $t = -1$ (not applicable)
The ball hits the ground at 2 s.

15. vertex: (0,3)
x-intercepts: (3,0) and (-3,0)
$y = a(x - 3)(x - (-3))$
$3 = a(0 - 3)(0 + 3)$
$a = -\frac{1}{3}$
The equation is $y = -\frac{1}{3}(x - 3)(x + 3)$.

16a. (Suggested answers)

Costs and Profits of Sweaters

b. vertex: (40,32)
x-intercepts: (0,0) and (80,0)
$y = a(x - 0)(x - 80)$
$32 = a(40 - 0)(40 - 80)$
$a = -0.02$
∴ $y = -0.02x(x - 80)$

c. $y = -0.02x(x - 80)$
$0 = -0.02x(x - 80)$
• zeros: $x = 0$ or $x - 80 = 0$
$x = 80$
• maximum value: $x = \frac{0 + 80}{2} = 40$
Mr. Jones would make no profit at the cost of $0 or $80.
He would make the maximum profit at the cost of $40.

5.3 Transformations of Quadratic Relations (1)

1. $y = x^2$

x	y
-2	4
-1	1
0	0
1	1
2	4

$y = 2x^2$

x	y
-2	8
-1	2
0	0
1	2
2	8

2. $y = x^2$

x	y
-2	4
-1	1
0	0
1	1
2	4

$y = \frac{1}{2}x^2$

x	y
-2	2
-1	$\frac{1}{2}$
0	0
1	$\frac{1}{2}$
2	2

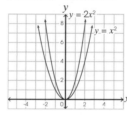

It is a vertical stretch.

It is a vertical compression.

3.
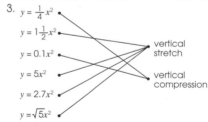

$y = \frac{1}{4}x^2$
$y = 1\frac{1}{2}x^2$
$y = 0.1x^2$
$y = 5x^2$
$y = 2.7x^2$
$y = \sqrt{5}x^2$

vertical stretch

vertical compression

4a. $4x^2$; $0.4x^2$; $1.5x^2$
b. Arrange the values of a from smallest to largest and match the most compressed graph with the relation that has the smallest value of a.

5a.

$y = -4x^2$ $y = -0.4x^2$ $y = -1.5x^2$

b. The graphs of $y = ax^2$ open upward and the graphs of $y = -ax^2$ open downward. They are reflections of one another in the x-axis.

ISBN: 978-1-77149-221-8

6a.

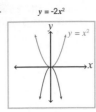

$y = -2x^2$ $y = -\frac{1}{2}x^2$

$y = -\frac{3}{2}x^2$ $y = -4x^2$

b. $y = -2x^2$:
vertically stretched by a factor of 2 and reflected in the x-axis

$y = -\frac{1}{2}x^2$:
vertically compressed by a factor of $\frac{1}{2}$ and reflected in the x-axis

$y = -\frac{3}{2}x^2$:
vertically stretched by a factor of $\frac{3}{2}$ and reflected in the x-axis

$y = -4x^2$:
vertically stretched by a factor of 4 and reflected in the x-axis

7. $y = -5x^2$ 8. $y = \frac{1}{4}x^2$

9. $y = \frac{2}{3}x^2$ 10. $y = -8\frac{3}{4}x^2$

5.4 Transformations of Quadratic Relations (2)

1.

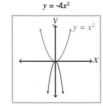

$y = x^2 + 2$		$y = x^2 - 2$	
x	y	x	y
-2	6	-2	2
-1	3	-1	-1
0	2	0	-2
1	3	1	-1
2	6	2	2

a. translate k units up   b. translate k units down
2. B ; A   3. B ; A
4. B ; A ; C
5.

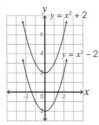

$y = (x - 1)^2$		$y = (x + 1)^2$	
x	y	x	y
-1	4	-3	4
0	1	-2	1
1	0	-1	0
2	1	0	1
3	4	1	4

a. translate h units to the right
b. translate h units to the left
6. D ; translated 3 units to the right
C ; translated 1.5 units to the right
A ; translated 4 units to the left
B ; translated 2 units to the left
7. The vertices are (-4,0), (-2,0), (1.5,0), and (3,0). The vertex of $y = (x - h)^2$ is $(h,0)$.

8.

$y = x^2$ $y = x^2 + 1$ $y = (x - 2)^2 + 1$

It is a translation of 1 unit up and 2 units to the right.

9.

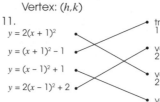

	upward or downward	stretched or compressed	vertex
$y = 2(x - 1)^2 + 2$	upward	stretched	(1,2)
$y = -\frac{1}{2}(x - 2)^2 + 1$	downward	compressed	(2,1)
$y = -2(x + 1)^2 - 1$	downward	stretched	(-1,-1)
$y = (x - 2)^2 + 1$	upward	none	(2,1)

$y = -\frac{1}{2}(x - 2)^2 + 1$;
$y = 2(x - 1)^2 + 2$;
$y = -2(x + 1)^2 - 1$;
$y = (x - 2)^2 + 1$

10. Parameter a:
upward ; downward ; stretched ; compressed
Parameter h: right ; left
Parameter k: up ; down
Vertex: (h,k)

11.

$y = 2(x + 1)^2$ → translated 1 unit to the left and 1 unit down
$y = (x + 1)^2 - 1$ → vertically stretched by a factor of 2 and translated 2 units up
$y = (x - 1)^2 + 1$ → vertically stretched by a factor of 2 and translated 1 unit to the left
$y = 2(x - 1)^2 + 2$ → vertex at (1,1)

12.

$y = -3(x - 1)^2 + 2$ → vertically compressed by a factor of $\frac{1}{2}$ and reflected in the x-axis
$y = -\frac{1}{2}(x - 1)^2 + 1$ → vertically stretched by a factor of 3 and translated 1 unit to the left
$y = 3(x + 1)^2 + 2$ → vertically compressed by a factor of $\frac{1}{2}$ and translated 1 unit to the left
$y = \frac{1}{2}(x + 1)^2$ → vertex at (1,2)

13. $y = (x - 2)^2 + 1$ $y = (x + 3)^2 - 4$ $y = (x - 1)^2 - 2$

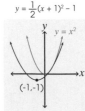

$y = 2(x + 1)^2 - 3$ $y = \frac{1}{3}(x - 3)^2$ $y = \frac{1}{2}(x + 1)^2 - 1$

14. $y = 2(x + 8)^2 + 1$ 15. $y = -\frac{1}{3}(x + 4)^2 + 2$
16. $y = -5(x - 2)^2 - 5$ 17. $y = -\frac{1}{4}x^2 + 3$
18. $y = -0.5x^2$ 19. $y = (x + 4)^2$

5.5 Modelling Quadratic Relations

Try This (p. 98)

$$y = a(x - (-2))^2 + (-1)$$
$$y = a(x + 2)^2 - 1$$
$$3 = a(2 + 2)^2 - 1$$
$$a = \frac{1}{4}$$
$$y = \frac{1}{4}(x + 2)^2 - 1$$

$$y = a(x - 2)^2 + (-1)$$
$$4 = a(-1 - 2)^2 - 1$$
$$a = \frac{5}{9}$$
$$y = \frac{5}{9}(x - 2)^2 - 1$$

1. A: vertex: (-3,2)
$$y = a(x - (-3))^2 + 2$$
$$y = a(x + 3)^2 + 2$$
$$\therefore y = \frac{1}{2}(x + 3)^2 + 2$$

   point: (-5,4)
$$4 = a(-5 + 3)^2 + 2$$
$$a = \frac{1}{2}$$

   B: vertex: (4,-2)
$$y = a(x - 4)^2 - 2$$
$$\therefore y = \frac{7}{4}(x - 4)^2 - 2$$

   point: (6,5)
$$5 = a(6 - 4)^2 - 2$$
$$a = \frac{7}{4}$$

   C: vertex: (0,1)
$$y = a(x - 0)^2 + 1$$
$$y = ax^2 + 1$$
$$\therefore y = -\frac{3}{4}x^2 + 1$$

   point: (2,-2)
$$-2 = a(2 - 0)^2 + 1$$
$$a = -\frac{3}{4}$$

2. C ; A ; B
   F ; E ; D

3. vertex: (1,-1)
   point: (-1,1)
$$y = a(x - 1)^2 - 1$$
$$1 = a(-1 - 1)^2 - 1$$
$$a = \frac{1}{2}$$
$$\therefore y = \frac{1}{2}(x - 1)^2 - 1$$

x	y
-2	3.5
-1	1
0	-0.5
1	-1
2	-0.5

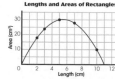

4. vertex: (-1,2)
   point: (0,3)
$$y = a(x + 1)^2 + 2$$
$$3 = a(0 + 1)^2 + 2$$
$$a = 1$$
$$\therefore y = (x + 1)^2 + 2$$

x	y
-3	6
-2	3
-1	2
0	3
1	6

5. vertex: (-1,3)
   point: (0,1)
$$y = a(x + 1)^2 + 3$$
$$1 = a(0 + 1)^2 + 3$$
$$a = -2$$
$$\therefore y = -2(x + 1)^2 + 3$$

x	y
-3	-5
-2	1
-1	3
0	1
1	-5

6. vertex: (-1,3)
   point: (1,2)
$$y = a(x + 1)^2 + 3$$
$$2 = a(1 + 1)^2 + 3$$
$$a = -\frac{1}{4}$$
$$\therefore y = -\frac{1}{4}(x + 1)^2 + 3$$

x	y
-5	-1
-3	2
-1	3
1	2
3	-1

7a. F   b. T   c. T   d. T

8-9. (Suggested answers)

8a.
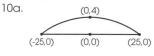

b. vertex: (5.5,30.25)
   point: (2,18)
$$y = a(x - 5.5)^2 + 30.25$$
$$18 = a(2 - 5.5)^2 + 30.25$$
$$a = -1$$
$$\therefore y = -(x - 5.5)^2 + 30.25$$

c. $y = -(6.5 - 5.5)^2 + 30.25 = 29.25$
   The area is 29.25 cm².

9a.

b. vertex: (3.5,4)
   point: (0,2)
$$y = a(x - 3.5)^2 + 4$$
$$2 = a(0 - 3.5)^2 + 4$$
$$a = -\frac{8}{49}$$
$$\therefore y = -\frac{8}{49}(x - 3.5)^2 + 4$$

c. $y = -\frac{8}{49}(5.75 - 3.5)^2 + 4 \doteq 3.17$
   Yes, it is.

10a.
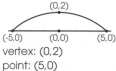

b. vertex: (0,4)
   point: (25,0)
$$y = a(x - 0)^2 + 4$$
$$y = ax^2 + 4$$
$$0 = a(25)^2 + 4$$
$$a = -\frac{4}{625}$$
$$\therefore y = -\frac{4}{625}x^2 + 4$$

11a.
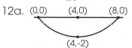
   vertex: (0,2)
   point: (5,0)
$$y = a(x - 0)^2 + 2$$
$$y = ax^2 + 2$$
$$0 = a(5)^2 + 2$$
$$a = -\frac{2}{25}$$
$$\therefore y = -\frac{2}{25}x^2 + 2$$

b. vertex: (0,2)
   point: (4,0)
$$y = ax^2 + 2$$
$$0 = a(4)^2 + 2$$
$$a = -\frac{1}{8}$$
   The equation will be
$$y = -\frac{1}{8}x^2 + 2.$$

12a.

   vertex: (4,-2)
   point: (8,0)
$$y = a(x - 4)^2 - 2$$
$$0 = a(8 - 4)^2 - 2$$
$$a = \frac{1}{8}$$
$$\therefore y = \frac{1}{8}(x - 4)^2 - 2$$

b. vertex: (4,-3.5)
   point: (8,0)
$$y = a(x - 4)^2 - 3.5$$
$$0 = a(8 - 4)^2 - 3.5$$
$$a = \frac{7}{32}$$
   The equation would be
$$y = \frac{7}{32}(x - 4)^2 - 3.5.$$

6 Solving Quadratic Equations

6.1 Standard Form to Factored Form

Try This (p. 102)

$$(x - 3)(x - 4) = 0$$
$$x - 3 = 0 \text{ or } x - 4 = 0$$
$$x = 3 \qquad x = 4$$
The roots are $x = 3$ and $x = 4$.

1. $(x - 3)(x + 2) = 0$
$$x - 3 = 0 \text{ or } x + 2 = 0$$
$$x = 3 \qquad x = -2$$

2. $(x - 7)(x + 3) = 0$
$$x - 7 = 0 \text{ or } x + 3 = 0$$
$$x = 7 \qquad x = -3$$

3. $(x + 6)(x + 1) = 0$
$$x + 6 = 0 \text{ or } x + 1 = 0$$
$$x = -6 \qquad x = -1$$

4. $(2x - 1)(x - 5) = 0$
$$2x - 1 = 0 \text{ or } x - 5 = 0$$
$$x = \frac{1}{2} \qquad x = 5$$

5. $x^2 + 4x - 12 = 0$
$$(x + 6)(x - 2) = 0$$
$$x + 6 = 0 \text{ or } x - 2 = 0$$
$$x = -6 \qquad x = 2$$

6. $x^2 - 6x - 16 = 0$
$$(x - 8)(x + 2) = 0$$
$$x - 8 = 0 \text{ or } x + 2 = 0$$
$$x = 8 \qquad x = -2$$

7. $3x^2 + 16x - 12 = 0$
$(3x - 2)(x + 6) = 0$
$3x - 2 = 0$ or $x + 6 = 0$
$x = \frac{2}{3}$ $\quad$ $x = -6$

8. $6x^2 - 7x - 5 = 0$
$(3x - 5)(2x + 1) = 0$
$3x - 5 = 0$ or $2x + 1 = 0$
$x = \frac{5}{3}$ $\quad$ $x = -\frac{1}{2}$

9. $4x^2 - 4x - 3 = 0$
$(2x + 1)(2x - 3) = 0$
$2x + 1 = 0$ or $2x - 3 = 0$
$x = -\frac{1}{2}$ $\quad$ $x = \frac{3}{2}$

10. $4x^2 - 3x - 5x - 21 = 0$
$4x^2 - 8x - 21 = 0$
$(2x + 3)(2x - 7) = 0$
$2x + 3 = 0$ or $2x - 7 = 0$
$x = -\frac{3}{2}$ $\quad$ $x = \frac{7}{2}$

11. $6x^2 + 25x - 5 - 4 = 0$
$6x^2 + 25x - 9 = 0$
$(3x - 1)(2x + 9) = 0$
$3x - 1 = 0$ or $2x + 9 = 0$
$x = \frac{1}{3}$ $\quad$ $x = -\frac{9}{2}$

12. $4x^2 + 12x - 27 = 0$
$(2x + 9)(2x - 3) = 0$
$2x + 9 = 0$ or $2x - 3 = 0$
$x = -\frac{9}{2}$ $\quad$ $x = \frac{3}{2}$

For $x = -\frac{9}{2}$,
$(-\frac{9}{2})(4(-\frac{9}{2}) + 12) = 27$
For $x = \frac{3}{2}$,
$(\frac{3}{2})(4(\frac{3}{2}) + 12) = 27$

13. $3x^2 + 15x + 4x - 14 = 0$
$3x^2 + 19x - 14 = 0$
$(3x - 2)(x + 7) = 0$
$3x - 2 = 0$ or $x + 7 = 0$
$x = \frac{2}{3}$ $\quad$ $x = -7$

For $x = \frac{2}{3}$,
$3(\frac{2}{3})(\frac{2}{3} + 5) = 11\frac{1}{3}$
$-4(\frac{2}{3}) + 14 = 11\frac{1}{3}$
For $x = -7$,
$3(-7)(-7 + 5) = 42$
$-4(-7) + 14 = 42$

14. $2x^2 - 2 + 8x^2 + x = 0$
$10x^2 + x - 2 = 0$
$(5x - 2)(2x + 1) = 0$
$5x - 2 = 0$ or $2x + 1 = 0$
$x = \frac{2}{5}$ $\quad$ $x = -\frac{1}{2}$

For $x = \frac{2}{5}$,
$2((\frac{2}{5})^2 - 1) = -1\frac{17}{25}$
$-(\frac{2}{5})(8(\frac{2}{5}) + 1) = -1\frac{17}{25}$
For $x = -\frac{1}{2}$,
$2((-\frac{1}{2})^2 - 1) = -\frac{3}{2}$
$-(-\frac{1}{2})(8(-\frac{1}{2}) + 1) = -\frac{3}{2}$

15. $5x^2 + x + 7x^2 - 1 = 0$
$12x^2 + x - 1 = 0$
$(4x - 1)(3x + 1) = 0$
$4x - 1 = 0$ or $3x + 1 = 0$
$x = \frac{1}{4}$ $\quad$ $x = -\frac{1}{3}$

For $x = \frac{1}{4}$,
$\frac{1}{4}(5(\frac{1}{4}) + 1) = \frac{9}{16}$
$-7(\frac{1}{4})^2 + 1 = \frac{9}{16}$
For $x = -\frac{1}{3}$,
$(-\frac{1}{3})(5(-\frac{1}{3}) + 1) = \frac{2}{9}$
$-7(-\frac{1}{3})^2 + 1 = \frac{2}{9}$

16. $4x^2 - x - 25 = 3x + 10$
$4x^2 - 4x - 35 = 0$
$(2x + 5)(2x - 7) = 0$
$2x + 5 = 0$ or $2x - 7 = 0$
$x = -\frac{5}{2}$ $\quad$ $x = \frac{7}{2}$
For $x = -\frac{5}{2}$, $y = 3(-\frac{5}{2}) + 10 = \frac{5}{2}$
For $x = \frac{7}{2}$, $y = 3(\frac{7}{2}) + 10 = \frac{41}{2}$
∴ The points are $(-\frac{5}{2}, \frac{5}{2})$ and $(\frac{7}{2}, \frac{41}{2})$.

17. $2x^2 + 3x - 1 = -8x^2 - 30x + 6$
$10x^2 + 33x - 7 = 0$
$(5x - 1)(2x + 7) = 0$
$5x - 1 = 0$ or $2x + 7 = 0$
$x = \frac{1}{5}$ $\quad$ $x = -\frac{7}{2}$
For $x = \frac{1}{5}$, $y = 2(\frac{1}{5})^2 + 3(\frac{1}{5}) - 1 = -\frac{8}{25}$
For $x = -\frac{7}{2}$, $y = 2(-\frac{7}{2})^2 + 3(-\frac{7}{2}) - 1 = 13$
∴ The points are $(\frac{1}{5}, -\frac{8}{25})$ and $(-\frac{7}{2}, 13)$.

18. $2x^2 - 4x + 1 = -x^2 - 3x + 15$
$3x^2 - x - 14 = 0$
$(3x - 7)(x + 2) = 0$
$3x - 7 = 0$ or $x + 2 = 0$
$x = \frac{7}{3}$ $\quad$ $x = -2$
For $x = \frac{7}{3}$, $y = 2(\frac{7}{3})^2 - 4(\frac{7}{3}) + 1 = \frac{23}{9}$
For $x = -2$, $y = 2(-2)^2 - 4(-2) + 1 = 17$
∴ The points are $(\frac{7}{3}, \frac{23}{9})$ and $(-2, 17)$.

19. $-2x^2 - 4x + 6 = 0$
$(-2x + 2)(x + 3) = 0$
$-2x + 2 = 0$ or $x + 3 = 0$
$x = 1$ $\quad$ $x = -3$
Vertex: $x = \frac{1 + (-3)}{2} = -1$
$y = -2(-1)(-1 + 2) + 6 = 8$
$(1,0)$ and $(-3,0)$; $(-1,8)$

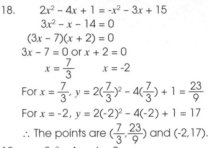

20. $-(x + 3)^2 + 4 = 0$
$-(x^2 + 6x + 9) + 4 = 0$
$-(x^2 + 6x + 5) = 0$
$-(x + 5)(x + 1) = 0$
$x + 5 = 0$ or $x + 1 = 0$
$x = -5$ $\quad$ $x = -1$
Vertex: $x = \frac{-5 + (-1)}{2} = -3$
$y = -(-3 + 3)^2 + 4 = 4$
$(-5,0)$ and $(-1,0)$; $(-3,4)$

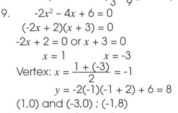

21. $8x^2 - 22x + 5 = 0$
$(4x - 1)(2x - 5) = 0$
$4x - 1 = 0$ or $2x - 5 = 0$
$x = \frac{1}{4}$ $\quad$ $x = \frac{5}{2}$
Vertex: $x = \frac{\frac{1}{4} + \frac{5}{2}}{2} = \frac{11}{8}$
$y = 8(\frac{11}{8})^2 - 22(\frac{11}{8}) + 5 = -\frac{81}{8}$
$(\frac{1}{4},0)$ and $(\frac{5}{2},0)$; $(\frac{11}{8}, -\frac{81}{8})$

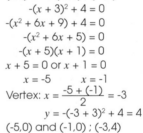

22. $x + x^2 = 240$
$x^2 + x - 240 = 0$
$(x + 16)(x - 15) = 0$
$x + 16 = 0$ or $x - 15 = 0$
$x = -16$ $\quad$ $x = 15$
(not applicable)
The number is 15.

23. $\frac{n(n + 1)}{2} = 153$
$n^2 + n - 306 = 0$
$(n + 18)(n - 17) = 0$
$n + 18 = 0$ or $n - 17 = 0$
$n = -18$ $\quad$ $n = 17$
(not applicable)
n is 17.

24. $x^2 + (x + 2)^2 = 52$
$2x^2 + 4x - 48 = 0$
$2(x^2 + 2x - 24) = 0$
$2(x + 6)(x - 4) = 0$
$x + 6 = 0$ or $x - 4 = 0$
$x = -6$ $\quad$ $x = 4$
If $x = -6$, then $x + 2 = -4$.
If $x = 4$, then $x + 2 = 6$.
The numbers are 4
and 6, or -4 and -6.

25. $(x + 2)(x - 3) = 24$
$x^2 - x - 30 = 0$
$(x - 6)(x + 5) = 0$
$x - 6 = 0$ or $x + 5 = 0$
$x = 6$ $\quad$ $x = -5$
$\quad$ (not applicable)
Length: $6 + 2 = 8$
Width: $6 - 3 = 3$
The length is 8 cm and
the width is 3 cm.

ISBN: 978-1-77149-221-8

26.
$$x(3x - 2) = 133$$
$$3x^2 - 2x - 133 = 0$$
$$(3x + 19)(x - 7) = 0$$
$$3x + 19 = 0 \text{ or } x - 7 = 0$$
$$x = -\frac{19}{3} \quad x = 7$$
(not applicable)
Length: $3(7) - 2 = 19$ The length is 19 cm and the width is 7 cm.

27.
$$25 \times 20 - (25 - 2w)(20 - 2w) = 200$$
$$500 - (500 - 90w + 4w^2) - 200 = 0$$
$$-4w^2 + 90w - 200 = 0$$
$$-2(2w^2 - 45w + 100) = 0$$
$$-2(2w - 5)(w - 20) = 0$$
$$2w - 5 = 0 \text{ or } w - 20 = 0$$
$$w = 2.5 \qquad w = 20 \text{ (too large)}$$
Its thickness is 2.5 cm.

28.
$$b^2 + (2b + 2)^2 = (2b + 3)^2$$
$$b^2 + 4b^2 + 8b + 4 = 4b^2 + 12b + 9$$
$$b^2 - 4b - 5 = 0$$
$$(b - 5)(b + 1) = 0$$
$$b - 5 = 0 \text{ or } b + 1 = 0$$
$$b = 5 \qquad b = -1 \text{ (not applicable)}$$
The length of the base is 5 cm.

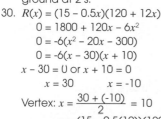

29.
$$6 = -(t - 2)^2 + 6$$
$$-(t - 2)^2 = 0$$
$$t - 2 = 0$$
$$t = 2$$
The ball was 6 m above the ground at 2 s.

30. $R(x) = (15 - 0.5x)(120 + 12x)$
$$0 = 1800 + 120x - 6x^2$$
$$0 = -6(x^2 - 20x - 300)$$
$$0 = -6(x - 30)(x + 10)$$
$$x - 30 = 0 \text{ or } x + 10 = 0$$
$$x = 30 \qquad x = -10$$
Vertex: $x = \frac{30 + (-10)}{2} = 10$
$$y = (15 - 0.5(10))(120 + 12(10)) = 2400$$
Cost: $15 - 0.5(10) = 10$
Each T-shirt should be sold at $10 to maximize revenue.

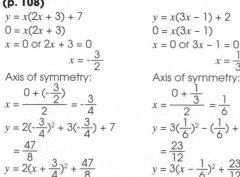

6.2 Partial Factoring

Try This (p. 107)

$y = x(x + 4) - 3$ $y = x(x - 1) + 8$
1. $y = x(x + 3) - 16$ 2. $y = (x + 7)(x - 2)$
3. $y = x(x + 5) - 12$ 4. $y = (x - 10)(x + 1)$
5. $y = x(x - 1) + 6$ 6. $y = -x(x - 2) - 9$
7. $y = -(x - 9)(x + 3)$ 8. $y = 2x(x - 2) - 7$
9. $y = x(2x + 1) + 1$ 10. $y = x(2x - 5) + 9$
11. $y = (2x + 7)(x + 3)$ 12. $y = -x(2x - 1) - 7$
13. $y = x(3x - 4) + 11$ 14. $y = -(2x + 3)(x - 5)$
15. $y = x(3x + 5) + 1$ 16. $y = x(x + 6) + 7$
17. $y = (2x - 5)(x - 5)$ 18. $y = x(3x - 1) + 5$

Try This (p. 108)

$y = x(2x + 3) + 7$ $y = x(3x - 1) + 2$
$0 = x(2x + 3)$ $0 = x(3x - 1)$
$x = 0 \text{ or } 2x + 3 = 0$ $x = 0 \text{ or } 3x - 1 = 0$
          $x = -\frac{3}{2}$ $x = \frac{1}{3}$
Axis of symmetry: Axis of symmetry:
$x = \frac{0 + (-\frac{3}{2})}{2} = -\frac{3}{4}$ $x = \frac{0 + \frac{1}{3}}{2} = \frac{1}{6}$
$y = 2(-\frac{3}{4})^2 + 3(-\frac{3}{4}) + 7$ $y = 3(\frac{1}{6})^2 - (\frac{1}{6}) + 2$
$\quad = \frac{47}{8}$ $\quad = \frac{23}{12}$
$y = 2(x + \frac{3}{4})^2 + \frac{47}{8}$ $y = 3(x - \frac{1}{6})^2 + \frac{23}{12}$

19. $y = 3x(x + 4) - 2$
$$0 = 3x(x + 4)$$
$$x = 0 \text{ or } x + 4 = 0$$
$$x = -4$$
Axis of symmetry:
$$x = \frac{0 + (-4)}{2} = -2$$
$$y = 3(-2)^2 + 12(-2) - 2$$
$$= -14$$
$$y = 3(x + 2)^2 - 14$$

20. $y = 2x(x + 4) + 2$
$$0 = 2x(x + 4)$$
$$x = 0 \text{ or } x + 4 = 0$$
$$x = -4$$
Axis of symmetry:
$$x = \frac{0 + (-4)}{2} = -2$$
$$y = 2(-2)^2 + 8(-2) + 2$$
$$= -6$$
$$y = 2(x + 2)^2 - 6$$

21. $y = x(x + 4) - 2$
$$0 = x(x + 4)$$
$$x = 0 \text{ or } x + 4 = 0$$
$$x = -4$$
Axis of symmetry:
$$x = \frac{0 + (-4)}{2} = -2$$
$$y = (-2)^2 + 4(-2) - 2$$
$$= -6$$
$$y = (x + 2)^2 - 6$$

22. $y = x(2x - 3) + 7$
$$0 = x(2x - 3)$$
$$x = 0 \text{ or } 2x - 3 = 0$$
$$x = \frac{3}{2}$$
Axis of symmetry:
$$x = \frac{0 + \frac{3}{2}}{2} = \frac{3}{4}$$
$$y = 2(\frac{3}{4})^2 - 3(\frac{3}{4}) + 7$$
$$= \frac{47}{8}$$
$$y = 2(x - \frac{3}{4})^2 + \frac{47}{8}$$

23. $y = -x(x - 6) - 1$
$$0 = -x(x - 6)$$
$$x = 0 \text{ or } x - 6 = 0$$
$$x = 6$$
Axis of symmetry:
$$x = \frac{0 + 6}{2} = 3$$
$$y = -(3)^2 + 6(3) - 1$$
$$= 8$$
$$y = -(x - 3)^2 + 8$$

24. $y = -2x(x - 1) - 3$
$$0 = -2x(x - 1)$$
$$x = 0 \text{ or } x - 1 = 0$$
$$x = 1$$
Axis of symmetry:
$$x = \frac{0 + 1}{2} = \frac{1}{2}$$
$$y = -2(\frac{1}{2})^2 + 2(\frac{1}{2}) - 3$$
$$= -\frac{5}{2}$$
$$y = -2(x - \frac{1}{2})^2 - \frac{5}{2}$$

25. $y = x(x - 6) - 1$
$$0 = x(x - 6)$$
$$x = 0 \text{ or } x - 6 = 0$$
$$x = 6$$
Axis of symmetry:
$$x = \frac{0 + 6}{2} = 3$$
$$y = 3^2 - 6(3) - 1$$
$$= -10$$
$$\therefore y = (x - 3)^2 - 10$$

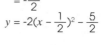

26. $y = 2x(x + 1) - 5$
$$0 = 2x(x + 1)$$
$$x = 0 \text{ or } x + 1 = 0$$
$$x = -1$$
Axis of symmetry:
$$x = \frac{0 + (-1)}{2} = -\frac{1}{2}$$
$$y = 2(-\frac{1}{2})^2 + 2(-\frac{1}{2}) - 5$$
$$= -\frac{11}{2}$$
$$\therefore y = 2(x + \frac{1}{2})^2 - \frac{11}{2}$$

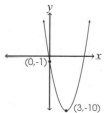

27. $y = x(x + k) + l$
$$0 = x(x + k)$$
$$x = 0 \text{ or } x + k = 0$$
$$x = -k$$
Axis of symmetry:
$$x = \frac{0 + (-k)}{2} = -\frac{k}{2}$$

28. Axis of symmetry:
$$\frac{-2 + 5}{2} = -\frac{k}{2}$$
$$k = -3$$
Substitute $(-2, 0)$.
$$(-2)^2 + (-3)(-2) + l = 0$$
$$l = -10$$

ISBN: 978-1-77149-221-8

29a. When $t = 0$,
$h = -8(0)^2 + 16(0) + 11 = 11$
The bridge is 11 m above water.

b. $h = -8t(t - 2) + 11$
$0 = -8t(t - 2)$
$t = 0$ or $t - 2 = 0$
$\quad\quad\quad\quad\quad\;\; t = 2$
Axis of symmetry: $\frac{0 + 2}{2} = 1$
The rock reached its maximum height at 1 s.

c. $h = -8(1)^2 + 16(1) + 11 = 19$
The maximum height of the rock was 19 m.

30a. $A = -2l(l - 30) + 40$
$0 = -2l(l - 30)$
$l = 0$ or $l - 30 = 0$
$\quad\quad\quad\quad\quad l = 30$
Axis of symmetry: $l = \frac{0 + 30}{2} = 15$
$A = -2(15)^2 + 60(15) + 40 = 490$
The maximum total area is 490 m².

b. "40" represents the area of the old grazing pen.

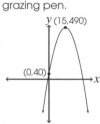

6.3 Completing the Square

Try This (p. 112)

$4 ; 4$
$x^2 - 4x + 4$
$= (x - 2)^2$

$6 ; 9$
$x^2 + 6x + 9$
$= (x + 3)^2$

1. $1 ; = (x - 1)^2$
2. $9 ; = (x - 3)^2$
3. $25 ; = (x - 5)^2$
4. $36 ; = (x - 6)^2$
5. $\frac{1}{4} ; = (x - \frac{1}{2})^2$
6. $\frac{9}{4} ; = (x - \frac{3}{2})^2$
7. $1 ; = 3(x - 1)^2$
8. $16 ; = 2(x - 4)^2$
9. $\frac{9}{4} ; = -(x + \frac{3}{2})^2$
10. $1 ; = 2(x - 1)^2$
11. $\frac{9}{4} ; = 4(x + \frac{3}{2})^2$
12. $\frac{25}{4} ; = -2(x + \frac{5}{2})^2$

Try This (p. 113)

$y = (x^2 - 2x + 1) - 1 + 7$
$y = (x - 1)^2 + 6$

13. $y = (x^2 - 4x + 4) - 4 - 1$
$y = (x - 2)^2 - 5$

14. $y = (x^2 - x + \frac{1}{4}) - \frac{1}{4}$
$y = (x - \frac{1}{2})^2 - \frac{1}{4}$

15. $y = (x^2 - 8x + 16) - 16 - 2$
$y = (x - 4)^2 - 18$

16. $y = (x^2 + 10x + 25) - 25 + 10$
$y = (x + 5)^2 - 15$

17. $y = (x^2 - 3x + \frac{9}{4}) - \frac{9}{4} + 8$
$y = (x - \frac{3}{2})^2 + 5\frac{3}{4}$

18. $y = (x^2 + 4x + 4) - 4 + 7$
$y = (x + 2)^2 + 3$

19. $y = (x^2 - 10x + 25) - 25 + 8$
$y = (x - 5)^2 - 17$

20. $y = (x^2 - 5x + \frac{25}{4}) - \frac{25}{4} + 1$
$y = (x - \frac{5}{2})^2 - 5\frac{1}{4}$

21. $y = 3(x^2 - 2x)$
$y = 3(x^2 - 2x + 1 - 1)$
$y = 3(x - 1)^2 - 3$

22. $y = 2(x^2 + 6x) - 15$
$y = 2(x^2 + 6x + 9 - 9) - 15$
$y = 2(x + 3)^2 - 33$

23. $y = -(x^2 - 6x) - 1$
$y = -(x^2 - 6x + 9 - 9) - 1$
$y = -(x - 3)^2 + 8$

24. $y = 3(x^2 - 10x) + 27$
$y = 3(x^2 - 10x + 25 - 25) + 27$
$y = 3(x - 5)^2 - 48$

25. $y = 5(x^2 - 2x) + 25$
$y = 5(x^2 - 2x + 1 - 1) + 25$
$y = 5(x - 1)^2 + 20$

26. $y = -2(x^2 - 7x) - 2$
$y = -2(x^2 - 7x + \frac{49}{4} - \frac{49}{4}) - 2$
$y = -2(x - \frac{7}{2})^2 + 22\frac{1}{2}$

27A: $y = -(x^2 - 6x) - 17$
$y = -(x^2 - 6x + 9 - 9) - 17$
$y = -(x - 3)^2 - 8$
$(3,-8)$

B: $y = 2(x^2 + 10x) + 51$
$y = 2(x^2 + 10x + 25 - 25) + 51$
$y = 2(x + 5)^2 + 1$
$(-5,1)$

C: $y = 3(x^2 + 2x) - 6$
$y = 3(x^2 + 2x + 1 - 1) - 6$
$y = 3(x + 1)^2 - 9$
$(-1,-9)$

D: $y = 2(x^2 - 6x) + 10$
$y = 2(x^2 - 6x + 9 - 9) + 10$
$y = 2(x - 3)^2 - 8$
$(3,-8)$

E: $y = -3(x^2 + 10x) - 74$
$y = -3(x^2 + 10x + 25 - 25) - 74$
$y = -3(x + 5)^2 + 1$
$(-5,1)$

F: $y = -(x^2 + 2x) - 10$
$y = -(x^2 + 2x + 1 - 1) - 10$
$y = -(x + 1)^2 - 9$
$(-1,-9)$

D ; E ; A ; B ; F ; C

28. If the coefficient of x^2 is positive, the parabola opens upward. If the coefficient is negative, the parabola opens downward.

29. $y = -(x^2 - 4x) - 8$ - reflection in the x-axis
$y = -(x^2 - 4x + 4 - 4) - 8$ - translation of 2 units to the
$y = -(x - 2)^2 - 4$ right and 4 units down

30. $y = 3(x^2 - 2x) + 1$ - vertical stretch by a factor
$y = 3(x^2 - 2x + 1 - 1) + 1$ of 3
$y = 3(x - 1)^2 - 2$ - translation of 1 unit to the
                       right and 2 units down

31. $y = -2(x^2 + 12x) - 73$
$y = -2(x^2 + 12x + 36 - 36) - 73$
$y = -2(x + 6)^2 - 1$
- vertical stretch by a factor of 2
- reflection in the x-axis
- translation of 6 units to the left and 1 unit down

32. $h = -3t^2 + 15t$
$h = -3(t^2 - 5t)$
$h = -3(t^2 - 5t + \frac{25}{4} - \frac{25}{4})$
$h = -3(t - \frac{5}{2})^2 + 18\frac{3}{4}$
Vertex: $(\frac{5}{2}, 18\frac{3}{4})$
The maximum height was $18\frac{3}{4}$ cm.

33. $h = x^2 - 5x + 3$
$h = (x^2 - 5x + \frac{25}{4}) - \frac{25}{4} + 3$
$h = (x - \frac{5}{2})^2 - 3\frac{1}{4}$ Vertex: $(\frac{5}{2}, -3\frac{1}{4})$
The greatest depth the swimmer reached was $3\frac{1}{4}$ m beneath the water surface.

34a. $P = -\frac{1}{3}(x^2 - 10x) - \frac{7}{3}$
$P = -\frac{1}{3}(x^2 - 10x + 25 - 25) - \frac{7}{3}$
$P = -\frac{1}{3}(x - 5)^2 + 6$
The maximum profit is $6000.
Vertex: $(5,6)$
Maximum profit:
$6 \times 1000 = 6000$

b. Number of units sold: $5 \times 1000 = 5000$
5000 units must be sold to obtain the maximum profit.

35. $A = l(\frac{40 - 2l}{2})$
$A = -l(20 - l)$
$A = -(l^2 - 20l)$
$A = -(l^2 - 20l + 100 - 100)$
$A = -(l - 10)^2 + 100$
Vertex: $(10,100)$
Maximum area: 100 units²
Length: 10
Width: $20 - 10 = 10$
The maximum area is 100 square units. The length and width in Popsicle sticks are both 10.

6.4 The Quadratic Formula

Try This (p. 117)

$x = \frac{-(-4) \pm \sqrt{(-4)^2 - 4(2)(1)}}{2(2)}$
$x = \frac{4 \pm \sqrt{8}}{4}$
$x \doteq 1.71$ and $x \doteq 0.29$

1. $2 ; 3 ; 1$

$$x = \frac{-3 \pm \sqrt{3^2 - 4(2)(1)}}{2(2)}$$

$$x = \frac{-3 \pm \sqrt{1}}{4}$$

$x = -0.5$ and $x = -1$

2. $1 ; -3 ; 1$

$$x = \frac{-(-3) \pm \sqrt{(-3)^2 - 4(1)(1)}}{2(1)}$$

$$x = \frac{3 \pm \sqrt{5}}{2}$$

$x \doteq 2.62$ and $x \doteq 0.38$

3. $-2 ; 8 ; -1$

$$x = \frac{-8 \pm \sqrt{8^2 - 4(-2)(-1)}}{2(-2)}$$

$$x = \frac{-8 \pm \sqrt{56}}{-4}$$

$x \doteq 0.13$ and $x \doteq 3.87$

4. $-1 ; 5 ; -2$

$$x = \frac{-5 \pm \sqrt{5^2 - 4(-1)(-2)}}{2(-1)}$$

$$x = \frac{-5 \pm \sqrt{17}}{-2}$$

$x \doteq 0.44$ and $x \doteq 4.56$

5. $x = \dfrac{-(-7) \pm \sqrt{(-7)^2 - 4(5)(1)}}{2(5)}$

$$x = \frac{7 \pm \sqrt{29}}{10}$$

$x \doteq 1.24$ and $x \doteq 0.16$

6. $x = \dfrac{-6 \pm \sqrt{6^2 - 4(-2)(-3)}}{2(-2)}$

$$x = \frac{-6 \pm \sqrt{12}}{-4}$$

$x \doteq 0.63$ and $x \doteq 2.37$

7. $x = \dfrac{-(-3) \pm \sqrt{(-3)^2 - 4(-1)(-1)}}{2(-1)}$

$$x = \frac{3 \pm \sqrt{5}}{-2}$$

$x \doteq -2.62$ and $x \doteq -0.38$

8. $x = \dfrac{-6 \pm \sqrt{6^2 - 4(4)(1)}}{2(4)}$

$$x = \frac{-6 \pm \sqrt{20}}{8}$$

$x \doteq -0.19$ and $x \doteq -1.31$

9. $x = \dfrac{-5 \pm \sqrt{5^2 - 4(-1)(-3)}}{2(-1)}$

$$x = \frac{-5 \pm \sqrt{13}}{-2}$$

$x \doteq 0.70$ and $x \doteq 4.30$

10. $x = \dfrac{-8 \pm \sqrt{8^2 - 4(6)(-1)}}{2(6)}$

$$x = \frac{-8 \pm \sqrt{88}}{12}$$

$x \doteq 0.12$ and $x \doteq -1.45$

11. $x = \dfrac{-9 \pm \sqrt{9^2 - 4(-3)(2)}}{2(-3)}$

$$x = \frac{-9 \pm \sqrt{105}}{-6}$$

$x \doteq -0.21$ and $x \doteq 3.21$

12. $x = \dfrac{-(-10) \pm \sqrt{(-10)^2 - 4(3)(-4)}}{2(3)}$

$$x = \frac{10 \pm \sqrt{148}}{6}$$

$x \doteq 3.69$ and $x \doteq -0.36$

13. $2x^2 - 2x + 3 = 5x - 1$
$2x^2 - 7x + 4 = 0$

$$x = \frac{-(-7) \pm \sqrt{(-7)^2 - 4(2)(4)}}{2(2)}$$

$$x - \frac{7 \pm \sqrt{17}}{4}$$

$x \doteq 2.78$ and $x \doteq 0.72$

14. $2x^2 - 5x - 5 = -6(x^2 - 2x + 1)$
$2x^2 - 5x - 5 = -6x^2 + 12x - 6$
$8x^2 - 17x + 1 = 0$

$$x = \frac{-(-17) + \sqrt{(-17)^2 - 4(8)(1)}}{2(8)}$$

$$x = \frac{17 \pm \sqrt{257}}{16}$$

$x \doteq 2.06$ and $x \doteq 0.06$

15. $4x^2 + 8x = -7x^2 + 14 - 12$
$11x^2 + 8x - 2 = 0$

$$x = \frac{-8 \pm \sqrt{8^2 - 4(11)(-2)}}{2(11)}$$

$$x = \frac{-8 \pm \sqrt{152}}{22}$$

$x \doteq 0.20$ and $x \doteq -0.92$

16. $2(x^2 - 2x + 1) = 5x^2 + 6x + 1$
$2x^2 - 4x + 2 = 5x^2 + 6x + 1$
$-3x^2 - 10x + 1 = 0$

$$x = \frac{-(-10) \pm \sqrt{(-10)^2 - 4(-3)(1)}}{2(-3)}$$

$$x = \frac{10 \pm \sqrt{112}}{-6}$$

$x \doteq -3.43$ and $x \doteq 0.10$

17A: $x = \dfrac{-8 \pm \sqrt{8^2 - 4(3)(-5)}}{2(3)}$

$$x = \frac{-8 \pm \sqrt{124}}{6}$$

$x \doteq 0.52$ and $x \doteq -3.19$

B: $x = \dfrac{-(-7) \pm \sqrt{(-7)^2 - 4(-2)(-6)}}{2(-2)}$

$$x = \frac{7 \pm \sqrt{1}}{-4}$$

$x = -2$ and $x = -1.5$

C: $x = \dfrac{-13 \pm \sqrt{13^2 - 4(-10)(2)}}{2(-10)}$

$$x = \frac{-13 \pm \sqrt{249}}{-20}$$

$x \doteq -0.14$ and $x \doteq 1.44$

D: $x = \dfrac{-5 \pm \sqrt{5^2 - 4(-0.5)(4)}}{2(-0.5)}$

$$x = \frac{-5 \pm \sqrt{33}}{-1}$$

$x \doteq -0.74$ and $x \doteq 10.74$

E: $x = \dfrac{-0.8 \pm \sqrt{0.8^2 - 4(-1.6)(5)}}{2(-1.6)}$

$$x = \frac{-0.8 \pm \sqrt{32.64}}{-3.2}$$

$x \doteq -1.54$ and $x \doteq 2.04$

F: $x = \dfrac{-1.6 \pm \sqrt{1.6^2 - 4(-2.75)(2)}}{2(-2.75)}$

$$x = \frac{-1.6 \pm \sqrt{24.56}}{-5.5}$$

$x \doteq -0.61$ and $x \doteq 1.19$

C ; A ; F
B ; E ; D

18. $-x^2 + 7x = -6x^2 - x + 3$
$5x^2 + 8x - 3 = 0$

$$x = \frac{-8 \pm \sqrt{8^2 - 4(5)(-3)}}{2(5)}$$

$$x = \frac{-8 \pm \sqrt{124}}{10}$$

$x \doteq 0.31$ and $x \doteq -1.91$
$x = 0.31$, $y = -(0.31)^2 + 7(0.31) \doteq 2.07$
$x = -1.91$, $y = -(-1.91)^2 + 7(-1.91) \doteq -17.02$
$(0.31, 2.07)$; $(-1.91, -17.02)$

19. $3x^2 - 7x - 1 = -x^2 + 2x + 3.25$
$4x^2 - 9x - 4.25 = 0$

$$x = \frac{-(-9) \pm \sqrt{(-9)^2 - 4(4)(-4.25)}}{2(4)}$$

$$x = \frac{9 \pm \sqrt{149}}{8}$$

$x \doteq 2.65$ and $x \doteq -0.40$
$x = 2.65$, $y = 3(2.65)^2 - 7(2.65) - 1 \doteq 1.52$
$x = -0.40$, $y = 3(-0.40)^2 - 7(-0.40) - 1 = 2.28$
$(2.65, 1.52)$; $(-0.40, 2.28)$

20. $x^2 - 5x + 3 = -2(0.6x^2 - x + 1)$
$x^2 - 5x + 3 = -1.2x^2 + 2x - 2$
$2.2x^2 - 7x + 5 = 0$

$$x = \frac{-(-7) \pm \sqrt{(-7)^2 - 4(2.2)(5)}}{2(2.2)}$$

$$x = \frac{7 \pm \sqrt{5}}{4.4}$$

$x \doteq 2.10$ and $x \doteq 1.08$
$x = 2.10$, $y = (2.10)^2 - 5(2.10) + 3 = -3.09$
$x = 1.08$, $y = (1.08)^2 - 5(1.08) + 3 \doteq -1.23$
$(2.10, -3.09)$; $(1.08, -1.23)$

21. $x^2 + 3x + 1 = 3x^2 - 4x - 2$
$-2x^2 + 7x + 3 = 0$

$$x = \frac{-7 \pm \sqrt{7^2 - 4(-2)(3)}}{2(-2)}$$

$$x = \frac{-7 \pm \sqrt{73}}{-4}$$

$x \doteq -0.39$ and $x \doteq 3.89$
$x = -0.39$, $y = (-0.39)^2 + 3(-0.39) + 1 \doteq -0.02$
$x = 3.89$, $y = (3.89)^2 + 3(3.89) + 1 \doteq 27.80$
$(-0.39, -0.02)$; $(3.89, 27.80)$

22. $3(x^2 - x - 1) = -x(x - 6)$
$3x^2 - 3x - 3 = -x^2 + 6x$
$4x^2 - 9x - 3 = 0$

$$x = \frac{-(-9) \pm \sqrt{(-9)^2 - 4(4)(-3)}}{2(4)}$$

$$x = \frac{9 \pm \sqrt{129}}{8}$$

$x \doteq 2.54$ and $x \doteq -0.29$
$x = 2.54$, $y = -2.54(2.54 - 6) \doteq 8.79$
$x = -0.29$, $y = -(-0.29)(-0.29 - 6) \doteq -1.82$
$(2.54, 8.79)$; $(-0.29, -1.82)$

23. by quadratic formula:

$$x = \frac{-(-10) \pm \sqrt{(-10)^2 - 4(1)(25)}}{2(1)}$$

$$x = \frac{10}{2}$$

$x = 5$

by factoring:
$(x - 5)^2 = 0$
$x - 5 = 0$
$x = 5$

(Individual answer)

24. by quadratic formula:

$$x = \frac{-29 \pm \sqrt{29^2 - 4(6)(-42)}}{2(6)}$$

$$x = \frac{-29 \pm 43}{12}$$

$x \doteq 1.17$ and $x = -6$

by factoring:
$(6x - 7)(x + 6) = 0$
$6x - 7 = 0$ or $x + 6 = 0$
$x = \dfrac{7}{6}$ $x = -6$
$x \doteq 1.17$

(Individual answer)

25. (Suggested answer)
An advantage of using the quadratic formula is that it is applicable to all quadratic equations, but a disadvantage is that it could involve more calculations.

26. (Suggested answers)
a. F   b. Q   c. Q   d. Q
e. F   f. Q   g. Q   h. F

27. $x + y = -1 \rightarrow x = -y - 1$
$xy = -306$
$(-y - 1)(y) = -306$
$-y^2 - y = -306$
$y^2 + y - 306 = 0$
$y = \dfrac{-1 \pm \sqrt{1^2 - 4(1)(-306)}}{2(1)}$
$y = \dfrac{-1 \pm 35}{2}$
$y = 17$ and $y = -18$
$x = -17 - 1 = -18$
$x = -(-18) - 1 = 17$
The numbers are 17 and -18.

28. $x^2 + (x + 1)^2 + (x + 2)^2 = 677$
$x^2 + x^2 + 2x + 1 + x^2 + 4x + 4 = 677$
$3x^2 + 6x - 672 = 0$
$x = \dfrac{-6 \pm \sqrt{6^2 - 4(3)(-672)}}{2(3)}$
$x = \dfrac{-6 \pm 90}{6}$
$x = 14$ (not negative) and $x = -16$
$x + 1 = -15$
$x + 2 = -14$
The integers are -16, -15, and -14.

29. $w(w + 9) = 52$
$w^2 + 9w - 52 = 0$
$w = \dfrac{-9 \pm \sqrt{9^2 - 4(1)(-52)}}{2(1)}$
$w = \dfrac{-9 \pm 17}{2}$
$w = 4$ and $w = -13$ (not applicable)
Length: $4 + 9 = 13$
The dimensions of the net are 13 cm and 4 cm.

30. $h^2 + (h - 2)^2 = (h + 16)^2$
$h^2 + h^2 - 4h + 4 = h^2 + 32h + 256$
$h^2 - 36h - 252 = 0$
$h = \dfrac{-(-36) \pm \sqrt{(-36)^2 - 4(1)(-252)}}{2(1)}$
$h = \dfrac{36 \pm 48}{2}$
$h = 42$ and $h = -6$ (not applicable)
$h - 2 = 42 - 2 = 40$
$h + 16 = 42 + 16 = 58$
The side lengths are 40 cm, 42 cm, and 58 cm.

31. $-x^2 + 4x + 1 = x - 12$
$-x^2 + 3x + 13 = 0$
$x = \dfrac{-3 \pm \sqrt{3^2 - 4(-1)(13)}}{2(-1)}$
$x = \dfrac{-3 \pm \sqrt{61}}{-2}$
$x \doteq -2.41$ and $x \doteq 5.41$
$x = -2.41,\ y = -2.41 - 12 = -14.41$
$x = 5.41,\ y = 5.41 - 12 = -6.59$
They will intersect at (-2.41,-14.41) and (5.41,-6.59).

6.5 Nature of Roots

Try This (p. 123)
$b^2 - 4ac = 2^2 - 4(1)(1) = 0$
The discriminant is 0.

1A: $b^2 - 4ac = (-12)^2 - 4(1)(35)$
$= 4$
$x = \dfrac{-(-12) \pm \sqrt{4}}{2(1)}$
$x = 7$ and $x = 5$
2 ; >

B: $b^2 - 4ac = (-6)^2 - 4(1)(9)$
$= 0$
$x = \dfrac{-(-6) \pm 0}{2(1)}$
$x = 3$
1 ; =

C: $b^2 - 4ac = 5^2 - 4(-6)(6)$
$= 169$
$x = \dfrac{-5 \pm \sqrt{169}}{2(-6)}$
$x \doteq -0.67$ and $x = 1.5$
2 ; >

D: $b^2 - 4ac = (-2)^2 - 4(1)(5)$
$= -16$
$x = \dfrac{-(-2) \pm \sqrt{-16}}{2(1)}$
no real roots
0 ; <

E: $b^2 - 4ac = 5^2 - 4(1)(-36)$
$= 169$
$x = \dfrac{-5 \pm \sqrt{169}}{2(1)}$
$x = 4$ and $x = -9$
2 ; >

F: $b^2 - 4ac = 10^2 - 4(1)(25)$
$= 0$
$x = \dfrac{-10 \pm 0}{2(1)}$
$x = -5$
1 ; =

If the discriminant is greater than 0, there are 2 real roots. If the discriminant is 0, there is 1 real root. If the discriminant is less than 0, there are no real roots.

Try This (p. 124)
$b^2 - 4ac = (-8)^2 - 4(-1)(2) = 72 > 0$
The relation has 2 real roots.

2. $b^2 - 4ac = 10^2 - 4(1)(64)$
$= -156 < 0$
0

3. $b^2 - 4ac = (-1)^2 - 4(2)(-3)$
$= 25 > 0$
2 real roots

4. $b^2 - 4ac = (-1)^2 - 4(3)(1)$
$= -11 < 0$
0 real roots

5. $b^2 - 4ac = (-12)^2 - 4(4)(9)$
$= 0$
1 real root

6. $b^2 - 4ac = (-8)^2 - 4(-1)(17)$
$= 132 > 0$
2 real roots

7. $b^2 - 4ac = (-6)^2 - 4(-8)(-1)$
$= 4 > 0$
2 real roots

8A: $2x^2 + 9x + 1 = 0$
$b^2 - 4ac = 9^2 - 4(2)(1)$
$= 73 > 0$
✔ ; 2

B: $5x^2 + 10x + 5 = 0$
$b^2 - 4ac = 10^2 - 4(5)(5)$
$= 0$
✔ ; 1

C: $3x^2 - 6x + 1 = 0$
$b^2 - 4ac = (-6)^2 - 4(3)(1)$
$= 24 > 0$
✔ ; 2

D: $4x^2 - 3x + 17 = 0$
$b^2 - 4ac = (-3)^2 - 4(4)(17)$
$= -263 < 0$
0

E: $4x^2 - 12x + 9 = 0$
$b^2 - 4ac = (-12)^2 - 4(4)(9)$
$= 0$
✔ ; 1

F: $x^2 + 2x + 6 = 0$
$b^2 - 4ac = 2^2 - 4(1)(6)$
$= -20 < 0$
0

9. $y = 2(x^2 - 6x + 9)$
$y = 2x^2 - 12x + 18$
$b^2 - 4ac = (-12)^2 - 4(2)(18)$
$= 0$
∴ 1 real root

10. $y = -(x^2 - 20x + 100)$
$y = -x^2 + 20x - 100$
$b^2 - 4ac = 20^2 - 4(-1)(-100)$
$= 0$
∴ 1 real root

11. $y = -3(x^2 - 2x + 1) + 1$
$y = -3x^2 + 6x - 2$
$b^2 - 4ac = 6^2 - 4(-3)(-2)$
$= 12 > 0$
∴ 2 real roots

12. $y = 4x^2 + 3x - 1 - 5$
$y = 4x^2 + 3x - 6$
$b^2 - 4ac = 3^2 - 4(4)(-6)$
$= 105 > 0$
∴ 2 real roots

$-(10 - x)^2$; $y = (4x - 1)(x + 1) - 5$;
$y = 2(x - 3)^2$; $y = -3(x - 1)^2 + 1$

13a. $b^2 - 4ac = b^2 - 4(1)(36)$
$= b^2 - 144$
$b^2 - 144 < 0$
$b^2 < 144$
$-12 < b < 12$

b. $b^2 - 144 > 0$
$b^2 > 144$
$b > 12$ or $b < -12$

14a. $b^2 - 4ac = 6^2 - 4(2)(k)$
   $= 36 - 8k$
   $36 - 8k = 0$
   $k = 4.5$

b. $y = 2x^2 + 6x + 4.5$
   $0 = 2x^2 + 6x + 4.5$
   $x = \dfrac{-6 \pm \sqrt{0}}{2(2)} = -1.5$
   The x-intercept is (-1.5,0)

15a. $-x^2 + 2x + 3 = kx + 3$
   $-x^2 + (2 - k)x = 0$
   $b^2 - 4ac = (2 - k)^2 - 4(-1)(0)$
   $= (2 - k)^2$
   $(2 - k)^2 = 0$
   $k = 2$

b. $-x^2 + 2x + 3 = 2x + 3$
   $-x^2 = 0$
   $x = 0$
   $y = 2(0) + 3 = 3$
   The point of intersection is (0,3).

16a. $x^2 + 4x - 12 = 3x - 14$
   $x^2 + x + 2 = 0$
   $b^2 - 4ac = 1^2 - 4(1)(2)$
   $= -7 < 0$
   There are no real roots.
   ∴ There are no points of intersection.

b. $y = x^2 + 4x - 12$
   $y = 3x - 14$

17. $700 = -75c(c - 6)$
   $75c^2 - 450c + 700 = 0$
   $b^2 - 4ac = (-450)^2 - 4(75)(700) = -7500 < 0$
   There are no real roots.
   No, it is not possible to make a $700 profit.

18. $2.7 = -0.3(t + 1)(t - 5)$
   $2.7 = -0.3(t^2 - 4t - 5)$
   $0.3t^2 - 1.2t + 1.2 = 0$
   $b^2 - 4ac = (-1.2)^2 - 4(0.3)(1.2) = 0$
   There is 1 real root.
   The ball reaches a height of 2.7 m once.

19. $xy = 18$
   $x + y = 8 \rightarrow x = -y + 8$
   $(-y + 8)(y) = 18$
   $-y^2 + 8y - 18 = 0$
   $b^2 - 4ac = 8^2 - 4(-1)(-18) = -8 < 0$
   There are no real roots.
   Cleo is correct.

20a. Denny:
   $d^2 - 5d + 6$
   $d^2 - 5d - 6 = 0$
   $b^2 - 4ac = (-5)^2 - 4(1)(-6)$
   $= 49 > 0$

   Belinda:
   $b^2 = 10b - 24$
   $b^2 - 10b + 24 = 0$
   $b^2 - 4ac = (-10)^2 - 4(1)(24)$
   $= 4 > 0$

   There are 2 solutions for each person.

b. Denny:
   $d = \dfrac{-(-5) \pm \sqrt{49}}{2(1)}$
   $d = 6$ and $d = -1$

   Belinda:
   $b = \dfrac{-(-10) \pm \sqrt{4}}{2(1)}$
   $b = 6$ and $b = 4$

   Denny is 6 years old and Belinda is either 4 or 6 years old. The negative solutions are not applicable because ages cannot be negative.

7 Triangles and Trigonometry

7.1 Congruent and Similar Triangles

1. $\angle A = \angle X$
   $AB = XY$
   $\angle B = \angle Y$
   $\triangle ABC \cong \triangle XYZ$ (by ASA)

2. $\angle J = \angle H$
   $JI = HI$
   $\angle JIK = \angle HIG$
   $\triangle JIK \cong \triangle HIG$ (by ASA)

3. $MO = PO$
   $NM = NP$
   $NO = NO$
   $\triangle NMO \cong \triangle NPO$ (by SSS)

4. $DE = DG$
   $DF = DF$
   Both are right triangles.
   $\triangle DEF \cong \triangle DGF$ (by RHS)

5. $\angle RPS = \angle QSP$
   $PS = SP$
   $\angle RSP = \angle QPS$
   $\triangle RPS \cong \triangle QSP$ (by ASA)

6. $\angle EDF = \angle HGF$
   $DE = GH$
   $\angle DEF = \angle GHF$
   $\cong$; ASA

7. Not congruent

8. $\angle PQR = \angle STR$
   $QR = TR$
   $\angle QRP = \angle TRS$
   $\triangle PQR \cong \triangle STR$ (by ASA)

9. $\angle MNO = \angle PQO$
   $NO = QO$
   $\angle NOM = \angle QOP$
   $\triangle MNO \cong \triangle PQO$ (by ASA)

10. Not congruent

11. $\angle ACB = 180° - 85° - 35° = 60°$
   $\angle EDF = 180° - 60° - 85° = 35°$
   $\angle ACB = \angle DFE$
   $\angle BAC = \angle EDF$
   $\angle ABC = \angle DEF$
   $\triangle ABC \sim \triangle DEF$

   $\dfrac{AB}{DE} = \dfrac{6}{3} = 2$
   $\dfrac{AC}{DF} = \dfrac{7}{3.5} = 2$
   $\dfrac{BC}{EF} = \dfrac{4}{2} = 2$

12. $\angle UWV = 180° - 45° - 103° = 32°$
   $\angle XZY = 180° - 32° - 103° = 45°$
   $\angle ZXY = \angle UWV$
   $\angle ZYX = \angle UVW$
   $\angle XZY = \angle WUV$
   $\triangle XYZ \sim \triangle WVU$

   $\dfrac{XZ}{WU} = \dfrac{22}{11} = 2$
   $\dfrac{XY}{WV} = \dfrac{16}{8} = 2$
   $\dfrac{YZ}{VU} = \dfrac{12}{6} = 2$

Try This (p. 130)

$\angle GIH = \angle IJH$
$\angle HGI = \angle HIJ$
$\angle GHI = \angle IHJ$
The scale factor is 1.25.

$\dfrac{IJ}{GI} = \dfrac{8.75}{7} = 1.25$
$\dfrac{HJ}{HI} = \dfrac{6.25}{5} = 1.25$
$\dfrac{HI}{HG} = \dfrac{5}{4} = 1.25$

13. $\angle WUX = \angle YZX$
   $\angle UWX = \angle ZYX$
   $\angle UXW = \angle ZXY$
   The scale factor is 2.
   $\triangle UWX \sim \triangle ZYX$

   $\dfrac{YZ}{WU} = \dfrac{8}{4} = 2$
   $\dfrac{XY}{XW} = \dfrac{6}{3} = 2$
   $\dfrac{XZ}{XU} = \dfrac{5}{2.5} = 2$

14. $\angle QPR = 180° - 120° - 30° = 30°$
   $\angle SPR = 180° - 68° - 30° = 82°$
   The triangles are not similar.

15. $\angle JIK = 180° - 115° - 27° = 38°$
   $\angle LMN = 180° - 115° - 42° = 23°$
   The triangles are not similar.

16. $\angle EGF = \angle ECD$
   $\angle EFG = \angle EDC$
   $\angle FEG = \angle DEC$
   The scale factor is 2.
   $\triangle EFG \sim \triangle EDC$

   $\dfrac{EF}{ED} = \dfrac{9}{4.5} = 2$
   $\dfrac{FG}{DC} = \dfrac{8}{4} = 2$
   $\dfrac{EG}{EC} = \dfrac{5}{2.5} = 2$

17. $XW = ZW$
   $WY = WY$
   $XY = ZY$
   congruent ; 1

   $\dfrac{XW}{ZW} = \dfrac{6}{6} = 1$
   $\dfrac{XY}{ZY} = \dfrac{5}{5} = 1$
   $\dfrac{WY}{WY} = \dfrac{3}{3} = 1$

18. $\angle ACB = 180° - 60° - 60° = 60°$
   $\angle BCD = 180° - 75° - 30° = 75°$
   neither

19. $\angle NMO = \angle PMQ$
   $\angle MNO = \angle MPQ$
   $\angle NOM = \angle PQM$
   similar ; $\dfrac{2}{3}$

   $\dfrac{MN}{MP} = \dfrac{6}{6 + 3} = \dfrac{2}{3}$
   $\dfrac{NO}{PQ} = \dfrac{5}{7.5} = \dfrac{2}{3}$
   $\dfrac{MO}{MQ} = \dfrac{7.8}{7.8 + 3.9} = \dfrac{2}{3}$

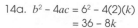

20. $GI = KI$

$HI = JI$

$GH = KJ$

$\dfrac{GI}{KI} = \dfrac{6}{6} = 1$

$\dfrac{GH}{KJ} = \dfrac{6}{6} = 1$

$\dfrac{HI}{JI} = \dfrac{7}{7} = 1$

congruent ; 1

21. $\dfrac{ST}{RS} = \dfrac{4}{3}$

$\dfrac{TU}{ST} = \dfrac{4.5}{4} = \dfrac{9}{8}$

$\dfrac{SU}{RT} = \dfrac{3}{2.6} = \dfrac{15}{13}$

neither

22. $\angle PQR = \angle QSR$

$\angle QPR = \angle SQR$

$\angle QRP = \angle SRQ$

similar ; 1.5

$\dfrac{QR}{PR} = \dfrac{1.5}{1} = 1.5$

$\dfrac{SR}{QR} = \dfrac{2.25}{1.5} = 1.5$

$\dfrac{QS}{PQ} = \dfrac{2.7}{1.8} = 1.5$

23. Congruent triangles have a scale factor of 1.

24. Yes, all congruent triangles are also similar triangles. The corresponding angles are equal and the corresponding sides have the scale factor of 1.

25. $a + 62° + 62° = 180°$

$a = 56°$

$\triangle ABC$ is an isosceles triangle.

$b = 8$ cm

56° ; 8 cm

26. $d + 45° + 90° = 180°$

$d = 45°$

Both are isosceles triangles.

$e^2 + e^2 = 10^2$

$e^2 = 50$

$e \doteq 7.07$

45° ; 7.07 cm

27. $i + 60° + 90° = 180°$

$i = 30°$

$(\dfrac{10}{2})^2 + 10^2 = j^2$

$j \doteq 11.18$

30° ; 11.18 cm

28. $l + 45° + 90° = 180°$

$l = 45°$

$\dfrac{MN}{ON} = \dfrac{ML}{OP}$

$\dfrac{10}{5} = \dfrac{7}{OP}$

$OP = 3.5$

$5^2 - 3.5^2 = m^2$

$m \doteq 3.57$

45° ; 3.57 cm

29. $\angle SRQ = \angle QRP$

$\angle SQR = \angle QPR$

$\angle QSR = \angle PQR$

$\angle PQS + \angle QPR = 180°$

$100° + p + p = 180°$

$p = 40°$

$\dfrac{QR}{SR} = \dfrac{PR}{QR}$

$\dfrac{6}{4} = \dfrac{q}{6}$

$q = 9$

40° ; 9 cm

30a. $\angle RQP = \angle SPQ$

$\angle TQP = \angle TPQ$

$\therefore \triangle PQT$ is an isosceles triangle.

b. $PT = QT$

$\angle PTR = \angle QTS$

$RT = RQ - TQ$

$= SP - TP$

$= ST$

$\therefore \triangle PRT \cong \triangle QST$ (by SAS)

31a. $\angle BAC = \angle XAE$

$\angle AXE = \angle CDE = \angle ABC$

$\angle BCA = \angle DEC = \angle XEA$

$\therefore \triangle ABC \sim \triangle AXE$

b. $AE = AC + CE = 2AC$

$AX = AB + BX = AB + CD = 2AB$

$XE = XD + DE = BC + DE = 2BC$

$\therefore$ The scale factor is 2.

$\dfrac{AE}{AC} = 2$

$\dfrac{AX}{AB} = 2$

$\dfrac{XE}{BC} = 2$

32a. $WY = ZY$

$\therefore \triangle WYZ$ is an isosceles triangle.

b. $\angle VWY = \angle XZY$

$\angle UWX = \angle UZV$

$WX = WY + YX = ZY + YV = ZV$

$\angle WXU = 180° - \angle ZXY = 180° - \angle WVY = \angle ZVU$

$\therefore \triangle UWX \cong \triangle UZV$ (by ASA)

33a. $MO = QO$

$\angle MOP = \angle QON$

$PO = NO$

$\therefore \triangle MOP \cong \triangle QON$ (by SAS)

$\therefore \triangle MOP \sim \triangle QON$

b. $MN = QP$

$\angle MNP = \angle QPN$

$NP = PN$

$\therefore \triangle MNP \cong \triangle QPN$ (by SAS)

7.2 Solving Problems on Similar Triangles

1. $\angle MLN + 76° + 62° = 180°$

$\angle MLN = 42°$

$\dfrac{OP}{MN} = \dfrac{LP}{LN}$

$\dfrac{8.4}{7} = \dfrac{LN + 2}{LN}$

$LN = 10$

42° ; 10 cm

2. $\angle CDE + 35° + 90° = 180°$

$\angle CDE = 55°$

$\angle CAB = \angle CDE = 55°$

$\dfrac{DC}{AC} = \dfrac{DE}{AB}$

$\dfrac{4.5}{3} = \dfrac{DE}{5.2}$

$DE = 7.8$

55° ; 7.8 cm

3. $\angle HGF + 57° + 105° = 180°$

$\angle HGF = 18°$

$\angle EDF = \angle HGF = 18°$

$\dfrac{FG}{FD} = \dfrac{GH}{DE}$

$\dfrac{6}{5} = \dfrac{5}{DE}$

$DE \doteq 4.17$

18° ; 4.17 cm

4. $\angle IJK + 27° + 90° = 180°$

$\angle IJK = 63°$

$\angle ILM = \angle IJK = 63°$

$\dfrac{LM}{JK} = \dfrac{IL}{IJ}$

$\dfrac{4}{2.5} = \dfrac{JL + 5.5}{5.5}$

$JL = 3.3$

63° ; 3.3 cm

5. $\angle PQR + \angle PRQ + 114° = 180°$

$2\angle PQR = 66°$

$\angle PQR = 33°$

$\angle QST = \angle PQR = 33°$

$\angle PRQ + \angle QRT = 180°$

$\angle QRT = 180° - 33° = 147°$

$PS = PT = 5.4 + 1.62 = 7.02$

33° ; 1.62 cm ; 147° ; 7.02 cm

$\dfrac{ST}{QR} = \dfrac{PT}{PR}$

$\dfrac{9.1}{7} = \dfrac{5.4 + RT}{5.4}$

$RT = 1.62$

6. $\angle PMO = \angle MNO = 55°$

$\angle NMO + 55° + 90° = 180°$

$\angle NMO = 35°$

$\angle MPO = \angle NMO = 35°$

$\dfrac{MP}{NM} = \dfrac{OP}{OM}$

$\dfrac{8.7}{6} = \dfrac{OP}{5}$

$OP = 7.25$

$\dfrac{MP}{NM} = \dfrac{MO}{NO}$

$\dfrac{8.7}{6} = \dfrac{5}{NO}$

$NO \doteq 3.45$

55° ; 7.25 cm ; 35° ; 3.45 cm

7. $\dfrac{45}{5} = \dfrac{35}{a}$

$a \doteq 3.89$

$\dfrac{45}{5} = \dfrac{72}{b}$

$b = 8$

a is 3.89 cm and b is 8 cm.

8. Side length of original triangle: $\sqrt{5^2 \div 2} \doteq 3.54$

Side length of cut-out: $\sqrt{2^2 \div 2} \doteq 1.41$

$x = \dfrac{3.54 - 1.41}{2} \doteq 1.065$

x is 1.065 cm.

9a. $\dfrac{h}{1.2} = \dfrac{1 + 0.8}{0.8}$

$h = 2.7$

The height of the street light is 2.7 m.

b. $\dfrac{2.7}{1.2} = \dfrac{s + 1.5}{s}$

$s = 1.2$

Her shadow is 1.2 m.

c. $\dfrac{2.7}{1.2} = \dfrac{t + 3}{t}$

$t = 2.4$

Her shadow is 2.4 m.

10. A
$$\frac{0.54}{0.3} = \frac{l}{3.6}$$
$$l = 6.48$$
The length of the ramp is 6.48 m.

11. A
$$\frac{4}{h} = \frac{4.76}{1.36}$$
$$h \doteq 1.14$$
She is 1.14 m tall.

12. A
$$\frac{60}{15} = \frac{s}{30}$$
$$s = 120$$
Ian climbed 120 steps.

13. B
$$\frac{0.4}{0.8} = \frac{d}{0.86 + d}$$
$$d = 0.86$$
They are 0.86 m apart.

14A: $\frac{l}{14.3} = \frac{12.2}{17.4}$
$$l \doteq 10.03$$
The pencil is 10.03 cm long.

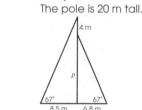

B: $\frac{a}{0.5} = \frac{0.5}{1}$
$$a = 0.25$$
$$l = \sqrt{(0.5^2 + 1^2)} + \sqrt{(0.25^2 + 0.5^2)} \doteq 1.68$$
The length of the board is 1.68 m.

C: $\frac{w}{1.4} = \frac{3}{1}$
$$w = 4.2$$
The approximated width is 4.2 m.

15. $\frac{h}{1.4} = \frac{4}{1}$
$$h = 5.6$$
The tree was 5.6 m tall.

16. $\frac{p}{p-4} = \frac{8.5}{6.8}$
$$6.8p = 8.5p - 34$$
$$p = 20$$
The pole is 20 m tall.

17. $\frac{3}{2} = \frac{x - 3.5}{3.5}$
$$x = 8.75$$
They are 8.75 m apart.

18. $\frac{h-9}{6.3} = \frac{6.3}{9}$
$$h = 13.41$$
It is 13.41 m tall.

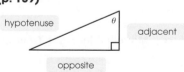

7.3 The Primary Trigonometric Ratios (1)

Try This (p. 139)

1a. BC ; $A'C'$
AC ; $B'C'$
AB ; $A'B'$

b. XY ; $Y'Z'$
YZ ; $X'Y'$
XZ ; $X'Z'$

2. GHI ; LMN
HI ; LN
GH ; MN
GI ; LM

3. $\frac{4.8}{6.2} \doteq 0.77$; $\frac{7.2}{9.3} \doteq 0.77$
$\frac{4}{6.2} \doteq 0.65$; $\frac{6}{9.3} \doteq 0.65$
$\frac{4.8}{4} = 1.2$; $\frac{7.2}{6} = 1.2$

4. $\frac{3.46}{3.6} \doteq 0.96$; $\frac{1.73}{1.8} \doteq 0.96$
$\frac{1}{3.6} \doteq 0.28$; $\frac{0.5}{1.8} \doteq 0.28$
$\frac{3.46}{1} = 3.46$; $\frac{1.73}{0.5} = 3.46$

5. Similar triangles have the same ratios of $\frac{\text{opposite}}{\text{hypotenuse}}$, $\frac{\text{adjacent}}{\text{hypotenuse}}$, and $\frac{\text{opposite}}{\text{adjacent}}$.

6. $\frac{4}{a} = 2$
$$a = 2$$
$$b = \sqrt{2^2 + 4^2} \doteq 4.47$$
2 m ; 4.47 m

7. $\frac{y}{5} = \frac{3}{5}$
$$y = 3$$
$$x = \sqrt{5^2 - 3^2} = 4$$
4 m ; 3 m

8. $\frac{5.14}{m} = 0.64$
$$m \doteq 8.03$$
$$n = \sqrt{8.03^2 - 5.14^2} \doteq 6.17$$
8.03 m ; 6.17 m

9. F   10. T   11. F
12. T   13. F

14a. $\frac{L}{8} = \frac{3}{6}$
$$L = 4$$
The ramp is 4 m long.

b. $\frac{r}{2.65} = \frac{8}{4}$
$$r = 5.3$$
The rise is 5.3 cm.

15. $s = \sqrt{1^2 + 0.15^2} \times 4 \doteq 4.04$
s is 4.04 m.

Yes, they have the same slope because the rise and run are from the similar triangles.

7.4 The Primary Trigonometric Ratios (2)

Try This (p. 142)

$$\sin \theta = \frac{DE}{DF} \qquad \cos \theta = \frac{EF}{DF} \qquad \tan \theta = \frac{DE}{EF}$$

1. 5.6 ; 6 ; 0.93 ; $\frac{2}{6}$; 0.33 ; $\frac{5.6}{2}$; 2.8

2. $\sin \theta = \frac{1.9}{2} = 0.95$
$\cos \theta = \frac{0.7}{2} = 0.35$
$\tan \theta = \frac{1.9}{0.7} \doteq 2.71$

3. $\sin \theta = \frac{5}{10.7} \doteq 0.47$
$\cos \theta = \frac{9.4}{10.7} \doteq 0.88$
$\tan \theta = \frac{5}{9.4} \doteq 0.53$

4. Ratios for a:
$\sin a = \frac{6}{19.4} \doteq 0.31$
$\cos a = \frac{18.5}{19.4} \doteq 0.95$
$\tan a = \frac{6}{18.5} \doteq 0.32$

Ratios for b:
$\sin b = \frac{18.5}{19.4} \doteq 0.95$
$\cos b = \frac{6}{19.4} \doteq 0.31$
$\tan b = \frac{18.5}{6} \doteq 3.08$

5. Ratios for x:
$\sin x = \frac{6.9}{8} \doteq 0.86$
$\cos x = \frac{4}{8} = 0.5$
$\tan x = \frac{6.9}{4} \doteq 1.73$

Ratios for y:
$\sin y = \frac{4}{8} = 0.5$
$\cos y = \frac{6.9}{8} \doteq 0.86$
$\tan y = \frac{4}{6.9} \doteq 0.58$

6. sine: 0.5 ; 0.71 ; 0.81 ; 1 ; 0.26
cosine: 0.5 ; 0.16 ; 0.26 ; 0.74 ; 0.88
tangent: 0.58 ; 0.84 ; 4.70 ; 3.73 ; 1.38 ; 1

7. 0.54 ; 0.54 ; 0.84 ; 0.65 ; 0

8. 0.64 ; 0.64 ; 0.77 ; 0.77 ; 0.84 ; 0.84

9. $\sin 25° \doteq 0.42$ $\frac{\text{opposite}}{\text{hypotenuse}} \doteq 0.42$
$\cos 25° \doteq 0.91$ $\frac{\text{adjacent}}{\text{hypotenuse}} \doteq 0.91$
$\tan 25° \doteq 0.47$ $\frac{\text{opposite}}{\text{adjacent}} \doteq 0.47$

10. $\sin 70° \doteq 0.94$ $\frac{\text{opposite}}{\text{hypotenuse}} = 0.94$
$\cos 70° \doteq 0.34$ $\frac{\text{adjacent}}{\text{hypotenuse}} \doteq 0.34$
$\tan 70° \doteq 2.75$ $\frac{\text{opposite}}{\text{adjacent}} \doteq 2.75$

ANSWERS

11. The trigonometric ratios and the specified ratios are equal.

12. It means that the opposite side and the adjacent side have the same length. So, the triangle is an isosceles triangle.

13.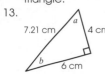

14.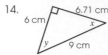

15.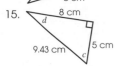

16.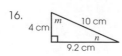

17.

18.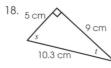

19. 2.1

20. 3.73 ; 11.19

21. 0.82 ; 8.2

22. $0.74 \doteq \frac{4}{y}$
    $y \doteq 5.41$

23. $3.08 \doteq \frac{9}{k}$
    $k \doteq 2.92$

24. $0.99 \doteq \frac{b}{10}$
    $b \doteq 9.9$

25. $0.18 \doteq \frac{j}{15}$
    $j \doteq 2.7$

26. $0.03 \doteq \frac{12}{y}$
    $y \doteq 400$

27. $0.62 \doteq \frac{n}{7}$
    $n \doteq 4.34$

28. $0.44 \doteq \frac{i}{9}$
    $i \doteq 3.96$

29. $0.38 \doteq \frac{6}{d}$
    $d \doteq 15.79$

30. $0.45 \doteq \frac{g}{20}$
    $g \doteq 9$

Try This (p. 145)

$\sin 55° = \frac{a}{4}$

$0.82 \doteq \frac{a}{4}$

$a \doteq 3.28$

31. $\cos 35° = \frac{x}{20}$
    $0.82 \doteq \frac{x}{20}$
    $x \doteq 16.4$

32. $\tan 65° = \frac{x}{4}$
    $2.14 \doteq \frac{x}{4}$
    $x \doteq 8.56$

33. $\sin 52° = \frac{6}{x}$
    $0.79 \doteq \frac{6}{x}$
    $x \doteq 7.59$

34. $\cos 75° = \frac{2}{x + 2.5}$
    $0.26 \doteq \frac{2}{x + 2.5}$
    $x \doteq 5.19$

35. $\sin 53° = \frac{x}{3}$
    $0.80 \doteq \frac{x}{3}$
    $x \doteq 2.4$

36. $\theta \doteq 53°$

37. $\theta \doteq 60°$

38. $\theta \doteq 30°$

39. $\theta \doteq 51°$

40. $\theta \doteq 73°$

41. $\theta \doteq 18°$

42. $\theta \doteq 27°$

43. $\theta \doteq 67°$

44. $\theta \doteq 48°$

Try This (p. 146)

$\tan \theta = \frac{2}{4.1}$

$\theta = \tan^{-1}\left(\frac{2}{4.1}\right)$

$\theta \doteq 26°$

$\cos \theta = \frac{1.5}{3}$

$\theta = \cos^{-1}\left(\frac{1.5}{3}\right)$

$\theta \doteq 60°$

45. A
    $\theta = \tan^{-1}\left(\frac{5}{2.66}\right)$
    $\theta \doteq 62°$

46. A
    $\theta = \sin^{-1}\left(\frac{1.88}{4}\right)$
    $\theta \doteq 28°$

47. A
    $\theta = \cos^{-1}\left(\frac{2}{4.92}\right)$
    $\theta \doteq 66°$

48. B
    $\theta = \cos^{-1}\left(\frac{6}{7.83}\right)$
    $\theta \doteq 40°$

49. A
    $\theta = \sin^{-1}\left(\frac{10}{17.88}\right)$
    $\theta \doteq 34°$

50. B
    $\theta = \cos^{-1}\left(\frac{5}{8.31}\right)$
    $\theta \doteq 53°$

51. $\tan \theta = 1$
    $\theta = \tan^{-1}(1)$
    $\theta = 45°$

52. $\tan \theta = \frac{2x}{x}$
    $\theta = \tan^{-1}(2)$
    $\theta \doteq 63°$

53. $\cos 30° = \frac{a}{8}$
    $0.87 \doteq \frac{a}{8}$
    $a \doteq 6.96$
    $\sin b = \frac{6.96}{8}$
    $b = \sin^{-1}\left(\frac{6.96}{8}\right)$
    $b \doteq 60°$
    6.96 cm ; 60°

54. $\cos 68° = \frac{1.8}{m}$
    $0.37 \doteq \frac{1.8}{m}$
    $m \doteq 4.86$
    $\sin n = \frac{1.8}{4.86}$
    $n = \sin^{-1}\left(\frac{1.8}{4.86}\right)$
    $n \doteq 22°$
    4.86 cm ; 22°

55. $\sin x = \frac{3.42}{4.6}$
    $x = \sin^{-1}\left(\frac{3.42}{4.6}\right)$
    $x \doteq 48°$
    $\cos 48° = \frac{y}{4.6}$
    $0.67 \doteq \frac{y}{4.6}$
    $y \doteq 3.08$
    48° ; 3.08 cm

56. $\tan i = \frac{6.4}{2.19}$
    $i = \tan^{-1}\left(\frac{6.4}{2.19}\right)$
    $i \doteq 71°$
    $\sin 71° = \frac{6.4}{j}$
    $0.95 \doteq \frac{6.4}{j}$
    $j \doteq 6.74$
    71° ; 6.74 cm

57. $\cos 65° = \frac{1}{p}$
    $0.42 \doteq \frac{1}{p}$
    $p \doteq 2.38$
    $\tan 65° = \frac{q}{1}$
    $2.14 \doteq \frac{q}{1}$
    $q \doteq 2.14$
    2.38 cm ; 2.14 cm

58. $\cos u = \frac{5.18}{20}$
    $u = \cos^{-1}\left(\frac{5.18}{20}\right)$
    $u \doteq 75°$
    $\sin 75° = \frac{v}{20}$
    $0.97 \doteq \frac{v}{20}$
    $v \doteq 19.4$
    75° ; 19.4 cm

59. $\sin 38° = \frac{h}{20}$
    $0.62 \doteq \frac{h}{20}$
    $h \doteq 12.4$
    14.09 cm ; 12.4 cm

    $\sin 62° = \frac{12.4}{a}$
    $0.88 \doteq \frac{12.4}{a}$
    $a \doteq 14.09$

60. $\sin 38° = \frac{3}{a}$
    $0.62 \doteq \frac{3}{a}$
    $a \doteq 4.84$
    $\tan 60° = \frac{4.84}{c}$
    $1.73 \doteq \frac{4.84}{c}$
    $c \doteq 2.80$
    4.84 cm ; 5.56 cm ; 2.80 cm

    $\sin 60° = \frac{4.84}{b}$
    $0.87 \doteq \frac{4.84}{b}$
    $b \doteq 5.56$

61. $\sin p = \frac{3}{5}$
    $p = \sin^{-1}\left(\frac{3}{5}\right)$
    $p \doteq 37°$
    37° ; 3.75 cm

    $\tan 37° = \frac{q}{5}$
    $0.75 \doteq \frac{q}{5}$
    $q \doteq 3.75$

7.5 Solving Problems Modelled by Right Triangles

1. D
   $\sin 57° = \frac{x}{2.5}$
   $0.84 \doteq \frac{x}{2.5}$
   $x \doteq 2.1$
   The entrance of the attic is 2.1 m from the floor.

2. B
   $\sin 30° = \frac{x}{2}$
   $0.5 = \frac{x}{2}$
   $x = 1$
   The slide is 1 m tall.

3. A
   $\sin 65° = \frac{x}{13}$
   $0.91 \doteq \frac{x}{13}$
   $x \doteq 11.83$
   The tree is 11.83 m tall.

4. C
   $\tan 40° = \frac{x}{2}$
   $0.84 \doteq \frac{x}{2}$
   $x \doteq 1.68$
   The squirrel has to climb 1.68 m.

ISBN: 978-1-77149-221-8

5. $\tan 36.9° = \dfrac{h-1.2}{7.6}$

$0.75 \doteq \dfrac{h-1.2}{7.6}$

$5.7 \doteq h-1.2$

$h \doteq 6.9$

The height of the flagpole is 6.9 m.

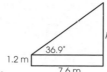

6. $\tan 23.75° = \dfrac{t-1.4}{5}$

$0.44 \doteq \dfrac{t-1.4}{5}$

$2.2 \doteq t-1.4$

$t \doteq 3.6$

The treehouse is 3.6 m from the ground.

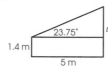

7. $\tan 30° = \dfrac{2.6}{d}$ $\tan 41° = \dfrac{h-2.6}{4.48}$

$0.58 \doteq \dfrac{2.6}{d}$ $0.87 \doteq \dfrac{h-2.6}{4.48}$

$d \doteq 4.48$ $h \doteq 6.50$

The ceiling is 6.5 m high.

8. $\cos 40° = \dfrac{k}{40}$ $\cos 50° = \dfrac{j}{40}$

$0.77 \doteq \dfrac{k}{40}$ $0.64 \doteq \dfrac{j}{40}$

$k \doteq 30.8$ $j \doteq 25.6$

$k - j = 30.8 - 25.6 = 5.2$

Jane's house is closer to the park by 5.2 km.

9. $\tan 48° = \dfrac{d}{2.7}$

$1.11 \doteq \dfrac{d}{2.7}$

$d \doteq 3$

The vertical distance is 3 m.

10. $\tan x = \dfrac{60-1.4}{15}$

$x = \tan^{-1}\left(\dfrac{60-1.4}{15}\right)$

$x \doteq 76°$

The angle of elevation is 76°.

11. $\tan 3° = \dfrac{e-1.48}{1.2}$

$0.05 \doteq \dfrac{e-1.48}{1.2}$

$e \doteq 1.54$

Ella is 1.54 m tall.

12. $\tan a = \dfrac{3}{2}$

$a = \tan^{-1}\left(\dfrac{3}{2}\right)$

$a \doteq 56°$

bearing: $360° - 56° = 304°$

The bearing is 304°.

13.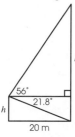

a. $\tan 21.8° = \dfrac{h}{20}$

$0.4 \doteq \dfrac{h}{20}$

$h \doteq 8$

The height is 8 m.

b. $\tan 56° = \dfrac{b-8}{20}$

$1.48 \doteq \dfrac{b-8}{20}$

$b \doteq 37.6$

The height is 37.6 m.

14.

a. $\tan 82.4° = \dfrac{d-2.4}{6}$

$7.49 \doteq \dfrac{d-2.4}{6}$

$d \doteq 47.34$

The dog is 47.34 m above the ground.

b. $\tan 66° = \dfrac{c-2.4}{6}$

$2.25 \doteq \dfrac{c-2.4}{6}$

$c \doteq 15.9$

The cat is 15.9 m above the ground.

8 Acute Triangle Trigonometry

8.1 The Sine Law

Try This (p. 152)

$\dfrac{15.4}{\sin 38°} = \dfrac{c}{\sin 64°}$

$\dfrac{15.4}{0.62} \doteq \dfrac{c}{0.9}$

$c \doteq 22.35$

22.35 cm

1. 16.83 cm   2. 8.31 cm   3. 2.78 cm
4. 80°   5. 66°   6. 67°
7. 6.00 m ; 6.39 m   8. 6.68 cm ; 5.29 cm   9. 10.09 cm ; 9.15 cm
10. 1.75 m ; 2.16 m   11. 4.60 cm ; 6.27 cm   12. 15.47 cm ; 10.35 cm
13. 3.77 m ; 7.08 m   14. 8.42 cm ; 7.05 cm   15. 14.70 cm ; 16.47 cm
16. 50° ; 90°   17. 73° ; 32°   18. 54° ; 36°
19. 75° ; 57°   20. 72° ; 55°   21. 43° ; 73°
22. 31° ; 35°   23. 35° ; 43°   24. 35° ; 19°
25. 57° ; 76°

26. $\dfrac{4}{\sin \theta} = \dfrac{4.5}{\sin 50°}$

$\theta \doteq 43°$

$\alpha = 180° - 50° - 43° = 87°$

$\dfrac{y}{\sin 87°} = \dfrac{4.5}{\sin 50°}$

$y \doteq 5.87$

87° ; 43° ; 5.87 cm

27. $\dfrac{y}{\sin 50°} = \dfrac{15}{\sin 68°}$

$y \doteq 12.39$

$\theta = 180° - 50° - 68° = 62°$

$\dfrac{x}{\sin 62°} = \dfrac{15}{\sin 68°}$

$x \doteq 14.28$

62° ; 14.28 cm ; 12.39 cm

28. $\dfrac{7.8}{\sin \theta} = \dfrac{8.3}{\sin 64°}$

$\theta \doteq 58°$

$\alpha = 180° - (180° - 116°) - 58°$

$= 58°$

$\dfrac{y}{\sin 58°} = \dfrac{7.8}{\sin 58°}$

$y \doteq 7.8$

58° ; 58° ; 7.8 cm

29. $\dfrac{x}{\sin 70°} = \dfrac{6.2}{\sin 42°}$

$x \doteq 8.71$

$\dfrac{y}{\sin 68°} = \dfrac{6.2}{\sin 42°}$

$y \doteq 8.59$

$\dfrac{7.6}{\sin 58°} = \dfrac{8.71}{\sin 65°}$

$\theta \doteq 52°$

52° ; 8.71 cm ; 8.59 cm

30. $\dfrac{x}{\sin 50°} = \dfrac{19.4}{\sin 65°}$

$x \doteq 16.40$

$\dfrac{y}{\sin 115°} = \dfrac{10}{\sin 21°}$

$y \doteq 25.29$

$\theta = 180° - 115° - 21° = 44°$

44° ; 16.40 cm ; 25.29 cm

8.2 Solving Problems Using the Sine Law

1. $\dfrac{b}{\sin 65°} = \dfrac{15}{\sin 70°}$ $\dfrac{c}{\sin 45°} = \dfrac{15}{\sin 70°}$

$b \doteq 14.47$ $c \doteq 11.29$

$b = 14.47$ cm, $c = 11.29$ cm, $\angle C = 45°$

2. $\dfrac{p}{\sin 71°} = \dfrac{8.4}{\sin 42°}$ $\dfrac{r}{\sin 67°} = \dfrac{8.4}{\sin 42°}$

$p \doteq 11.87$ $r \doteq 11.56$

$p = 11.87$ cm, $r = 11.56$ cm, $\angle P = 71°$

3. $\dfrac{b}{\sin 47°} = \dfrac{5}{\sin 51°}$ $\dfrac{c}{\sin 82°} = \dfrac{5}{\sin 51°}$

$b \doteq 4.71$ $c \doteq 6.37$

$b = 4.71$ cm, $c = 6.37$ cm, $\angle A = 51°$

4. $\dfrac{10}{\sin R} = \dfrac{12}{\sin 76°}$ $\dfrac{p}{\sin 50°} = \dfrac{12}{\sin 76°}$

$R \doteq 54°$ $p \doteq 9.47$

$\angle P = 180° - 76° - 54° = 50°$

$p = 9.47$ cm, $\angle P = 50°$, $\angle R = 54°$

5.

She is correct.

Applying the sine law:

$\dfrac{a}{\sin A} = \dfrac{b}{\sin B}$

$a \sin B = b \sin A$

ISBN: 978-1-77149-221-8

6. Sine law in any acute triangle: $\dfrac{a}{\sin A} = \dfrac{b}{\sin B} = \dfrac{c}{\sin C}$

$\dfrac{a}{\sin A} = \dfrac{b}{\sin B}$ $\dfrac{b}{\sin B} = \dfrac{c}{\sin C}$

$a \sin B = b \sin A$ $b \sin C = c \sin B$

$\dfrac{\sin B}{b} = \dfrac{\sin A}{a}$ $\dfrac{\sin C}{c} = \dfrac{\sin B}{b}$

$\therefore \dfrac{\sin A}{a} = \dfrac{\sin B}{b} = \dfrac{\sin C}{c}$

7. To calculate an unknown side length (b), she needs the measures of at least 1 side and 2 angles where one of them is opposite the unknown side.

$\dfrac{a}{\sin A} = \dfrac{\boxed{b}}{\sin B}$

To calculate an angle measure (B), she needs the measures of at least 2 sides and 1 angle opposite one of the sides.

$\dfrac{a}{\sin A} = \dfrac{b}{\boxed{\sin B}}$

8. In △ABD,
$\sin B = \dfrac{AD}{c}$
$AD = c \sin B$
$\therefore c \sin B = b \sin C$
$\dfrac{c}{\sin C} = \dfrac{b}{\sin B}$

    In △ACD,
$\sin C = \dfrac{AD}{b}$
$AD = b \sin C$

In △AEB,
$\sin A = \dfrac{BE}{c}$
$BE = c \sin A$
$\therefore c \sin A = a \sin C$
$\dfrac{c}{\sin C} = \dfrac{a}{\sin A}$

    In △BEC,
$\sin C = \dfrac{BE}{a}$
$BE = a \sin C$

$\therefore \dfrac{a}{\sin A} = \dfrac{b}{\sin B} = \dfrac{c}{\sin C}$ All the ratios are equal.

9. $\dfrac{p}{\sin 40°} = \dfrac{18}{\sin 70°}$ $\dfrac{r}{\sin 30°} = \dfrac{16}{\sin 75°}$ $\dfrac{s}{\sin 90°} = \dfrac{10}{\sin 45°}$

$p \doteq 12.31$ $r \doteq 8.28$ $s \doteq 14.14$

The rhombus has the shortest diagonal.

10a. 84° ; 23 cm ; 50° ; 32 cm   b. 54° ; 19 cm ; 14 cm
   c. 52° ; 19 cm ; 95° ; 22 cm

11. $48.75 = \dfrac{1}{2} \times BC \times 5$ $\dfrac{19.5}{\sin 65°} = \dfrac{AB}{\sin 38°}$ $\dfrac{19.5}{\sin 65°} = \dfrac{AC}{\sin 77°}$

$BC = 19.5$ $AB \doteq 13.25$ $AC \doteq 20.96$

Perimeter: $19.5 + 13.25 + 20.96 = 53.71$
The perimeter is 53.71 cm.

12. $\dfrac{a}{\sin 58°} = \dfrac{18}{\sin 75°}$ $\dfrac{b}{\sin 47°} = \dfrac{18}{\sin 75°}$

$a \doteq 15.80$ $b \doteq 13.63$

Swimmer B is closer to the starfish.

13. $\dfrac{j}{\sin 38°} = \dfrac{150}{\sin 70°}$ $\dfrac{s}{\sin 72°} = \dfrac{150}{\sin 70°}$

$j \doteq 98.28$ $s \doteq 151.81$

Joe is 98.28 m away from the ship and Sue is 151.81 m away.

14. $\dfrac{x}{\sin 45°} = \dfrac{125}{\sin 50°}$

$x \doteq 115.38$

Airplane B is 115.38 km away from the airport.

15. $\dfrac{x}{\sin 60.5°} = \dfrac{12}{\sin 52°}$

$x \doteq 13.25$

The airplanes are 13.25 km apart.

16. $\dfrac{12}{\sin 75°} = \dfrac{x}{\sin 43°}$ $\dfrac{8.47}{\sin 85°} = \dfrac{y}{\sin 70°}$

$x \doteq 8.47$ $y \doteq 7.99$

Ship B is 7.99 km from the port.

17. $\dfrac{b}{\sin 49°} = \dfrac{125}{\sin 84°}$ $\dfrac{a}{\sin 47°} = \dfrac{125}{\sin 84°}$

$b \doteq 94.86$ $a \doteq 91.92$

Bird A is closer to the nest.

18. Length of the rope: $23 \times 4 = 92$
6:8:9:23 = 24:32:36:92
∴ The side lengths are 24 cm, 32 cm, and 36 cm.

$\dfrac{32}{\sin \theta} = \dfrac{36}{\sin 78.6°}$
$\theta \doteq 60.6°$
$\alpha = 180° - 78.6° - 60.6° = 40.8°$
The angles are 60.6° and 40.8°.

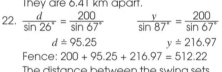

19.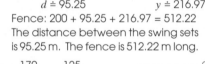

$\dfrac{40 - 2y}{\sin 50°} = \dfrac{y}{\sin 65°}$ $\dfrac{40 - 2y}{\sin 80°} = \dfrac{y}{\sin 50°}$
$0.91(40 - 2y) \doteq 0.77y$ $0.77(40 - 2y) \doteq 0.98y$
$y \doteq 14.05$ $y \doteq 12.22$

The side lengths are 14.05 cm, 14.05 cm, and 11.9 cm.   The side lengths are 12.22 cm, 12.22 cm, and 15.56 cm.

20. $\dfrac{4}{\sin \theta} = \dfrac{3.7}{\sin 71°}$
$\sin \theta \doteq 1.02$ ← no possible solutions
No triangles can be formed with the given measurements.

21. Distance travelled by Sam in 5 min:
$\dfrac{60 \text{ km}}{60 \text{ min}} \times 5 \text{ min} = 5 \text{ km}$
$\dfrac{d}{\sin 65°} = \dfrac{5}{\sin 45°}$
$d \doteq 6.41$
They are 6.41 km apart.

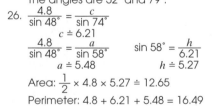

22. $\dfrac{d}{\sin 26°} = \dfrac{200}{\sin 67°}$ $\dfrac{y}{\sin 87°} = \dfrac{200}{\sin 67°}$
$d \doteq 95.25$ $y \doteq 216.97$
Fence: $200 + 95.25 + 216.97 = 512.22$
The distance between the swing sets is 95.25 m. The fence is 512.22 m long.

23. $\dfrac{170}{\sin 55°} = \dfrac{125}{\sin \theta}$
$\theta \doteq 37°$
The angle formed is 37°.

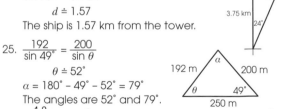

24. Distance travelled in 15 min: $15 \div 4 = 3.75$ (km)
$\dfrac{3.75}{\sin 76°} = \dfrac{d}{\sin 24°}$
$d \doteq 1.57$
The ship is 1.57 km from the tower.

25. $\dfrac{192}{\sin 49°} = \dfrac{200}{\sin \theta}$
$\theta \doteq 52°$
$\alpha = 180° - 49° - 52° = 79°$
The angles are 52° and 79°.

26. $\dfrac{4.8}{\sin 48°} = \dfrac{c}{\sin 74°}$
$c \doteq 6.21$
$\dfrac{4.8}{\sin 48°} = \dfrac{a}{\sin 58°}$ $\sin 58° = \dfrac{h}{6.21}$
$a \doteq 5.48$ $h \doteq 5.27$

Area: $\dfrac{1}{2} \times 4.8 \times 5.27 \doteq 12.65$
Perimeter: $4.8 + 6.21 + 5.48 = 16.49$
The area is 12.65 cm² and the perimeter is 16.49 cm.

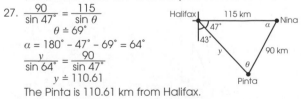

27. $\dfrac{90}{\sin 47°} = \dfrac{115}{\sin \theta}$
$\theta \doteq 69°$
$\alpha = 180° - 47° - 69° = 64°$
$\dfrac{y}{\sin 64°} = \dfrac{90}{\sin 47°}$
$y \doteq 110.61$
The Pinta is 110.61 km from Halifax.

28.

P

7.8 cm   9 cm ≤ q ≤ 10.2 cm

72°

Q R

If q = 9 cm,
$$\frac{9}{\sin 72°} = \frac{7.8}{\sin R}$$
$R \doteq 56°$

If q = 10.2 cm,
$$\frac{10.2}{\sin 72°} = \frac{7.8}{\sin R}$$
$R \doteq 47°$

The greatest measure of $\angle R$ is 56° when q is 9 cm.

29. Kevin 450 m Wayne

60° 72°

x 48° y

$$\frac{450}{\sin 48°} = \frac{x}{\sin 72°}$$
$x \doteq 575.90$
$$\frac{450}{\sin 48°} = \frac{y}{\sin 60°}$$
$y \doteq 524.41$

Kevin is 575.9 m from the nest and Wayne is 524.41 m from it.

8.3 The Cosine Law

Try This (p. 162)

$c^2 = 5^2 + 5^2 - 2(5)(5) \cos 50°$
$c^2 \doteq 17.86$
$c \doteq 4.23$

The length of c is about 4.23 cm.

1. B
$x^2 \doteq 56.74$
$x \doteq 7.53$

2. A
$s^2 \doteq 3.61$
$s \doteq 1.9$

3. B
$m^2 \doteq 38.29$
$m \doteq 6.19$

4. A
$y^2 \doteq 323.97$
$y \doteq 18$

5. B
$p^2 \doteq 108.33$
$p \doteq 10.41$

6. Circle: A, C, E, F, G

Triangle A: $x^2 = 6^2 + 5.8^2 - 2(6)(5.8) \cos 33°$
$x^2 \doteq 11.27$
$x \doteq 3.36$

Triangle C: $6^2 = 6^2 + 3.21^2 - 2(6)(3.21) \cos a$
$-10.3041 = -38.52 \cos a$
$\cos a = 0.2675$
$a = \cos^{-1} (0.2675)$
$a \doteq 75°$

Triangle E: $y^2 = 4^2 + 8.5^2 - 2(4)(8.5) \cos 78°$
$y^2 \doteq 74.11$
$y \doteq 8.61$

Triangle F: $5^2 = 3.89^2 + 3.89^2 - 2(3.89)(3.89) \cos n$
$-5.2642 = -30.2642 \cos n$
$\cos n \doteq 0.17$
$n \doteq \cos^{-1} (0.17)$
$n \doteq 80°$

Triangle G: $8.5^2 = 6.5^2 + 7.7^2 - 2(6.5)(7.7) \cos i$
$-29.29 = -100.1 \cos i$
$\cos i \doteq 0.29$
$i \doteq \cos^{-1} (0.29)$
$i \doteq 73°$

7. $BC^2 = 6^2 + 5^2 - 2(6)(5) \cos 89°$
$BC^2 \doteq 59.95$
$BC \doteq 7.74$
$5^2 = 6^2 + 7.74^2 - 2(6)(7.74) \cos B$
$\cos B \doteq 0.76$
$B \doteq 40°$
7.74 cm ; 40°

8. $13^2 = 12.5^2 + 6^2 - 2(12.5)(6) \cos R$
$\cos R = 0.155$
$R \doteq 81°$
$6^2 = 12.5^2 + 13^2 - 2(12.5)(13) \cos Q$
$\cos Q = 0.89$
$Q \doteq 27°$
81° ; 27°

9. $YZ^2 = 5.7^2 + 10^2 - 2(5.7)(10) \cos 66°$
$YZ^2 \doteq 86.12$
$YZ \doteq 9.28$
$5.7^2 = 10^2 + 9.28^2 - 2(10)(9.28) \cos Z$
$\cos Z \doteq 0.83$
$Z \doteq 34°$
9.28 cm ; 34°

10. $EF^2 = 9^2 + 7.72^2 - 2(9)(7.72) \cos 33°$
$EF^2 \doteq 24.06$
$EF \doteq 4.91$
$7.72^2 = 9^2 + 4.91^2 - 2(9)(4.91) \cos E$
$\cos E \doteq 0.51$
$E \doteq 59°$
4.91 cm ; 59°

11. $MN^2 = 5.6^2 + 7.4^2 - 2(5.6)(7.4) \cos 54°$
$MN^2 \doteq 37.40$
$MN \doteq 6.12$
$5.6^2 = 7.4^2 + 6.12^2 - 2(7.4)(6.12) \cos M$
$\cos M \doteq 0.67$
$M \doteq 48°$
6.12 cm ; 48°

12. $RT^2 = 6.2^2 + 7^2 - 2(6.2)(7) \cos 57°$
$RT^2 \doteq 40.17$
$RT \doteq 6.34$
$7^2 = 6.2^2 + 6.34^2 - 2(6.2)(6.34) \cos R$
$\cos R \doteq 0.38$
$R \doteq 68°$
68° ; 6.34 cm

13. $8.5^2 = 8^2 + 5.1^2 - 2(8)(5.1) \cos I$
$\cos I \doteq 0.22$
$I \doteq 77°$
$8^2 = 8.5^2 + 5.1^2 - 2(8.5)(5.1) \cos J$
$\cos J \doteq 0.40$
$J \doteq 66°$
77° ; 66°

14. $9.2^2 = 8.8^2 + 5^2 - 2(8.8)(5) \cos V$
$\cos V \doteq 0.20$
$V \doteq 78°$
$8.8^2 = 9.2^2 + 5^2 - 2(9.2)(5) \cos W$
$\cos W = 0.35$
$W \doteq 70°$
78° ; 70°

15. Yes   16. No   17. Yes
18. Yes   19. No   20. Yes
21a. $\angle A$; c b. b ; a and c
22a. $b^2 = 7^2 + 16^2 - 2(7)(16) \cos 90°$
$b^2 = 305$
$b \doteq 17.46$

b. The cosine law is identical to the Pythagorean theorem when the angle in the cosine law is a right angle. This is because cos 90° is 0.

8.4 Solving Problems Using the Cosine Law

Try This (p. 166)

$DE^2 = 5^2 + 4.3^2 - 2(5)(4.3) \cos 35°$
$DE^2 \doteq 8.27$
$DE \doteq 2.88$
The length of DE is 2.88 cm.

1. $XZ^2 = 4^2 + 3.16^2 - 2(4)(3.16) \cos 40°$
$XZ^2 \doteq 6.62$
$XZ \doteq 2.57$

2. $LM^2 = 12^2 + 15.66^2 - 2(12)(15.66) \cos 65°$
$LM^2 \doteq 230.40$
$LM \doteq 15.18$

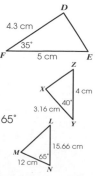

3. $6^2 = 7^2 + 4.5^2 - 2(7)(4.5) \cos I$
    $\cos I \doteq 0.53$
    $I \doteq 58°$

4. $5^2 = 12.5^2 + 12^2 - 2(12.5)(12) \cos P$
    $\cos P \doteq 0.9175$
    $P \doteq 23°$

5. $x^2 = 8^2 + 5.4^2 - 2(8)(5.4) \cos 37°$
    $x^2 \doteq 24.16$
    $x \doteq 4.92$
    $5.4^2 = 4.92^2 + 8^2 - 2(4.92)(8) \cos y$
    $\cos y \doteq 0.75$
    $y \doteq 41°$
    4.92 cm ; 41°

6. $a^2 = 4.5^2 + 4.1^2 - 2(4.5)(4.1) \cos 84°$
    $a^2 \doteq 33.20$
    $a \doteq 5.76$
    $5.76^2 = 6^2 + 6^2 - 2(6)(6) \cos b$
    $\cos b \doteq 0.5392$
    $b \doteq 57°$
    5.76 cm ; 57°

7. $m^2 = 6^2 + 4.1^2 - 2(6)(4.1) \cos 68°$
    $m^2 \doteq 34.38$
    $m \doteq 5.86$
    $9^2 = 7.5^2 + 5.86^2 - 2(7.5)(5.86) \cos n$
    $\cos n \doteq 0.11$
    $n \doteq 84°$
    5.86 cm ; 84°

8. $13^2 = 10.9^2 + 13.8^2 - 2(10.9)(13.8) \cos i$
    $\cos i \doteq 0.47$
    $i \doteq 62°$
    $j^2 = 4.5^2 + 3^2 - 2(4.5)(3) \cos 62°$
    $j^2 \doteq 16.57$
    $j \doteq 4.07$
    62° ; 4.07 cm

9. $r^2 = 6.9^2 + 9^2 - 2(6.9)(9) \cos 41°$
    $r^2 \doteq 34.88$
    $r \doteq 5.91$
    $(5.91 + 8.69)^2 = (6.9 + 2.5)^2 + 17.3^2 - 2(6.9 + 2.5)(17.3) \cos s$
    $\cos s \doteq 0.54$
    $s \doteq 57°$
    5.91 cm ; 57°

10. $p^2 = 7^2 + 12^2 - 2(7)(12) \cos 54°$
    $p^2 \doteq 94.25$
    $p \doteq 9.71$
    $q^2 = 12^2 + (4.23 + 9.71)^2 - 2(12)(4.23 + 9.71) \cos 36°$
    $q^2 \doteq 67.66$
    $q \doteq 8.23$
    9.71 cm ; 8.23 cm

11. $5^2 = 8^2 + 8^2 - 2(8)(8) \cos a$
    $\cos a \doteq 0.8047$
    $a \doteq 36°$
    $8^2 = 8^2 + 5^2 - 2(8)(5) \cos b$
    $\cos b \doteq 0.3125$
    $b \doteq 72°$
    The measures of its angles are 36°, 72°, and 72°.

12. $x^2 = 3^2 + 7^2 - 2(3)(7) \cos 68°$
    $x^2 \doteq 42.27$
    $x \doteq 6.50$
    The lengths of each triangle are
    3 cm, 6.5 cm, and 7 cm.

13. $5^2 = 5^2 + 3^2 - 2(5)(3) \cos A$
    $\cos A = 0.3$
    $A \doteq 73°$
    The measure of $\angle A$ is 73°.

14. $c^2 = 4^2 + 4^2 - 2(4)(4) \cos 30°$
    $c^2 \doteq 4.29$
    $c \doteq 2.07$
    $2.07^2 = 6^2 + 6^2 - 2(6)(6) \cos a$
    $\cos a \doteq 0.94$
    $a \doteq 20°$
    $b = (180° - 20°) \div 2 = 80°$
    The measure of the angles in the
    big triangle are 20°, 80°, and 80°.

15a. $9.18^2 = 12^2 + 12^2 - 2(12)(12) \cos a$
    $\cos a \doteq 0.71$
    $a \doteq 45°$
    $b = (180° - 45°) \div 2 = 67.5°$
    The measures of the angles are 45°, 67.5°, and 67.5°.

  b. $(n - 2) \times 180° = n \times (b + b)$
    $180n - 360° = 135n$
    $45n = 360°$
    $n = 8$
    The polygon has 8 sides.

16. $7.32^2 = 4.5^2 + 6^2 - 2(4.5)(6) \cos a$
    $\cos a = 0.05$
    $a \doteq 87°$
    Melissa should shoot within 87° to score.

17. $x^2 = 11^2 + 7^2 - 2(11)(7) \cos 45°$
    $x^2 \doteq 61.11$
    $x \doteq 7.82$
    The distance is 7.82 cm.

18. $d^2 = 14^2 + 14^2 - 2(14)(14) \cos 62°$
    $d^2 \doteq 207.97$
    $d \doteq 14.42$
    The width of the ravine is 14.42 m.

19. $d^2 = 150^2 + 199^2 - 2(150)(199) \cos 65°$
    $d^2 \doteq 36\,870.69$
    $d \doteq 192.02$
    Ada and Ellen are 192.02 m apart.

20. $l^2 = 1^2 + 1.1^2 - 2(1)(1.1) \cos 81°$
    $l^2 \doteq 1.87$
    $l \doteq 1.37$
    The stick is 1.37 m long.

21. $35^2 = x^2 + x^2 - 2(x)(x) \cos 70°$
    $1225 \doteq 2x^2 - 0.68x^2$
    $1225 \doteq 1.32x^2$
    $x^2 \doteq 928.03$
    $x \doteq 30.46$
    Each island is 30.46 km away from the treasure chest.

22. $3^2 = 2.5^2 + 2^2 - 2(2.5)(2) \cos a$
    $\cos a = 0.125$
    $a \doteq 83°$
    The measure of the largest angle is 83°.

23. $d^2 = 18^2 + 30^2 - 2(18)(30) \cos (30° + 50°)$
    $d^2 \doteq 1036.46$
    $d \doteq 32.19$
    The stands are 32.19 m apart.

24. Amy's distance: $60 \times 2 = 120$
    Juno's distance: $70 \times 2 = 140$
    $d^2 = 120^2 + 140^2 - 2(120)(140) \cos 80°$
    $d^2 \doteq 28\,165.42$
    $d \doteq 167.83$
    They will be 167.83 km apart.

25. $d^2 = 12^2 + 16^2 - 2(12)(16) \cos 36°$
    $d^2 \doteq 89.34$
    $d \doteq 9.45$
    The girls are 9.45 m apart.

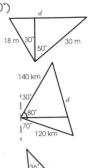

26. $d^2 = 50^2 + 50^2 - 2(50)(50) \cos 110°$
   $d^2 \doteq 6710.10$
   $d \doteq 81.92$
   The dolphins are 81.92 m apart.

27. $d^2 = 2^2 + 10^2 - 2(2)(10) \cos 36°$
   $d^2 \doteq 71.64$
   $d \doteq 8.46$
   Andrei ran 8.46 km.

28. $x^2 = 1^2 + 2.5^2 - 2(1)(2.5) \cos 67°$
   $x^2 \doteq 5.30$
   $x \doteq 2.30$
   Perimeter: $1 + 2.5 + 2.3 = 5.8$
   The perimeter of the flag is 5.8 m.

29. $\frac{x}{4} = \sin 73.4°$
   $x = 4 \sin 73.4°$
   $x \doteq 3.83$
   Area: $3.83 \times 7 = 26.81$
   The area of the parallelogram is 26.81 cm².

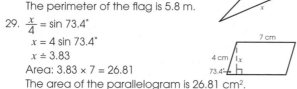

8.5 Applying the Sine Law and the Cosine Law

Try This (p. 172)
$XY^2 = 4.6^2 + 5^2 - 2(4.6)(5) \cos 47°$
$XY^2 \doteq 14.79$
$XY \doteq 3.85$
The length of XY is 3.85 cm.

1. B
   $3^2 = 5.18^2 + 5.07^2 - 2(5.18)(5.07) \cos C$
   $\cos C \doteq 0.83$
   $C \doteq 34°$

2. A
   $\frac{DE}{\sin 41°} = \frac{4.8}{\sin 60°}$
   $DE \doteq 3.64$

3. B
   $5.8^2 = 5.2^2 + 3^2 - 2(5.2)(3) \cos P$
   $\cos P \doteq 0.08$
   $P \doteq 85°$

4. A
   $\frac{MN}{\sin 26°} = \frac{4.8}{\sin 85°}$
   $MN \doteq 2.11$

5. A
   $\frac{3.7}{\sin J} = \frac{8.1}{\sin 82°}$
   $\sin J \doteq 0.45$
   $J \doteq 27°$

6. B
   $VW^2 = 6^2 + 6.1^2 - 2(6)(6.1) \cos 85°$
   $VW^2 \doteq 66.83$
   $VW \doteq 8.17$

7. $\frac{x}{\sin 68°} = \frac{10}{\sin 57°}$
   $x \doteq 11.06$
   $y^2 = 11.06^2 + 9.54^2 - 2(11.06)(9.54) \cos 70°$
   $y^2 \doteq 141.16$
   $y \doteq 11.88$

8. $\frac{x}{\sin 64°} = \frac{6}{\sin 84°}$
   $x \doteq 5.42$
   $5.42^2 = 4.67^2 + 6.17^2 - 2(4.67)(6.17) \cos y$
   $\cos y \doteq 0.53$
   $y \doteq 58°$

9. $x^2 = 8^2 + 5.86^2 - 2(8)(5.86) \cos 60°$
   $x^2 \doteq 51.4596$
   $x \doteq 7.17$
   $\frac{6.46}{\sin y} = \frac{7.17}{\sin 74°}$
   $\sin y \doteq 0.87$
   $y \doteq 60°$

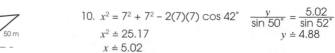

10. $x^2 = 7^2 + 7^2 - 2(7)(7) \cos 42°$ $\frac{y}{\sin 50°} = \frac{5.02}{\sin 52°}$
   $x^2 \doteq 25.17$ $y \doteq 4.88$
   $x \doteq 5.02$

11. $5^2 = 5.74^2 + 4.17^2 - 2(5.74)(4.17) \cos x$
   $\cos x \doteq 0.53$
   $x \doteq 58°$
   $y^2 = 5.74^2 + 5.74^2 - 2(5.74)(5.74) \cos (90° - 58°)$
   $y^2 \doteq 10.01$
   $y \doteq 3.16$

12. $\frac{2}{\sin x} = \frac{1.79}{\sin 60°}$ $2.69^2 = 2^2 + 1.9^2 - 2(2)(1.9) \cos y$
   $\sin x \doteq 0.97$ $\cos y \doteq 0.05$
   $x \doteq 76°$ $y \doteq 87°$

13a. $DE^2 = 5^2 + 6^2 - 2(5)(6) \cos 48°$
    $DE^2 \doteq 20.85$
    $DE \doteq 4.57$

  b. $BC^2 = 10^2 + 12^2 - 2(10)(12) \cos 48°$
    $BC^2 \doteq 83.41$
    $BC \doteq 9.13$
    $\frac{10}{\sin C} = \frac{9.13}{\sin 48°}$
    $\sin C \doteq 0.81$
    $C \doteq 54°$

14a. $10^2 = XZ^2 + XY^2 - 2(XZ)(XY) \cos 40°$
    $100 \doteq 2XY^2 - 1.53XY^2$
    $XY \doteq 14.59$

  b. $XM^2 = 14.59^2 - 5^2$
    $XM \doteq 13.71$
    Area: $10 \times 13.71 \div 2 = 68.55$

15. $2.7^2 = 3.1^2 + 1.8^2 - 2(3.1)(1.8) \cos \theta$
   $\cos \theta \doteq 0.50$
   $\theta \doteq 60°$
   The angle of the routes diverged at the theatre is 60°.

16. $l^2 = 21^2 + 18^2 - 2(21)(18) \cos 83°$
   $l^2 \doteq 672.87$
   $l \doteq 25.94$
   The length of the picture is 25.94 cm.

17. Last angle: $180° - 80° - 63° = 37°$
   $\frac{2.5}{\sin 63°} = \frac{l}{\sin 37°}$
   $l \doteq 1.69$
   The length of the stairs is 1.69 m.

18. $\frac{d}{\sin 60°} = \frac{10}{\sin 35°}$
   $d \doteq 15.10$
   Difference: $15.1 - 10 = 5.1$
   Lifeguard B was 5.1 m closer than Lifeguard A.

19. $2.86^2 = 3^2 + 1.67^2 - 2(3)(1.67) \cos \angle COD$
   $\cos \angle COD \doteq 0.36$
   $\angle COD \doteq 69°$
   $\frac{AB}{\sin 69°} = \frac{2.5}{\sin 83°}$
   $AB \doteq 2.35$
   Students A and B are 2.35 m apart.

20. $a^2 = 6^2 + 6^2 - 2(6)(6) \cos 70°$
   $a^2 \doteq 47.37$
   $a \doteq 6.88$
   $\frac{b}{\sin 53°} = \frac{7.96}{\sin 90°}$
   $b \doteq 6.36$
   Height: $a + b = 6.88 + 6.36 = 13.24$
   The height of the wooden tower is 13.24 cm.

21. $24^2 = 20^2 + 18^2 - 2(20)(18) \cos a$
   $\cos a \doteq 0.21$
   $a \doteq 78°$
   $a + b = 180°$
   $b = 102°$
   The sizes of the angles are 78°, 102°, 78°, and 102°.

ISBN: 978-1-77149-221-8

22. $\tan 27° = \dfrac{h}{10}$

$h = 10 \tan 27°$

$h \doteq 5.10$

$\tan 29° = \dfrac{h+c}{10}$

$h + c = 10 \tan 29°$

$c = 10 \tan 29° - 5.1$

$c \doteq 0.44$

The chimney is 0.44 m tall.

23. $2.2^2 = l^2 + l^2 - 2(l)(l) \cos 75°$

$4.84 \doteq 2l^2 - 0.52l^2$

$4.84 \doteq 1.48l^2$

$l \doteq 1.81$

The length of the swing is 1.81 m.

24. $d^2 = 10^2 + 5^2 - 2(10)(5) \cos 35°$

$d^2 \doteq 43.08$

$d \doteq 6.56$

Ken is 6.56 km away from home.

25. $\dfrac{x}{\sin 85°} = \dfrac{53}{\sin 56°}$

$x \doteq 63.69$

$\dfrac{y}{\sin 39°} = \dfrac{63.69}{\sin 90°}$

$y \doteq 40.08$

Stanley's house and the building are 40.08 m apart.

Cumulative Review

1a. B ; C b. B c. D d. C e. A

2a. A b. B ; C c. C

3. C 4. A 5. C 6. C

7a. B b. C 8. C 9. A ; B

10a. A b. C c. D

11. T 12. T 13. F 14. F 15. T

16. T 17. T

18. $2(x - 4)(x + 1)$

19. $-12(x + 1)^2$

20. $(b - 6)(b + 6)$

21. $(a - 2)(a + 2)(a^2 + 4)$

22. $\dfrac{1}{6}(x - 6)(x + 3)$

23. $(3a^3 + 1)(a^3 - 2)$

24a. $y = \dfrac{1}{2}x + 3$ b. $y = -2x - 1$ c. $y = \dfrac{2}{5}x - 2$

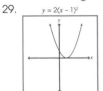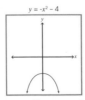

25. The centroid is at (-5,-2).

26. The orthocentre is at (0,3).

27. The area of $\triangle PQR$ is 3 square units.

28. $IK = 12.5$, $JK = 10$, $IJ = 7.5$, $IJ \perp JK$

$\triangle IJK$ is a right scalene triangle.

29. $y = 2(x - 1)^2$ $y = -2x^2 - x + 1$ $y = -x^2 - 4$

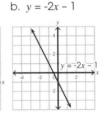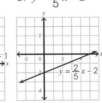

30a. $y = 2(x - 1)^2$ has a minimum because the parabola opens upward.

b. $y = -x^2 - 4$ has no solutions because the parabola does not intersect the x-axis.

31. $y = -2x^2 + 4$ 32. $y = 0.5(x + 5)^2 - 4.5$

33. $y = -\dfrac{1}{5}(x - 3)^2 + 5$ 34. $y = -(x + 2)^2 + 4$

35. $y = -\dfrac{7}{16}(x - 4)^2 + 7$ 36. $y = 20(x - \dfrac{5}{2})^2 - 5$

37. $a \doteq 3.44$ cm 38. $r \doteq 2.47$ cm

$b \doteq 4.06$ cm $s \doteq 22°$

39. $p \doteq 50°$ 40. $x = 6$ cm

$q \doteq 78°$ $y \doteq 7.21$ cm

41. $m \doteq 3.3$ cm

$n \doteq 54°$

42. Similar triangles have the same corresponding angles and the corresponding sides have the same ratio. (Circle the triangles in Questions 39 and 40.)

43. The measure of the angle opposite the unknown side is needed.

44. Yes. When two angles are known, the third angle can be found using angles in a triangle. The known side and all 3 angles can then be used with the sine law to find the remaining sides.

45. $y = -2(x - 4)^2 + 5$

Stretch vertically by a factor of 2. Reflect in the x-axis. Translate 4 units to the right and 5 units up.

46. $y = \dfrac{1}{2}x^2 - 2$

Compress vertically by a factor of $\dfrac{1}{2}$. Translate 2 units down.

47a. The new relation is $y = (x - 1)^2 + 3$.

b. It is a reflection in the x-axis and a translation of 1 unit to the right and 3 units up.

c. It is a reflection in the x-axis and a translation of 1 unit to the left and 3 units down.

48. intersect at (-1,3)

49. The lines are parallel.

50. The lines coincide.

51. 12 cookies and 6 doughnuts cost $21.

52. Karen needs 1.6 L of 10%-sugar juice and 6.4 L of 20%-sugar juice.

53. Elle jogged for 25 min and walked for 5 min.

54. Lines A and D have the same slope. Lines A and D are either parallel or they coincide. There are either no solutions or an infinite number of solutions.

55a. $-24 < k < 24$

b. $k > 24$ or $k < -24$

56. The graph cannot be a parabola. In a parabola, the vertex must lie on the axis of symmetry, which has an equal distance from both zeros. The axis of symmetry should be $x = \dfrac{2 + 6}{2} = 4$, but the vertex is at (3,2). Therefore the graph is not a parabola.

57. The width must be 22.5 m.

58. Her brother is 1.59 m tall.

59. The revenue will be maximized at a price of $4.75.

60a. The building is 14.3 m tall.

b. The difference is 4.5°.

61. The angles are 74°, 53°, and 53°.

62. The drive will be 0.43 h long.

63. She will have to run 4.87 km N75°W.